THE TROUBLE WITH MARRIAGE

GENDER AND JUSTICE

Edited by Claire M. Renzetti

This University of California Press series explores how the experiences of offending, victimization, and justice are profoundly influenced by the intersections of gender with other markers of social location. Cross-cultural and comparative, series volumes publish the best new scholarship that seeks to challenge assumptions, highlight inequalities, and transform practice and policy.

THE TROUBLE

WITH MARRIAGE

FEMINISTS CONFRONT LAW

AND VIOLENCE IN INDIA

Srimati Basu

⊞ UNIVERSITY OF CALIFORNIA PRESS

University of California Press, one of the most distinguished
university presses in the United States, enriches lives around
the world by advancing scholarship in the humanities, social
sciences, and natural sciences. Its activities are supported by
the UC Press Foundation and by philanthropic contributions
from individuals and institutions. For more information, visit
www.ucpress.edu.

University of California Press
Oakland, California

Portions of this book have been adapted from the following
publications: "Judges of Normality: Mediating Marriage in the
Family Courts of Kolkata, India," in *Signs* 37 (2): 469–92;
"Impossible Translation: Beyond the Legal Body in Two South
Asian Family Courts," in *Law, Culture and the Humanities* 7 (3):
358–75; "Sexual Property: Staging Rape and Marriage in Indian
Law and Feminist Theory," in *Feminist Studies* 37 (1): 185–211;
"Playing Off Courts: The Negotiation of Divorce and Violence
in Plural Legal Settings in Kolkata, India," in *Journal of Legal
Pluralism and Unofficial Law* 52: 41–75; "Family Law
Organizations and the Mediation of Resources and Violence in
Kolkata, India," in *New South Asian Feminisms: Paradoxes and
Possibilities*, ed. Srila Roy (London: Zed Books, 2012); and "The
Legal Structures of Kinship: Re-Working Affinity, Residence
and Entitlement in the Kolkata Family Court," in *Histories of
Intimacy and Situated Ethnography*, ed. Karen Isaksen Leonard,
Gayatri Reddy, and Ann Grodzins Gold (New Delhi: Manohar
Publications, 2010).

All photographs by Srimati Basu.

Library of Congress Cataloging-in-Publication Data

Basu, Srimati, author.
    The trouble with marriage : feminists confront law and
violence in India / Srimati Basu.
        pages   cm
    Includes bibliographical references and index.
    ISBN 978-0-520-28244-5 (cloth : alk. paper)
    ISBN 978-0-520-28245-2 (pbk. : alk. paper)
    ISBN 978-0-520-95811-1 (ebook)
    1. Women—India—Social conditions.   2. Marriage law—
India.   3. Women's rights—India.   4. Rape—Law and
legislation—India.   5.—Family violence—Law and legislation—India.   I. Title.
    HQ1742.B394   2015
    306.840954—dc23   2014024133

Manufactured in the United States of America

24   23   22   21   20   19   18   17   16   15
10   9   8   7   6   5   4   3   2   1

To my maternal great-grandfather, Nripendra Nath Sircar, and my maternal grandmother, Juthika Sircar (Bose)—whose lives speak to me of the power of law, the abjection of violence, and the silences in kinship

CONTENTS

ILLUSTRATIONS

ACKNOWLEDGMENTS

In the book that follows, I trace the complications of kinship and the perils of legal families—but let me start here with the joy of kin and community forged beyond the formulas of blood and marriage. In well over a decade, I have popped into all sorts of new spaces, routinely made incomprehensible requests of complete strangers and pestered friends with odd and quotidian requests and favors. Thank you, everyone, for your generosity, your curiosity, your affection, and your concern, for entertaining baffling queries, keeping me exceedingly well nourished in body and mind, and helping me think. While there are far too many credits to tabulate, here is a short list of starring roles deserving special mention.

The biggest thanks for this book go to the people who made me welcome in their workspaces in courts, police stations, and mediation groups. The Kolkata Family Court has come to be, indeed, a home away from home, where tea arrives and conversations pick up and court personnel drift in with big smiles as if I had not been gone for a good year. I am especially grateful to the counselors and judges for seamlessly including me in the easy warmth that is their signature, for allowing me watch them at work, and for taking me places: Minati Chakravarti and Sandhya Das above all, as well as Ronju Ghosh, Shukla Sen, Chitra Ghosh Dastidar, Judge Keya Basu, and Judge Bimalendu Basu feature at the top of the list. Others who similarly helped facilitate my research over shorter stretches include Sanjay Mukherjee, Damayanti Sen, Sukla Tarafdar, and Nilima Samaddar for the Kolkata Women's Grievance Cell and the Paribarik Shahayata Kendra, Sadhana Ramachandran at the Delhi

Mediation Centre, and Judge Amimul Ehasan at the Dhaka Family Court. A big thanks also goes out to those who entertained my request for interviews and conversations long and short, including judges and activists, and litigants and lawyers rendered anonymous in these pages.

Feminist groups and women's groups have been another vital source of learning. I particularly thank friends at the Women's Grievance Cell and the Paribarik Shahayata Kendra and interlocutors who facilitated my interactions with their organizations, energetically argued their positions, and shared their doubts: Flavia Agnes and Audrey D'Mello at Majlis Legal Centre (Mumbai), Rukmini Sen and Ruchira Goswami at Nari Nirjaton Pratirodh Mancha (Kolkata), Shipra Raha at Suraha Socio-Cultural Research Institute (Kolkata), Anchita Ghatak at Parichiti (Kolkata), A. Suneetha and Vasudha Nagaraj at Anveshi Research Centre for Women's Studies (Hyderabad), Salma Ali at Bangladesh National Women Lawyers Association (Dhaka), and Sara Hossain at Bangladesh Legal Aid Services Trust (Dhaka).

I am grateful for the opportunities and institutional support that provided time and funds to pursue fieldwork and writing, at both the institutions I have worked at: DePauw University and the University of Kentucky. I've been fortunate to have deans and provosts who have been unfailing champions, with special thanks to Neal Abraham and Mark Kornbluh. I've been encouraged by my departmental homes and would like to thank my faculty colleagues and especially the administrative staff, including Carol Cox, Krista Dahlstrom, Terry Bruner, Betty Pasley, and Michelle del Toro, for a million questions and favors. Welcome awards of support have included the Larz A. Whitcomb Faculty Fellowship at DePauw University, the Freeman Foundation Grant at DePauw University, College Research Activity Awards at the College of Arts & Sciences at the University of Kentucky, the Ms. Scholar Award (from Ms. Magazine Writer's Workshop), and the Fulbright-Nehru Senior Research Scholar Award. And the magical place where my notes and papers began becoming a book, the Bellagio Residency funded by the Rockefeller Foundation.

I am deeply thankful for the generosity and friendship of scholars across disciplines and generations, not only for quick turnarounds on letters and abstracts or thoughtful respondent comments, but as much for sharing their wealth of professional knowledge, their contacts established through long-seeded networks, down-to-earth advice, and exuberant, hilarious times. Those of us who do feminist work in South Asian studies are privileged to have a brilliant, nurturing cohort of senior scholars, among whom I am most indebted to Rajeswari Sunder Rajan, Geraldine Forbes, Sylvia Vatuk, and Mrinalini Sinha for their concern, support, and a whole lot of work on my behalf. I am equally fortunate in having been able to count on, learn from, and work and play with a range of inspiring thinkers in my various fields of interest, including Janaki Abraham, Pratiksha Baxi, Daniela Berti, Brinda Bose, Tamsin Bradley, Emily Burrill, Angana Chatterji, Indrani Chatterji, Elora Chowdhury, Molly Dragiewicz, Shelley Feldman, Bishnupriya Ghosh, Durba Ghosh, Shalini Grover, Anne Hardgrove, Sarah Hautzinger, Christine Helliwell, Dorothy Hodgson, Ravinder Kaur, Prabha Kotiswaran, Rochona Majumdar, Sameena Mulla, Rajni Palriwala, Kunal Parker, Barbara Ramusack, Raka Ray, Gayatri Reddy, Srila Roy, Bhaskar Sarkar, Rukmini Sen, Samita Sen, Mitra Sharafi, Sanjay Shrivastava, and Mytheli Sreenivas.

A special shoutout to those who read and commented on the book proposal or manuscript, including Sarasij Majumdar, Jyoti Puri, Debarati Sen, my much-missed once-only-an-office-away former colleague Lucinda Ramberg, and my present colleague extraordinaire Karen Tice, whose perceptive comments on the full draft shape many parts of the final approach. And most of all to Purnima Bose, for her enormous labor at reading through multiple drafts, her meticulous editorial eye, her focus on sanity and humor in academia, and for co-inventing writing bootcamp.

It has been a pleasure to have been at two academic institutions with colleagues across a range of disciplines who love to argue deep into the night, who integrate robust intellectual life, political energy, and everyday warmth and joy. Thanks in particular to Cristina Alcalde, Meryl Altman, Tamara Beauboeuf, Mona Bhan, Dwight Billings, Kate Black, Francie Chassen-Lopez, Lisa Cliggett, Patricia Ehrkamp, Kathi Kern, Diane King, Melynda Price, Suzanne Pucci, Claire Renzetti, Michael Sinowitz, Keiko Tanaka, Karen Tice, and Mark Whitaker for convoluted debates, patient elucidation, and sharing resources and insights.

Working through the material of this book has often involved thinking about family in terms of distress, power, property, and violence. But this also, thankfully, means recognizing the abundance of care (and thus of work) that transcends biological kin to families of affinity and alliance, to communities that started in school and work and neighborhoods and became so much more. I owe much of this book's existence to friends-family who have buoyed and challenged me, made me part of their homes, helped me out, and let me be: my parents Tapas and Sujata Basu, Tarit and Preeti Bose, Jyotsna and Jayant

Basu, Sheila Sengupta, Ashok Ravat, Maya Malatpure, Brinda Bose, Kinsuk Mitra, Bishnupriya Ghosh, Bhaskar Sarkar, Mita Datta, Tufan Ghosh, Huvida Marshall, Elina Mukherjee, Udayan Majumdar, Nirmalyo Ghoshal, Sunrita Hazra, Paroma and Subhamoy Roychowdhury, Dhruva Ghosh, Ranjan Bachawat, Abhijit and Aditi De, Naseem Ahmed, Michael Sinowitz, Robin Mendelsohn, Nancy Davis, Rob Robinson, Sherry Mou, Angana Chat· terji, Richard Schapiro, Lisa Beran, Jim and Amy Collins, Karen Tice, Dwight Billings, and our "platemates" Kate Black and Kathi Kern. For Tiku Ravat, my partner in trouble, adventure, respite, marriage, work, and law, big love for sharing my corner and traveling along.

And far from last on my mind, Maura Roessner has been the best of editors in her enthusiasm and clarity and presence, Claire Renzetti has been terrifically helpful and supportive as a series editor and a colleague, and Jack Young has shepherded the publication process along with exemplary alacrity.

CHAPTER I

Introduction

Law, Marriage, and Feminist Reform

Courts are notoriously difficult to represent. Photography is generally forbidden, as are audio and video recordings. Most commonly, the cacophony of court corridors comes to us in stiff legal language, in the form of parsed judgments (less often in ethnographic jottings, as in this book). One way of capturing the space, I thought, would be to look at the walls of a family court in India, keeping in mind that artifacts may be placed by design or without coordination, by different people over time. Here is a verbatim rendition of what ornamented the walls of the Mumbai Family Court in 2006, in no particular order:

- No mobile phones.
- 3 monkeys. Open your Eyes—Speak Out—The ACB Listens to You. Expose Corruption. (The Anti-Corruption Bureau)
- Men who think women are playthings deserve women who think men are generous bank accounts.
- Children are LITTLE people who need BIG rights. (Dr. Klaus Klankel, governor and federal minister of foreign affairs)
- A Lean Compromise is better than a FAT lawsuit.
- It is through women that order is maintained. Then why call her inferior from whom all great ones are born? (Guru Nanak)
- Woman-Friend-Wife
  Don't walk behind me—I may not lead
  Don't walk ahead of me—I may not follow
  Just walk beside me and be my friend and partner. (Albert Camus 1913–1968)
- A child has a right to love both parents—give your child that gift.

· Oh God, why can't a woman take stock of her destiny? Why does she have to stand by the roadside, head bowed, waiting patiently for a miracle in the morrow? (Rabindranath Tagore)
· The best gift a father can give his child is to *love* their mother.

The jumble of discourses in these sayings suggests the frameworks through which law, mediation, marriage, and feminism proliferate in contemporary India. They encapsulate the four primary zones of trouble explored in this book. First, disciplinary governmentality, marked in the instruction to turn off phones and the invitation to report corruption, follows the book's preoccupation with the force of law in the postcolonial state. Here, we see the state to be benevolent and stern, righteous and lofty, mimicking family discipline even as it attempts to transform it. Second, the seductive call for alternative dispute resolution (ADR), in which the "fat lawsuit" is pejoratively contrasted with the "lean compromise," suggesting trim efficiency and shedding the burden of law. This book interrogates the trend toward use of such alternate forums and their seemingly contradictory coexistence with expanded governmentality. A third trajectory pertains to the normative ideals of marriage and family in law: gendered discourses of male productivity (men as "generous bank accounts") and female sexuality (women as "playthings") are represented as unhealthy mirror images, and the optimal childrearing unit is presented as two-parental and "loving." These ideals suggest that companionate conjugal love is the basis of the ideal family, that children have rights, and thus that family law is a progressive space of liberal modernity, a vision of gender often different in practice from that articulated by judges and counselors.

Fourth, it would appear that the space is characterized by a broad, noble feminism, articulated through the marital ideals above, as well as the incongruent poetic (male) voices of Nobel laureates Rabindranath Tagore and Albert Camus, and Sikh religious leader Guru Nanak. Nanak's equation of the feminine with order (and hence the masculine with chaos) appears to honor women; however, it casts the feminine as a haven from the world of frenetic action, as difference from the norm. In contrast, Tagore's poem *Sabala* (The strong woman), written in the voice of a rebellious feminist subject, makes a powerful argument for equity and justice as part of the human condition, providing a sharp critique of patriarchy. Camus's presence is most ironic in this cohort, given his legendary dislike of marriage.[1] Best of all, in the quote in question, commonly misattributed to him,[2] the phrase "and partner" has been added only in this version; hence the marriage-averse Camus is here *invented* to represent marriage as a form of friendship. The lesson to be had by reading these together—that women deserve to be equals, friends, and companions—suggests marriage as a site of heteronormative harmony, in which discordant notes of power, hostility, and rebellion are muted.[3]

These walls serve as pedagogical frames for litigants, setting up what they might expect even before they encounter a court or a counselor. They are led to a notion of the ideal family, often at odds with the experiences of family that bring them to court, and to claims of gender equity that may not be borne out in adjudication. Most people conceive of law as a distant and formidable realm, often imagining it through popular literary or film renditions where moral order is dramatically restored and justice meted out with certitude. The discourses above advertise a new world of active negotiation, without intimating that it is one in which justice, order, and strategy are likely to be much murkier.

We will be lingering in such courts in this book, but also in other spaces where law is deployed formally or informally to work out marital trouble, including Women's Grievance Cells managed by the police to hear complaints of violence, and mediation agencies variously affiliated with the state and women's movements. Through encounters with family law, intimate violence, and mediation in contemporary India, this book will examine marriage as reflected and shaped through law and, conversely, provide an ethnographic portrait of everyday law as depicted through the governance of marriage. Accounts of marital discord serve as a diagnostic, as "trouble cases" in the classic legal anthropological sense of revealing cultural frameworks. Through them, we can contemplate the categorical trouble of marriage itself: an institution fused with "trouble and strife" by definition, persistently associated with conflict, deprivation, and exclusion.[4]

The legacies of global feminist legal reform, particularly the Indian women's movement of the late 1970s and 1980s, are another central node in this book. Has the heavy emphasis on law as the instrument of achieving gender equity been effective? We seek an answer in the workings of institutions that were founded as a result of local and global feminist campaigns since the UN Decade for Women (1976–85), looking for what has worked and what has emerged unexpectedly, what has caused conflicts within women's movements and what has been appropriated by other groups. The main Indian laws profiled relate to divorce and gender violence: the Family Courts Act (1984), S498A cases against domestic violence/"torture" added to the Indian Penal Code in 1985, and S376 of the Indian Penal Code against rape.

The following chapters consider how laws transform social being. If we all recognize that law provides neither stable nor predictable solutions, what do social movements, including feminist movements, gain by insistently turning to it? Litigants may find that law opens strategic spaces of negotiation, despite the practical limitations of legal remedies. New laws, created in response to political imperatives or social movements and filtered through legislatures, are applied by individuals and groups in both foreseen and unanticipated ways and are often connotatively transformed in the process. People "bargain in the shadow of the law," shaping it to their ends and building new legal cultures. This basic tenet of legal pluralism guides my approach: I find it pointless to debate whether the laws in question are "correctly used" or "misused," whether they are "good" or "bad" laws, whether feminist visions are adequately recognized. Rather we follow the ways they are utilized as new cultural horizons: to stretch the entitlements of marriage, calibrate the meanings of violence, or construct kinship. I focus on "the kind of society in which law operates," as opposed to the efficacy of particular rules or concepts, an anthropological rather than a legal reform approach (Moore 1969, 253).

Mediation (and alternative dispute resolution more generally), characterized as an end to the trouble represented by law and a mode of generating plural customized solutions, features prominently in these discussions. A popular feminist resource, it seems to offer a way around the oppressiveness of trials, interminable delays, and fuzzy legal language, setting up women as empowered agents in control of their narratives and transforming legal authority. The very ubiquity of mediation is the cause for worry here. Mediation, as law's Other, is ambivalent in the same ways as law: new spaces and new modes of speaking do not necessarily alter legal authority. Discourses of efficiency and resolution may be highlighted in mediation at the cost of working through questions of anger and power, thus becoming a form of "coercive harmony," to use Laura Nader's trenchant phrase (1997). As we will see, marriage mediation is particularly fraught, given the predominance of questions of power, property, and violence.

The following sections lay out the four main theoretical and thematic trajectories of the book: law as strategy and force, the possibilities and limitations of alternate dispute resolution, marriage as both privilege and deprivation, and the ambivalent effect of feminist jurisprudence in the gender-equality-friendly modern nation-state. The introduction then orients readers to the methodological framework of the book, the political and cultural locations of fieldwork, and the demographic context of Indian marriage and divorce.

LAW AND CULTURE

Law is the clothes men wear
Anytime, anywhere,
Law is Good morning and Good night.
—W. H. Auden, "Law Like Love" (1941)

This volume echoes Auden's parsing of law as encompassing shifting, contradictory areas of life: law as practice, custom, and habit ("the clothes men wear"); as orthodox and disciplinary ("Law is the Law"); as a product of political and historical specificities ("Law is only crimes / Punished by places and by times"); and even as being "like love," incommensurable and inexplicable, something through which one knows oneself and something that inevitably is tied with loss ("Like love we often weep / Like love we seldom keep"). The venues in and around law explored in this book will demonstrate each of these levels: we will track legal realms as normative, disciplinary, affective, and political—a force and a promise, triumph, love, and loss.

However, this broad approach makes it difficult to demarcate law as a separate object of study: is it coterminous with the space of culture itself?[5] Law has been theorized in the most expansive of terms as a basic "property of interaction" (Reisman 1999, 2), a diagnostic of the symbolic realm as "a distinctive manner of imagining the real" (Geertz 1983, 184), or a collective social conscience to Durkheim (Calavita 2001, 98). To some law and society scholars, law maps historically contingent practices: the "product of a specific moment in the history of a society"(Demian 2003, 99); "whatever people identify and treat through their social practices as 'law'" (Tamanaha 2000, 313); or a dynamic entity "constantly transformed given its mediation within a sociospatial context" (Blomley 1989, 516). In these "constitutive" perspectives (Blomley, Delaney, et al. 2001, xv), law is seen to affirm other cultural realms (Calavita 2001, 90). The conceptual problem here lies in the difficulty of delimitation: if we cannot find an "outside" to law, how do we draw the lines around it? In the following chapters, legal cultures do indeed help define kinship, class, marriage, governance, and politics. But we also want to ask of them: why are these conflicts expressed through *law*? What added value does law provide?

Unlike the work of scholars who have studied legal norms through everyday social moments (Reisman 1999), this book engages with law in its formal incarnations, as a form of state power. Auden vividly captures the regulatory force of law in formal settings:

> Law, says the judge as he looks down his nose,
> Speaking clearly and most severely,
> Law is as I've told you before,
> Law is as you know I suppose,
> Law is but let me explain it once more,
> Law is The Law.

Law operates with a sense of its own power ("Law is The Law"), authorizing the salience of precedent ("as I've told you before") and hegemonic consent ("as you know I suppose"). Legal personages are lofty and stern, enforcers of discipline. Derrida's riff on the terms *law, justice,* and *rights* ties them profoundly to force: "There are, to be sure, laws that are not enforced, but there is no law without enforceability, and no applicability or enforceability of the law without force, whether this force be direct or indirect, physical or symbolic, exterior or interior, brutal or subtly discursive and hermeneutic, coercive or regulative" (1992, 6).

In the modern nation-state, overt force seems to have been replaced by systems of governance, called "bureaucracy" and "legality" in Weber's account (2004, 133) and "governmentality" in Foucault's (1991). "Government" may be conflated with the notion of a watchful state "in the imagination and everyday practices of ordinary people" (Gupta 2012, 100, 43–44, parsing Abrams), but scholars like Gupta contend that governance is diffuse rather than centrally coordinated and works by evoking protection and regulation. This book takes a similar view—that an ethnographic approach to bureaucracy reveals the state to be "disaggregated" rather than "cohesive," to fail people in the contradictions and slippages between sectors and mechanisms (Gupta 2012, 33). The "state" and "law" in everyday contexts are experienced as "both distant and impersonal ideas as well as localized and personified institutions, . . . violent and destructive as well as benevolent and productive" (Hansen and Stepputat 2001, 4–5). In this vein, legal authorities personify abstract and yet intimate encounters with a state that is simultaneously protective and disciplinary. However, their authority is demystified and challenged when legal arbitrariness becomes evident, showing that law is also fractured, "deconstitutive" (Calavita 2001, 96).

Such fractures show that the power of law is mediated by resistance, even if power adapts to forms of resistance (Foucault 1978; Abu-Lughod 1990). As the field of critical legal studies has explored (e.g., White 1990), marginal subjects' use of legal tools can destabilize hegemonies or fail in the face of resilient norms (Lazarus-Black and Hirsch 1999, 9). People often imagine that engaging the legal realm typifies resistance, that bringing "real grievances" to light and getting better "justice" is a form of agency. But if we think of law, like other cultural realms, as a performative field in which people strategically conform to normative expectations, using law is after all a (powerful) attempt to conform to its rules, seeking an optimal outcome. Resistance may be seen as a residue, a (potentially useful) tear in such performance against the force of culture/law (Hirsch 1998, drawing on Butler).

These strategic uses of law, whether failures or successes, are demonstrated in the following chapters in the "off-label" uses of law, such as in the use of rape law to secure marriage, or domestic violence criminal prosecutions to assist in civil alimony suits. We seek to understand what determines a choice to use formal law and study the ways people can bargain *with* formal law in informal venues of legal pluralism.[6] Sometimes, legal cases are avoided at all costs so that questions of kinship or economics may be negotiated (Basu 1999), while elsewhere, people may turn to courts to pursue "justice" in both idealistic and situational ways (Merry 1986). Seeming manipulations to secure extralegal outcomes can thus be read as attempts to put law to complex use (Marshall and Barclay 2003). Legal realists contest this view of willy-nilly traffic, arguing that people "bargain in the shadow of the law," meaning formal law is a central determinant of decision making and not just one option (Jacob 1992, 566; Roberts 1994, 979). The counterargument to this view is that questions of social and economic capital are prime drivers of decisions, while law is but a "dim" shadow (Jacob 1992, 585, particularly relevant for divorce cases).[7] Importantly, law may be either used or avoided when decisions are made, in the "deliberate choice to step outside the local culture, to translate the subject matter from the language of local customs into the language of the formal legal system" (Engel 1980, 430–31).

We see in the following chapters many such examples of "legal pluralism" in the active, creative, strategic choices to move in and out of law, with mixed success depending on one's fallback position. Such systems are defined as "weak legal pluralism" when they describe the narrower strategy of simultaneously using legal and quasi-legal or informal options (as we see in chapter 7), sometimes anointed "forum-shopping" (von Benda-Beckmann 1981). More broadly, decisions to use or avoid law, or to reshape the cultural meaning of law, exemplify "strong legal pluralism." Lest we think of legal pluralism as a quaint traditional throwback or an awkward melding under colonial administrations, it is important to recognize it as crucial to the modern nation-state's claim to be benevolent, democratic, participatory, and multicultural (Chowdhury 2005), a critical "way in which the state organizes its own loss of centrality" (de Sousa Santos 2006, 44; see also Sieder and McNeish 2013, 11–15). The formal legal system deliberately functions alongside (and along with) informal venues of dispute resolution, whether customary or new.

The question here, for purposes of social justice, is whether legal pluralism expands gender or class or race equity, or whether it merely provides an array of options that cement prevailing ideologies. Boaventura de Sousa Santos's influential perspective champions plural systems as "palimpsests" that are incompletely ruptured from their past, characterized by "porosity" and "hybridity," able to "giv[e] rise to new forms of legal meaning and action" (2006, 46). Solanki, with similar optimism, argues that possibilities reside between the simultaneous processes of "centralization" (where the state supports formal institutions and norms of equity) and "decentralization" (in the space created by fragmented official application of laws and the "diverse ways in which social actors and institutions filter into the state judicial system" [2011, 61–63]). Given the omnipresence of legal pluralism, it may be most useful to notice how "rights and claims are made and responded to within a range of cultural, social, economic and political contexts" (Sieder and McNeish 2013, 2). Considering the question of gender, for example: "What strategies do men and women use to claim and obtain resources, protection, security and voice? How are rights and obligations understood and negotiated? Under what conditions are complex legal pluralities a factor in gendered forms of exclusion? And under what conditions do they constitute a resource for women—and men—to challenge their marginalization?" (Sieder and McNeish 2013, 2). The existence of legal pluralities opens up possibilities for negotiating solutions unavailable within formal law. The shadow of law might help feminist claims-making by building "a sense of entitlement, of the right to have rights" (Cornwall and Molyneux 2006, 1188) or by launching a space of discursive debate (Kapur and Cossman 1996; Suneetha and Nagaraj 2010).

In this book, we explore some of these directions in the study of law. We follow the ways laws make marriage, kinship, and violence legible, as well as the ordinary ways they work themselves into people's language and habitus. Yet laws often prove inadequate in translating deep-rooted problems, unable for example to transform marriage as a gendered institution of power and property. We will follow the work of agents of the state and the compliant and resistant strategies used by litigants, noticing both the force and elasticity of rules and processes and the permeability between legal and quasi-legal venues.

(ALTERNATIVE) DISPUTE REVOLUTION: THE OTHER OF LAW

Choose Mediation because . . .
    It immediately puts you in control of both the dispute and its resolution.
    The law mandates it, and the courts encourage and endorse it.
    Through it you can communicate in a real sense with the other side which you may not have done before.
    The process is confidential, the procedure is simple and the atmosphere is informal.
    It is voluntary and you can opt out of it at any time if it does not help.
    It saves precious time and energy.
    It saves costs on what usually becomes a prolonged litigation.
    It shows you the strengths and weaknesses of your case which helps find realistic solutions.
    It focuses on long-term interests and helps you create options for settlement.
    It restores broken relationships and focuses on improving the future, not dissecting the past.
    You opt for more by signing a settlement that works to benefit both you and your opponent.
    At the end of mediation you can actually shake hands with your opponents and wish them good health and happiness.
—Pamphlet from Samadhan, Delhi High Court Mediation and Conciliation Centre

As indicated in the previous discussion on legal pluralism, do-it-yourself law has become increasingly prized as a mode of bypassing a cumbersome state, and alternative dispute resolution (ADR) forums have mushroomed. The above bilingual, attractively illustrated pamphlet from the Delhi Mediation Centre exemplifies the conundrum posed by ADR as the optimal alternative to law. The pamphlet celebrates mediation (a form of ADR) as the smart solution to conflict, its principles oft repeated in the center's materials, from the annual calendar, to standard opening speeches by mediator-lawyers to clients, to the plaques and posters around the well-appointed new space. The center is called Samadhan, meaning "solution," thus promising an ending rather than perpetual legal process. It proudly draws upon the ultimate register of Indian respectability, Gandhi's words on mediation: "I had learnt the true practice of law. I had learnt to find out the better side of human nature and to enter men's hearts. . . . [A] large part of my time during my twenty years of practice as a lawyer was occupied in bringing about private compromises of hundreds of cases. I lost nothing thereby—not even money, certainly not my soul" (Samadhan 2011, 7). Media coverage reflects these ideologies in headlines such as "Come, Let's Sit and Talk Things Out" and "Stuck in Court? Try Mediation" (Samadhan 2011, 126–27). The impression is that law is alien, distant, and expensive, an evil modern infestation, while ADR provides more democratic access and better justice.

Mediation, or "dispute" resolution, is nostalgically associated with a grounding in local culture, as opposed to the forceful homogeneity of law. Depicted as being "away from judge- (and judgment-) oriented accounts" and focused on actors' "circumstances, goals, strategies and actions" (Comaroff and Roberts 1981, 14), it offers the possibility to more fruitfully engage with why people acted in a certain way and to construct a satisfying resolution. The systems considered in this book are not the small-scale disputing venues beloved of legal anthropologists but the hybrid institutions developed by modern nation-states as "popular justice" forums,[8] often depicted as veritable revolutions of participation and access. As the following chapters demonstrate, however, the problem is that mediation might work in turn through alternative repressive ideologies, posing disproportionately greater problems for marginal subjects.

Legal anthropologists who studied community forums (Bohannan 1957; Just 2000) highlighted local norms of transgression and compensation, in which the state appeared as a distant force; community sanctions twisted state categories of crime to fit their own sense of violation. ADR's appeal similarly lies in honoring community norms over the state: Merry and Milner profiled a U.S. program that offered "subordinate groups greater access to justice or greater control over its administration," "permeated by the values and rules of local communities" (1993, 8); Auerbach mapped "a persistent counter-tradition to legalism" through U.S. history via a variety of dispute resolution forums (1983, 4).

However, communities exercise their own forms of hegemonic regulation and can be poor venues for gender equity (Baxi 1986, 75–76). As studies of dispute resolution (many focused on marital trouble) have demonstrated, community power may even affect formal courts. In a study by Griffiths, women in Botswana who tried new legal strategies found they were constrained by the ways "social understandings, expectations and values" of property and labor related to marriage saturated both customary and Western law settings (1997, 222, 228). Kenyan Kadhi's courts, imagined as a religious alternative to the formal courts, allowed women to be creative protagonists but also "solidif[ied] gender differences and gender antagonisms" and could not displace the patriarchal grounding of the laws (Hirsch 1998, 243).[9] Erin Moore, narrating one Rajasthani woman's struggles in a range of legal venues from communities to formal legal forums, argues that law is a limited source of gender justice when it "legitimizes ideologies and asymmetrical power relations, particularly between genders" (1999, 30).

There is danger, too, in confusing efficiency with justice.[10] Owen Fisk, leading the critique, points out that representing mediation as a stranger's benign resolution of a neighborly dispute ignores potential harm and minimizes the problem. "Settlement," he argues passionately, "is a truce more than a true reconciliation. Settlement is for me the civil analogue of plea bargaining: consent is often coerced; the bargain may be struck by someone without authority; the absence of a trial and judgment renders subsequent judicial involvement troublesome; and although dockets are trimmed, justice may not be done" (1984, 1075). The deal is typically less favorable to the party with greater economic disadvantage, exemplifying a game theory axiom; future enforcement of settlement terms is also frequently difficult (Fisk 1984, 1076, 1084). While others describe more positive results, such as "a more personal and private approach," "high ratings of user satisfaction," "a sense of commitment to abide by the agreement," and "less damag[e] to relationships," they nonetheless recognize that there are "no consistent improvements in long-term compliance, spousal cooperation and relitigation" (Pearson and Thoeness 1988, 86–88). Laura Nader has stringently critiqued ADR for being "coercive, repressive and undemocratic," for highlighting discourses of communication, therapy, and healing and evading issues of "rights, remedies, injustice, prevention and unequal power" (1993, 5–6).

ADR's reputation for providing a better hearing and improved legal access made it very popular with women's movements, who depicted mediation as "a feminist alternative to the patriarchally inspired adversary system" (Nader 1993, 10). Nader describes the scenario as a perfect ideological storm in the United States: "It did not hurt that there was a close fit between the [ADR] rhetoric, the ethic of Christian harmony, the interests of corporations in cutting legal fees, psychologists and other therapists, the women's movement, and a myriad of vested interests" (1993, 7). However, feminist scholars have pointed out that ADR poses grave problems for women and economically marginal subjects, for whom the deliberate erasure of power relations, the disavowal of angry expression, and the injunction to forget the past generate dissatisfaction and injustice. Divorce, for example, involves "parties with lengthy, intimate and problem-ridden histories and deeply established behavioral patterns," such that "mediation cannot and does not address the underlying emotional problems of families" (Pearson and Thoeness 1988, 86–88). In recent years, restorative justice (RJ) has been recommended by some feminist scholars as an improved form of ADR: rather than assuming equivalence between parties, it focuses on remedying harm to victims and on offenders accepting responsibility, as a way of shortening the adversarial process (Daly and Stubbs 2006; Koss and Achilles 2008; Koss 2010; McGlynn, Westmarland, et al. 2012). Remarkably, RJ seems to have worked well for some sexual assault and sexual abuse cases but so far has proved difficult to apply to divorce and domestic violence.

The Samadhan pamphlet encapsulates these possibilities and limitations of mediation. It highlights the "lofty goals": control, customization, frugality, time-saving, confidentiality. It posits a firm end in sight for litigation and a conflict-free future. I have talked at length with one of the prime movers of this well-funded and efficient center about their careful work, which involves mainstreaming mediation by seeking judicial referrals, ensuring the buy-in of lawyers by acknowledging their expertise and paying for their participation, and most of all, incorporating complex kin and economic obligations into clients' decisions, being careful to balance women's safety and well-being. But as we will see in the following chapters, "shaking hands with your opponents and wishing them good health and happiness" and "restoring broken relationships" are difficult standards in divorce litigation, given structures of power located within marriage. In the rush to compromise and settlement, ADR ideologies may erase anger and violence, assuming that parties in conflict operate in a universe of balanced bargaining equity, again a poor fit with marriage.

FRACTURING MARRIAGE

After marriage, husband and wife become two sides of a coin; they just can't face each other, but still they stay together.

—Hemant Joshi

By all means marry. If you get a good wife, you'll be happy. If you get a bad one, you'll become a philosopher.

—Socrates

I had some words with my wife, and she had some paragraphs with me.

—Anonymous

I don't worry about terrorism. I was married for two years.

—Sam Kinison

There's a way of transferring funds that is even faster than electronic banking. It's called marriage.

—James Holt McGavran

I've had bad luck with both my wives. The first one left me and the second one didn't.

—Patrick Murray

My wife and I were happy for twenty years. Then we met.

—Rodney Dangerfield

A good wife always forgives her husband when she's wrong.

—Milton Berle

Marriage is the only war where one sleeps with the enemy.

—Anonymous

A man inserted an "ad" in the classifieds: "Wife wanted." The next day he received a hundred letters. They all said the same thing: "You can have mine."

—Anonymous

Marriage is shaped not just in religious ceremonies and rituals, courts and police stations, and mediation sessions, but in conversations and jokes and rumors, through media and ephemera. The epigraph is one such instantiation, both random and densely evocative. Excerpted from one of those relentless e-mail forwards that arrive like locusts despite one's best cyber-pesticides,[11] it carries the signature "Bilkisu Labaran, Country Director, BBC World Service Trust Nigeria," with the exhortation to "send this to all the guys to give them a good laugh . . . and those ladies with a sense of humor" (the female audience is supposed to be flattered, since being a feminist is feared to come with a humor lobotomy). The "funny" message circulates globally as a normalized discourse about marriage and the relationship between men and women, laced with resignation, desperation, and not a little hostility. Heterosexual sociality is the only scene there is, it suggests fatalistically and with full cross-cultural conviction, and it is characterized by men losing their money, their freedom, and all the arguments. What a buzz-kill it would be to counter with the oft-cited 1985 United Nations Human Development Report's statistic that women perform two-thirds of the world's labor hours, earn one-tenth of the world's income, and own one-hundredth of the world's property! Most interestingly for our purposes, the message poses marriage as an essential scene of conflict, of "trouble and strife"; it is akin to terrorism, a path both to bankruptcy and—remarkably—to philosophy. It posits implacable gender difference, assigning wives and husbands to unreasonable loquacity and pathetic compliance, respectively, and looks to the end of marriage/marriages with glee.

This book presents a portrait of marriage through the stress fractures of marital dissolution, where conflict and terror are often on display. But it views marriage as neither the inevitable locus of sociality, nor as marked by fixed gender difference. We follow the ways marriage institutes legitimacies and secures regimes of property and labor, as seen in legal strategies for negotiating alimony, violence, residence, or custody. Conflicts serve as a lens for putting marriage itself on trial, allowing us to examine it as a site of privilege, entitlement, and exclusion on the one hand, and of deprivation, vulnerability, and violence on the other.

Marriage tends to be represented as a transparent good, assuming at its center the universal cultural unit of the heterosexual couple. The popular paperback *A History of the Wife* suggests that "it is still 'a good thing' to have a wife and to be a wife" because "going through life as a member of a pair" means "being validated and strengthened through a long-term, loving union" (Yalom 2001, xvii), mirroring Giddens's influential theory that modernity is marked by the rise of romantic love (including within marriage) as the primary mode of personal satisfaction (1993; Cole and Thomas 2009). These perspectives erase the facts that most human cultures are nonmonogamous and marriage may not be the only basis for long-term or loving relationships. Contemporary forms of marriage might be one mode of "enhancing intimacy" and a locus of "social and political power," but the idea that marriage brings prosperity "is propaganda, not reason or social science" and hides "the gross favoritism that the government lavishes on marriage" (Bernstein 2003, 211–12).

Each culture has a "sex-gender system," to use Gayle Rubin's useful formulation (1975), in which marriage is part of a specific arrangement of labor, kinship, gender, and sexuality, producing subjectivities and socialities. Along these lines, critiquing the view that gender and kinship are stable and given categories in marriage, Borneman provocatively suggests that marriage is a "privilege that operates through a series of foreclosures and abjections, through the creation of an 'outside'" *because* it serves specific material and ideological purposes (1996, 225). He urges an analysis of the privileged links among marriage, gender, kinship, and erotic desire that would purposefully document "not only what asserts itself as presence and life, but also identify what is foreclosed, placed outside, or erased" (228). In parallel vein, Rubin seeks to "reimagine" marriage beyond the replication of intransigent patriarchal notions of kinship (1975).[12]

Contemporary movements to expand notions of conjugality and family in terms of recognition and rights, such as legalizing gay marriage, have newly animated these theoretical debates, proposing other reimaginations of the heteronormative contract. It is notable, though, that such movements do not necessarily subvert dominant configurations; as gay marriage becomes a rising ground of civil rights mobilization in the United States, it often works through forms of "homonormativity" that foreclose alternate sexualities and citizenships (Puar 2007). A more expansive vision is articulated by groups who advocate for recognition of a variety of marriage-like formations, such as Indian activists who support the broadest swath of "relationships in the nature of marriage." These include homosexual and heterosexual practices involving short- and long-term exchanges of labor, sex, and intimacy, of which the nuclear gay and lesbian family would be one small part (Partners for Law in Development 2010). Ashley Tellis contends that Indian feminists, too, have exclusively promoted marriage as the locus of entitlements and have failed to "create spaces for women outside marriage and family, outside the heterosexual imperative"; he argues for the need to imagine "spaces outside marriage within which same-sex subjects can breathe and imagine their lives the way they want" (2014, 348, 346). This book engages such invitations to expose the sutures of gender, erotics, labor, and kinship in the contemporary nation-state's representations of marriage.

Divorce is the literal unsuturing of the institution of marriage. As "the point at which the principles, assumptions, values, attitudes and expectations surrounding marriage, family and parenting are made explicit" (Simpson 1998, 27), it illuminates material and cultural negotiation among state, communities, and families. Rising divorce rates are most often evoked in terms of anxiety and pain (and there are plenty of examples in the following chapters to confirm the validity of such regrets). Rather than viewing it inevitably as fragmentation and loss, however, here we study it as a productive mode that "generates continuities in the way one generation passes on its status, property, identity and accumulated wisdom and folly to the next" (Simpson 1998, 2). Importantly, divorce has been a powerful mode of escaping physical and economic violence, as well as other interpersonal constraints. It is often experienced as a mixed bag of possibilities, with depression and strain balanced against greater economic independence and less dominance, a fuller identity, and better connections.[13] While there are only scant commonalities in causes of dissolution (Betzig 1989; Goode 1993),[14] divorce rates are most strongly correlated with whether one can afford to be divorced—that is, to social, economic, and political options in a given nation-state, such as gendered labor market patterns, public assistance within or outside marriage, and practices of remarriage and kin support for the divorced.[15] In this book, along similar lines, divorce is seen to generate both benefit and loss, while being a powerful diagnostic of the gendered distribution of labor, property, and social support.

Almost without exception,[16] however, the *economic* consequences of divorce for women in the contemporary nation-state are disproportionately difficult (despite some putative *social* trade-offs). The important distinction is between nominal and substantive gender equality (Molyneux 1985), in which the formal (nominal) gender equality in divorce laws is often at odds with, and blind to, the (substantive) economic consequences of divorce. Many women litigants face a contradiction between their status as seemingly empowered subjects who invoke laws with face-value equity, and the constraints of social and economic factors related to income and residence. That is, potential dissolution exposes the fundamental economic infrastructure of marriage: "Gender-structured marriage involves women in a cycle of socially caused and distinctly asymmetric vulnerability," meaning women "are made vulnerable by marriage itself" (Okin 1989, 138). Okin's legal analysis echoes a staple argument of socialist feminism, that ideologies of family (or familialism) anchored in heterosexual marriage and nuclear families are the root of economic subordination. These institutions systematically foster dependency, generating "inequality and asymmetry" in the gendered division of labor in both households and evolving labor markets (Young, Wolkowitz, et al. 1981, xvii).[17]

Several chapters of this book deal with the state's management of marriage, including adjudication of alimony or child support through the governance of behavior. I find it useful to see such management across state domains as "neither hegemonic nor monolithic" (Brown 1992, 29): the diffusion across disarticulated facets of the state is a form of power exercised through disparate interpretations from officials. Such diffusion, which together promotes an ideal conjugal family modulated by class, may even be mapped as the very hallmark of modernity in state governance (Donzelot 1997): Donzelot argues that the "interests of the child" were rhetorically mobilized to transform a range of labor practices, residential spaces, social work interventions, and notions of violence. In seeming contradiction, many scholars have suggested that recent changes to marriage and divorce laws demonstrate a loosening of state control over the marriage tie, marked by an assumption of equality among spouses and greater reliance on individual property (Glendon 1980; Buchhofer and Ziegert 1981; Fineman 1991; McIntyre 1995). In Brown and Donzelot's analyses, these are not contradictions; it is precisely consonant with the ideologies of the modern state not to appear heavy handed and to promote individual choice and well-being. The governance of family and marriage is often enforced through domains not necessarily related to divorce, such as children or population or health. It is of a piece with this indirect intervention and the illusion of choice in the private realm that systemic impoverishment related to marriage is diffusely dispersed across sites of governance.

Much of this book follows the state's governance of marriage, presenting the economic effects of seemingly gender-neutral divorce law, discourses of benevolent protectionism that reinscribe gender roles, and administrative operations that shore up marriage as an ultimate privilege. But it also purposefully decenters the state, emphasizing litigants' cultural negotiations, such as the use of law for contesting caste, class, religion, and kinship. A rich emergent body of ethnographic studies of marriage in India has tracked inventive practices of marriage in informal venues that manipulate categories of formal law (Holden 2008; Vatuk 2008; Grover 2010). However, before we celebrate resistance too gleefully, we might also remember that marriage law is deployed (often violently) to enforce adherence to community norms, such as to further religious majoritarianism. and caste and religious endogamy, by using kidnapping and rape laws to constrict marriage choice (Chowdhry 2007; Mody 2008). We will follow the various ways law is creatively used to shape marriage, with and against women's agency.

FEMINIST JURISPRUDENCE AND GOVERNANCE

Anita: Get down from your dais and go see people—see how happy the Indian wife can be with setting up her home [Hindustani aurat ghar basakey kitni sukhi ho sakti hai].

Sita Devi (feminist campaigner): They think slavery is happiness—what do they know of independence? [Wo ghulami ko sukh samajhti hai, wo kya jane azadi kaisi hoti hai?] I will teach them freedom as I have learned from women in Europe and America.

Anita: Those women will give you a lot to learn, like changing husbands four times.

—Mr. & Mrs. 55, dir. Guru Dutt (1955)

Feminist intervention in questions of marriage, body, sexuality, and violence is often, as in the above accusation, equated with the destruction of family, marriage, and love, and a feminist such as Sita Devi depicted as "a dangerous complainer who exposes family problems" (Hirsch 1998, 243). As the "typical" Indian woman, represented by Anita, complains, feminists are seen as substituting the rudeness of equity and independence for the satisfaction of compulsory heterosexuality, thus precipitating social chaos. Despite such fears (or as their measure), feminist reforms have been mainstreamed into state institutions since the 1970s. "Governance feminism," the "noticeable installation of feminists and feminist ideas in actual legal-institutional power," is a visible global force (Halley, Kotiswaran, et al. 2006, 340). Legal interventions have transformed workplaces and doctors' offices and sports arenas and police stations; rape is recognized as a war crime; sexual harassment constitutes employment discrimination; pregnancy cannot be cause for workplace termination; states have funded shelters and programs to combat various forms of intimate violence; and the "reasonable man" standard no longer counts as the sole criterion of considered judgment.

Since the mobilization following the UN Decade for Women (1976–85), global conversations around gender equity have included calls for improved legal access, including the creation of informal venues, as well as greater attention to violence against women and women's economic deprivation. The violence against women movement has been described as "perhaps the greatest success story of international mobilization around a specific human rights issue" because of the rapidity with which international norms, programs, and policies have been developed (Coomaraswamy 2005, 2). It was further spurred by the decision of the Committee on the Elimination of Discrimination against Women to count violence against women as a form of gender discrimination in 1991, the UN Declaration on the Elimination of Violence against Women in 1993 (Coomaraswamy 2005), and monitoring by a Special Rapporteur on Violence against Women, its Causes and Consequences through the UN Commission of Human Rights, which in 2011 sharply put states on notice to undertake concerted efforts at local and national levels to design programs and policies, "based on the premise that the human rights of women are universal, interdependent, and indivisible."[18]

The Indian women's movement (IWM), active since before independence, was especially influential in the 1970s and 1980s in bringing forms of gendered violence to legislative attention (Kumar 1993; Chaudhuri 2004; Khullar 2005). Subsequent IWM mobilization has included a prohibition on the results of amniocentesis tests to deter sex-selective abortions, provision of matrimonial maintenance through the Domestic Violence Act, and establishment of women's right to ancestral family property. The family courts analyzed in this book are among the new legal institutions that emerged in the wake of the UN Decade, designed to provide better access to law and attention to gendered violence and economic entitlements of marriage. S498A of the Indian Penal Code on "domestic torture" and the reform of rape law, also subjects of this book, are other legacies of the IWM. I study the effects of these legal and policy changes, along with emergent concerns of the contemporary women's movement, such as matrimonial property, the rising role of mediation, and the means of effectively addressing gendered violence.

This book focuses on the seeming successes of women's movements and the afterlife of feminist-inspired institutions. Legal reform has been a critical strategy for feminist movements, involving demands for change that affect material options as well as symbolic inscriptions (Smart and Brophy 1985; Kapur and Cossman 1996; Rai 1996; Johnson 2009).[19] But putting a law in place does not ensure satisfactory mainstreaming of gender justice (ideally also equity of race, caste, class, sexuality, ability, nation); law should be thought of "as the first thing and not the last thing," Spivak urges (2010)—an introductory gambit rather than a solution. Societal change and legal reform are mutually constitutive, ongoing processes of political negotiation. Legal categories created as a result of feminist demands are transformed as they pass through legislative and policy levels, further taking concrete shape in organizations and offices distant from movement rhetoric. Instead of stopping crimes or practices through law, as "governance feminism" seeks, reforms often generate new cultural repertoires (Halley, Kotiswaran, et al. 2006, 337).

Feminist reform often has a fundamentally ambivalent relationship with the state. It is favorably headlined when politically convenient, but only within particular "discursively available possibilities for representation and action" that fit state goals (Pringle and Watson 1992, 69). Moreover, apparent support for feminist issues can be channeled through patriarchal assumptions, in effect making the state "masculinist without intentionally or overtly pursuing the 'interests' of men" (Brown 1992, 14). For example, state responses to curbing sexual violence often recode solutions within patriarchal structures of power, missing the complexities of feminist analyses of violence (Menon 2004, 121, 133). Normative class and race orders also structure the logic of judgments (Crenshaw 1996; Mehra 1998). Interpretations of gender and sexuality in new policies often lead to unexpected criminalization of some people while routine violators are ignored (Halley, Kotiswaran, et al. 2006, 337). Even task forces instituted to remedy gender bias end up realizing that "not all women are similarly situated, and that gaining attention from legal patriarchal power on one kind of bias may well come at the expense of another" (Resnick 1996, 979). While the state thereby appears vigilant to gender equity because it has acted, no matter how misguidedly, frustration over poor implementation of laws gets directed to the women's movement. Indeed, the visibility of women's movements makes it difficult to argue that their power is limited, the irony being that "the conspicuous *success* of the women's movement in the field of legal reform [leads] to the doubts about its efficacy as strategy"(Rajan 2003, 32–33; see also Kelly 2005, 490–91). Thus feminist legal reform is best thought of as a way of making claims and space, rather than a force of change per se.[20]

Neither is gendered justice necessarily realized in institutions inspired by feminist lobbying. In evaluating Brazil's Delegacia de Proteção à Mulher, the women's police stations envisaged to remedy violence against women, Sarah Hautzinger concludes that "the specialized delegacias were created by feminists with strategic interests in mind, but largely carried out by policewomen enacting practical gender interests" (1997, 20). In the United States, scholars and advocates weighing the effects of domestic violence policies envisaged by feminists, such as mandatory arrest or comprehensive coordination, have concluded that these policies disempower those they were meant to help, disproportionately causing difficulties to women of color and immigrant women (Tsai 2000; Bebelaar, Caplow, et al. 2003; Sack 2004). Several ethnographies of the adjudication of violence (Merry 1999; Santos 2004; Hautzinger 2007; Lazarus-Black 2007) also indicate that the institutionalization of feminist principles through a variety of actors (including women) may be accompanied by the loss of foundational critiques of gender essentialism and of substantive gender equity. Moreover, litigants themselves strategize *with* law (and change it), making legal reform projects inherently unstable.

This book is poised in that space of reckoning. It is a tribute to institution building from feminist social movements and a recognition of the effectiveness of feminist tools for theorizing questions of power and violence. But it is also an evaluation of the problems that arise as feminist legal reforms are put to work, in the inevitable gap between seeding a process and the ways "it might live in the world on terms not wholly—sometimes not even approximately— our own" (Wiegman 2012, 37). In Spivak's evocative phrase (2010), legal reform might be functioning simultaneously as "poison and medicine," as a putative mode of healing that generates secondary infections, symptomatic of a larger crisis of feminist institutionalization.

A related problem is the coding of gender in feminist legal reform. Calls for overturning discrimination are typically based on a model of "legal protection" (Bumiller 1987, 422), inscribing femininity in terms of victimhood, or incipient motherhood, or other gendered codes of nurturance and fragility (rape law, especially statutory rape, protective rules in the workplace that "guard" women's reproduction, and keeping women away from war are stark instances). But gendered protection is highly ambivalent, creating women as a subsidiary category of dependence/difference incompatible with equity and hence full subjectivity, the latter carrying greater burdens and responsibilities (Williams 1997). Women themselves may avoid law as a way to resist such ascriptions (Bumiller 1987). This book grapples with the deployment of a language of gendered vulnerability in laws related to marriage and family violence, and its effects on legal subjectivity. In the afterlife of feminist policies, we observe women and men, as strategic actors in law, using the victim category creatively to claim kinship and property, constructing its place in law and policy.

CONTEXTS: THE URBAN "FIELD"

At the heart of this book is my ethnographic fieldwork in settings related to Indian family law, domestic violence, and marriage mediation, most frequently at the two family courts in Kolkata. Typically, I attended a day's legal proceedings from one of the rear benches in the court, taking furtive notes when possible. I conducted two extended periods of fieldwork in 2001 and 2004–5, and have continued ongoing annual investigations since then. In this time, ten judges have come and gone in the Kolkata courts (some for a couple of turns), counselors have found other jobs or doggedly hung on, court personnel have shuffled only slightly, and most remarkably, litigants whose cases I saw signed and sealed have reappeared in the court corridors with fresh disputes.

In addition, I sat in regularly on "in-camera" hearings in the judges' chambers and their consultations with counselors. I sometimes followed court counselors as they went about their tasks for the court, visiting litigants' homes and workplaces to determine the veracity of their claims or persuade them to modulate their positions. I also conducted formal interviews with counselors and judges, though not litigants (who mostly speak in this book through their public utterances and a few moments of interaction).[21] Other criminal and quasi-legal venues related to family law that I observed during multiple day-long visits include the Women's Grievance Cell at the Kolkata Police Headquarters, a family assistance cell affiliated with a police station in a city adjacent to Kolkata, and a variety of nongovernmental organizations. Here too, I most often observed and took notes on the proceedings, interviewing mediators and activists. In extended research, I also conducted shorter bits of fieldwork in family courts and mediation groups related to family law in other parts of India (Mumbai, Pune, and Hyderabad) and outside India (the longest stretch was in Dhaka, depicted in chapter 3).

The legal encounters described in this book are drawn from my observational and interview archive of 297 cases in the Indian venues, 234 of these from sites in Kolkata. These include accounts of cases I observed as well as cases drawn from counselors' and judges' accounts. Some are brief hearings or petitions in court. Others are extensive, over several months, some over multiple years (such cases are assigned a unique number so as to be counted only once). No sessions were recordable, and even note writing in court is cause for great suspicion, so my observations are based on quick jottings in court, filled out in trips to the corridor and developed later that day into full field notes.[22] Pseudonyms (preserving gender, religious, and caste markers) are used for all interviews (other than those interviewed in specific public roles) and for case data, despite the public nature of the legal proceedings.

Most of the fieldwork presented in the following chapters is located in Kolkata and its surroundings, formerly known as Calcutta to the world (though Kolkata to its residents). Kolkata as a location is an overdetermined signifier, between the etic depiction of the city as a mythic embodiment of crowds, poverty, and misery[23] and the emic celebration of radical politics, film and the arts, and a fanatic devotion to the local.[24] In trying to depict the city through sites where cultures and classes intersect, I find Roy's (2003) dynamic portrayal of the city as a space of political and socioeconomic negotiations, beyond hegemonic *bhadralok* culture or the abjection of poverty, to be useful. The courts and police stations and offices and homes depicted in this book—spaces of everyday life—are a reminder that this city, like others, embodies many contradictions and coexistences. Its spaces include beautiful old buildings (such as the court itself), fancy megamalls, narrow lanes in the old city with houses grouped around common courtyards, and flats in new developments; varied forms of transportation, from subway trains to old Ambassador cabs, shiny new cars, huge lumbering minibuses, and hand-drawn rickshaws; areas of religious and linguistic concentration; a range of sartorial and culinary styles; passionate public cultures; and marginalized groups hidden to civil society.

The population of Kolkata accounts for about 4.91 percent of the population of West Bengal. According to the 2011 census, there has been a drop in absolute population and population density in the last decade,[25] but the concentration of urban living is nonetheless intense. The metropolis is recorded as being twenty-four times as dense as the average population density of the state (already the most densely populated state, according to the 2001 census). It is also useful to supplement this data with a recognition of invisible populations, such as people who live on the streets or in squatter colonies and hidden quarters of elite buildings, and "rural-urban fringes" that reflect "rural dispossession," "distress migration," and "urban liberalization" (Roy 2003, 10; Banerjee and Mukherjee 2005; Ray and Qayum 2009). Similarly, the low workforce participation rate for women of 18.3 percent in West Bengal (2001 census)[26] does not include the large population of daily female commuters and the associated "feminization of the urban labor market" (Roy 2003, 72), which constitutes the growing, primarily feminized, informal sector workforce (Banerjee and Mukherjee 2005). Formally, only those who live in Kolkata "proper" are entitled to seek the services of the courts (the family court's jurisdiction is for people with a residence roughly in the northwest quadrant of the city) and the Lalbazar central police station, but in fact, people regularly came to mediation organizations, courts, and police stations from close-by and even far-off areas, following kin or patronage networks or recommendations.

The institutions profiled in this book, from courts and police stations to legal aid and community governance, reflect both the national and local political economy. The large and complex Indian nation-state is a "state of contradictions" on many levels (Kaviraj 2003): postcolonial socialist development goals and over two decades of intense economic liberalization; ruthless state authoritarianism and accommodation to social movements and local parties; deeply systematized corruption and the option of radical social intervention through public interest litigation.[27] Its practices of governance pervade the book. But as will become evident, the specific nature of the local state (here the left political regime in West Bengal, positioned for the last three decades in opposition to the [changing] central government) is also critical to understanding the people and spaces in this book.

In May 2011, West Bengal experienced the first change of political regime in thirty-four years, when the Left Front coalition led by the Communist Party of India (Marxist) lost to the Trinamul Party. From the perspective of the old regime, this had been a period of "stable Left Front government" with extensive land reform (Bagchi 2005, 15), indexed by better-than-national numbers for literacy levels, rates of life expectancy at birth, infant mortality, even sex-ratio accounting for migration. Critics point to problems with economic development, deep-seated corruption, and bureaucracy. Scholars of development who have studied the long-term governance of West Bengal by the Left Front emphasize that stereotypical understandings of "communist states" do not work well in this context (Majumder 2010): while certain elements of Marxist rhetoric provided strategic political frameworks, the party also had to work through complex rural and urban constituencies, as well as local and national political coalitions and economic opportunity structures (Roy 2003, 12; Chakrabarty 2011). It bears emphasis here that the very subjectivities and structures under consideration—counselors, judges, mediators in the Left Front or among radical feminists, courts, police, indeed forms of desire and comportment—are constituted, whether in alliance or opposition, through the mobilization, patronage, and power of the ruling government.

The following tables provide a demographic framework of marriage.[28] Importantly, census figures do not reflect registered marriages (or divorces), but rather self-reported religious-social marriages. For example, marriages below the official age could not be registered marriages (in the 2001 census, 2.4 percent of girls below eighteen are recorded as married, as are 2.7 percent of boys below twenty-one).[29] The tables 2–4 strongly emphasize the social ubiquity of marriage: only 4.4 percent of women and 14.1 percent of men over twenty-one are not married (table 2). Despite much media excitement and anxiety around growing rates of divorce in India,[30] only 0.3 percent of the population nationally (0.4 percent of the population of Kolkata) is *formally* counted as divorced or separated, based on household reporting (tables 1 and 3); figures on de facto separations or divorces cannot be known. This

TABLE I   MARITAL STATUS IN INDIA (2001 CENSUS)

	Number of Persons	% of Population	Never Married	% of Population	Married	% of Population	Widowed	% of Population	Divorced or Separated	% of Population
Total Persons	1,028,610,328	100	512,567,639	49.8	468,593,016	45.5	44,018,648	4.3	3,331,025	0.3
Rural	742,490,639	72.1	370,531,390	36.0	336,894,950	32.7	32,580,523	3.2	2,483,776	0.2
Urban	286,119,689	27.8	142,136,249	13.8	131,698,066	12.8	11,438,125	1.1	847,249	0.08
Men	532,156,772	51.7	289,619,359	28.1	231,820,399	22.5	9,728,919	0.9	988,095	0.09
Rural Men	381,602,674	37	208,231,522	20.2	164,990.657	16	7,634,502	0.74	745,993	0.07
Urban Men	150,554,098	14.6	81,387,837	7.9	66,829,742	6.5	2,094,417	0.2	242,102	0.02
Women	496,453,556	48.2	223,048,280	21.7	236,772,617	23	34,289,729	3.3	2,342,930	0.2
Rural Women	360,887,965	35	162,299,868	15.8	171,904,293	16.7	24,946,021	2.4	1,737,783	0.16
Urban Women	135,565,591	13.2	60,748,412	5.9	64,868,324	6.3	9,343,708	0.9	605,147	0.05
Persons over 21	536,416,422	52.1	50,084,911	4.9	439,598,583	42.7	43,672,242	4.2	3,060,686	0.29
Men over 21	274,133,609	26.6	38,633,770	3.8	224,948,447	21.9	9,658,671	0.9	912,721	0.08
Women over 21	262,282,813	25.5	11,451,141	1.1	214,650,136	20.8	34,053,571	3.3	2,147,965	0.2

SOURCE: Ministry of Home Affairs, Government of India, "Marital Status by Age and Sex," *Census of India 2001*, www.censusindia.gov.in/Tables_Published/C-Series/c_series_tables_2001.aspx.

TABLE 2   MARITAL STATUS IN INDIA BY GENDER (2001 CENSUS)

	Number of Persons	Never Married	% of Total	Married	% of Total	Widowed	% of Total	Divorced or Separated	% of Total
Men	532,156,772	289,619,359	54.4	231,820,399	43.6	9,728,919	1.8	988,095	0.2
Men over 21	274,133,609	38,633,770	14.1	224,948,447	82.0	9,638,671	3.5	912,721	0.3
Women	496,453,556	223,048,280	44.9	236,772,617	47.7	34,289,729	6.9	2,342,930	0.4
Women over 21	262,282,813	11,451,141	4.4	214,650,136	81.8	34,033,571	13.0	2,147,965	0.8

SOURCE: Ministry of Home Affairs, Government of India, "Marital Status by Age and Sex," *Census of India 2001*, www.censusindia.gov.in/Tables_Publ shed/C-Series/c_series_tables_2001.aspx.

TABLE 3   MARITAL STATUS IN KOLKATA (2001 CENSUS)

	Number of persons	% of Population	Never Married	% of Population	Married	% of Population	Widowed	% of Population	Divorced or Separated	% of Population
Total Persons	4,572,876	100	2,084,959	45.6	2,248,288	49.2	220,779	4.8	18,840	0.4
Men (% of men)	2,500,040	54.7	1,236,140 (49.4)	27.0	1,219,904 (48.8)	26.7	37,856 (1.5)	0.8	6,140 (0.2)	0.1
Women (% of women)	2,072,836	45.3	848,829 (40.9)	18.6	1,028,384 (49.6)	22.5	182,923 (8.8)	4.0	12,700 (0.6)	0.3

SOURCE: Ministry of Home Affairs, Government of India, "Marital Status by Age and Sex," *Census of India 2001*, www.censusindia.gov.in/Tables_Published/C-Series/c_series_tables_2001.aspx.

translates to 0.2 percent of men and 0.4 percent of women being divorced (table 2).[31] Among households nationally, 0.5 percent are reported to have a divorced or separated household head (of whom 0.2 percent are men and 0.3 percent are women), in comparison to 83.5 percent of households having "currently married" male household heads and 2.8 percent households having "currently married" female household heads (table 4).

Of note here is the way the characteristics of women-headed households reveal the inequalities of income and property generated by marriage. Households are deemed to be women-headed when "a resident and functional male head" is absent, "due to widowhood, separation or disability" or due to "migration of male members of the household for long periods"; that is, in the logic of patrilineality, households are male-centered by default and women-headed only as exception. They constitute about 10 percent of households in West Bengal (10.3 percent nationally, as shown in table 4) and are a "particularly disadvantaged segment" economically (Banerjee and Mukherjee 2005, 24). Married women are rarely registered as heads of household; most women heads of household are divorced or widowed, which is correlated with a worse economic situation. Cases of abandonment or desertion or (unofficial) bigamy—an effective head of household status for married women—are not even counted in this number; such women are typically counted as "currently married," meaning the percentage of women-headed households is effectively far larger. Widowed and divorced women also far outnumber men in those categories (tables 2–4), indicating greater possibilities of remarriage for men.[32] The poverty of women-headed households underlines the fact that women are rendered destitute by the lack or failure of marriage: ideologies of conjugality along with labor-market and property inequities systematically produce economic and social dependency for widowed, deserted, and divorced women, as the following chapters will further show.

ORGANIZATION OF THE BOOK

The new legal frontiers of marriage in India, from mediation to family courts to police cells to rape prosecutions, structure the content of this book. Chapter 2 sets out the historical legacy of law and policy on marriage critical to understanding contemporary uses of law (those reading this book for ethnographic content may move ahead to chapter 3). Chapter 3 considers the methodologies for interpreting law and the ethnographic study of law involving

TABLE 4   MARITAL STATUS OF HEADS OF HOUSEHOLD IN INDIA (2001 CENSUS)

	Number of Households	% of Households	Never Married	% of Households	Currently Married	% of Households	Widowed	% of Households	Divorced or Separated	% of Households
Total Households	193,119,360	100	5,431,023	2.8	166,686,561	86.3	19,912,899	10.3	1,089,417	0.5
Male Head	173,131,502	89.6	4,741,076	2.5	161,277,063	83.5	6,694,621	3.5	418,742	0.2
Female Head	19,987,858	10.3	689,947	0.3	5,408,958	2.8	13,218,278	6.8	670,675	0.3
Rural Households										
Male Head	123,618,395	64.0	3,096,411	1.6	114,916,260	59.5	5,277,273	2.7	328,951	0.17
Female Head	13,876,365	7.2	434,521	0.2	3,919,876	2.0	9,029,973	4.7	491,995	0.2
Urban Households										
Male Head	49,512,607	25.6	1,644,665	0.8	46,360,803	24.0	1,417,348	0.7	89,791	0.04
Female Head	6,111,493	3.2	255426	0.1	1,489,082	0.8	4,188,305	2.2	178,680	0.09

SOURCE: Ministry of Home Affairs, Government of India, "Marital Status by Age and Sex," Census of India 2001, www.censusindia.gov.in/Tables_Published/C-Series/c_series_tables_2001.aspx.

language, body, and mediation. Chapters 4 and 5 delineate the role of state institutions in fashioning kinship and conjugality, and the emergence of new cultural and legal subjectivities. Chapters 6 and 7 focus on the use of nonstate institutions or varied state forums against the grain. But that is only one way of sorting the book. The theoretical and political questions at its core—law in negotiation, effects of alternative dispute resolution, structural crises of marriage, and the constitutive role of violence—are in conversation across the chapters.

Chapter 2 provides a history of the anxieties around divorce and family violence by focusing on four critical colonial and postcolonial moments: the Muslim Dissolution of Marriage Bill debates (1939), the Hindu Code Bill debates (1949), the report of the Committee on the Status of Women in India (1974), and the Family Courts Bill debates (1984). A prequel to the contemporary workings of law portrayed in later chapters, it also provides a methodological contrast in its use of legislative and policy documents. Marriage law becomes the ground of contestation for liberal reformers, conservative opposition, and emergent feminist groups, who negotiate issues of gendered protection, caste, religious progressiveness, and nationalism consonant with their identity and politics. While divorce and marital violence find greater acknowledgment over time, the economic entitlements of marriage are persistently ignored, affecting women's access to property resources.

Chapter 3 explores questions of method and legibility in studying law, comparing ethnographic fieldwork with adjudication processes in two family courts in Kolkata and Dhaka where litigants directly present their cases to judges. It addresses the partiality of identities and inadequate attempts to translate lives into law by reading silences and taboo topics such as body, sex, or violence. Cases involving sexual consummation within marriage and mediation as optimal resolution are used to demonstrate that the idea of efficiency that drives these processes erases the indeterminacies of the sexual body and the presence of violence.

Chapter 4 depicts everyday life in the "lawyerless" Kolkata Family Court, by way of evaluating the workings of "alternative" modes of justice. Litigants, judges, counselors, and lawyers depict this experiment in terms of new subjectivities and possibilities of action that allow for more intimate interactions and customized solutions. But fundamental change is difficult given the formal hierarchies of law. The governance of marriage is embedded in structural gender inequities, as demonstrated in the preference for reconciliation as the optimal end to marital trouble. Despite the claim that such courts facilitate clients telling their own stories, speaking out is difficult even for those with cultural capital, and more so for the economically marginalized. Women's organizations' conflict over lawyer-free spaces, over whether fierce lawyer advocates or efficient mediators serve women better, points to problems with institutionalizing feminist legal reform.

Chapter 5 is a portrait of contemporary marriage in Kolkata, based on complaints brought to courts and counselors. New forms of kinship are created in court, even as the breakdown of kinship systems is diagnosed. The chapter maps optimal and dysfunctional conjugalities through the prevalent tension staged between the patrilocal joint family and modern companionate marriage, in conflicts over space, resources, and affective advantage. It tracks two forms of gendered embodiment in legal claims that express the conflict over generational distribution of resources: the disabled mind (or putative mental illness) of women and the able body (or the potential earning capacity) of men. The disavowal of mentally ill women by kin and the elaborate runarounds for small, irregular alimony highlight women's lack of access to both natal or matrimonial property, and thus their impoverishment and vulnerability.

Chapters 6 and 7 explore off-label uses of rape law and domestic violence law to solve issues of property and marriage. They trace the traffic between criminal laws on gendered violence and the economic and social entitlements of marriage available through civil law. In chapter 6, rape charges brought against men who refuse to turn sex into marriage despite earlier promises, offers of marriage from rapists to remedy violence, and rape charges filed against eloping partners to control exogamous marriage choice are three genealogically related scenarios that illustrate rape to be considered primarily a crime against kinship rather than a violation of bodily integrity. The harm appears to lie in closing off marriage to women, making sex largely a transactional resource that provides access to the material benefits of marriage, with consent irrelevant. These scenarios indicate the need to understand rape in terms of economies of alliance and property, and to critique protectionist laws that work to restore the patriarchal kinship order.

Chapter 7 evaluates legal pluralism by focusing on the criminal prosecution of domestic violence (S498A) alongside civil remedies and mediation. It follows litigants through formal and informal forums, including a Women's Grievance Cell run by the police, a state-sanctioned arbitration board, a politically influential nongovernmental organization, and an independent feminist organization. These sites allow people to both bypass and leverage family court maintenance settlements by raising the threat of criminal prosecution. However, S498A allegations meet with widespread cynicism, and the use of simultaneous venues is a delicate process fraught with confusion, contradictions, and failures. Across a range of political positions and institutional priorities, interventions end up supporting similar options: claims of violence are most often dismissed as a criminal category in favor of negotiating reconciliation or monetary compensation in divorce.

Chapter 8, in conclusion, calls for attention to the ways in which law materializes. Post-1980s legal interventions have enabled new ways of engaging the state, but their institutionalization through a variety of agents has had complicated effects. Feminist reliance on ideas of feminine vulnerability and state protection, and on marriage as the optimal socioeconomic harbor, have failed to fully imagine women as economic and sexual actors.

CHAPTER 2

Construction Zones

Marriage Law in Formation

"Nanny": *Rat din aurat ki azadi, mardon ka zulm, iske bina aur bhi kuch ata hai kya tumlogko? . . . Sabke sab Angrez ho gaye hain!* [Day and night, it's just "women's liberation, men's oppression." Isn't there anything else you all know? . . . Everyone has just become English/foreign!]

—*Mr. & Mrs. 55*, dir. Guru Dutt (1955)

Guru Dutt's engaging (and deeply antifeminist) film *Mr. & Mrs. 55* dramatizes the disaster brought upon the new postcolonial Indian state by feminist groups and their attempts to reshape family law. The "55" of the title invokes the Hindu Marriage Act (HMA) of 1955, provocatively called the "divorce bill" in the movie (though Muslim divorce laws in fact led the way in 1939). The HMA enacted a broad set of reforms for Hindus, mandating monogamy, specifying alimony, and enumerating grounds for divorce. In the film, a romantic couple triumphs against a feminist plot and successfully establishes that conjugality is about women's loving submission, beyond material considerations. The couple prevails against organized feminists, who are seen to equate marriage with slavery and view women's access to property as the path to relief from marriage. "If happiness with tasks in the home and keeping your husband happy [*ghar ke kam kaz me sukh pana, gharwalon ko khushi rakhna*] is slavery [*ghulami*], then I will take on that slavery a hundred times. The slavery that involves love between a husband and wife is far better than one's own independence," the educated, wealthy heroine declares at the end, ending her divorce case. The movie hammers the point that feminist policy demands were launched by elite Westernized subjects out of touch with the sensibilities of "real women," in contrast both to the simple village wife who revels in childbearing and doesn't mind occasional violence and to superficial feminist delegates who discuss the merits of face creams in the back row as fiery committee speeches wash over them.[1]

This straw feminist is a familiar figure throughout this book, the frequent focal point of anxieties about transgressions of culture and tradition involved in legal reform.[2] In this chapter, we follow these anxieties across four allegedly "radical" legislative and policy interventions in divorce that critically shape family law in India. This chapter thus serves as a prequel to later chapters, which present the legacies of these interventions. The contrast is methodological as well as temporal: this chapter presents a discursive analysis of policy and legislative debates, compared to the ethnographic method of the others. These four key moments, in chronological order, are the (pre-independence) Muslim Dissolution of Marriage Act (1939), the Hindu Code Bill debates in the 1950s, the 1974 Report of the Committee on the Status of Women in India, and the 1984 Lok Sabha debates around the Family Courts Bill.[3]

This chapter focuses on the construction of law in an effort to delineate who speaks in the name of gender, the transformations they seek to effect, and the gender ideologies at the heart of family law. Gendered rights often serve as the ground of debate for norms of religion, region, caste, and class, expressed by people both within and outside the identity groups they argue for. In conceptualizing modes of cultural and political engagement, Stuart Hall (1993) suggests the framework of "encoding/decoding" discourses: after an (artistic, media, political) text is put in place (encoded), it is read (decoded) not as a unitary document with fixed meaning but as a pliable space to which readers/users bring their own perspectives, agendas, and needs. Per Hall's model, this chapter falls neatly in the domain of "encoding" family law in its focus on legislation and policy, whereas later chapters portray forms of "decoding" through use and interpretation. The life of the law lies between reforms and their deployment. Or, as Veena Das (1996, 2412) puts it, this chapter deals with grammar (equivalent to "judicial grammar without content"), while the others are analyses of meaning/"semanticity" (adjudications provide "content" and "verification" to "judicial grammar"). However, we will see that contested meanings and conflicting agendas around political and cultural capital saturate debates of law and policy. That is, lawmaking involves both encoding and decoding, and grammar is inseparable from semantic significance.

In India, family law falls under the system of personal law,[4] according to which provisions for divorce, adoption, maintenance, custody, guardianship, and inheritance vary depending on one's religion (in some cases, on proving one belonging to a certain religion Basu 1999). There are separate codes for Hindus (Buddhists, Jains, and Sikhs are counted in this category), Muslims, Christians, and Zoroastrians, and a separate nonreligious act to govern inter-religious and other secular marriages, the Special Marriage Act (1954). The colonial claim that personal law was launched to demonstrate noninterference in "personal matters" (Williams 2006, 6) is dubious, given that the laws intro-duced broad codification, homogenization, and suppression of nonhegemonic practices within religions, in a process Spivak dubs "epistemic violence" (1988; see also Merry 1991, 897, on colonial invention of customary law; Williams 2006, 7). In fact, personal laws are closely tied to other categories of criminal, land, and commercial law (Williams 2006, 43).

Scholars such as Lata Mani (1990) and Janaki Nair (1996) have argued that women's interests were both foregrounded and systematically subverted in the colonial period. While women as victims were always good to talk "with" for making interventions (widow immolation and widow remarriage being the most spectacular colonial examples), their gains were ambivalent. This mode of arguing "with" the interests of women and religious minorities con-tinued in the postcolonial era, further worsening some hierarchies (Williams 2006, 53). Postcolonial reforms in the name of gender justice might be seen at best as "a modestly modernist strategy of making nation and family," using "idioms of modernization and national integration" drawn both from West-ern political theorists and Indian traditions (Subramanian 2010, 773). Family law has the dubious distinction of being the site of the greatest disagreement and compromise in this process (776), as postcolonial identity politics and democratic space were constituted *through* these claims: "Hindu nationalists defined the issue [of personal law] in terms of nationalism, Congress and religious minority groups defined it in terms of religious rights, minority rights and multiculturalism, and women's rights groups defined it in terms of gender" (Williams 2006, 56). Feminist scholars have pointed out that notwithstanding the rhetoric of social justice, there has been a steady consolidation of hege-monic high-caste Hindu male power through sustained compromises (Para-shar 1992; Agnes 1999), with placatory gestures to powerful interests in minority communities "supersed[ing] the rights of women and children" (Agnes 2005, 115).[5]

In thinking of the "political field" of family law in terms of "actors such as the state, political parties and social movement organizations, who are connected to each other in both friendly and antagonistic ways" (Ray 1999, 8), it is evident that the negotiation of "women's rights" occurs between state and nonstate actors from a variety of political positions. Proposals to institute divorce or property rights are treated by some influential social groups as cultural affronts—as outrageous overstepping and betrayal of national identity—although one might surmise that some shrill cultural claims deflect deeper concerns with asset distribution or religious hegemony. Divorce is variously represented as a preferred aspect of a liberal polity, a necessary part of a modernizing postcolonial nation, and contrarily, as a regrettable intrusion into traditional harmonies and a portent of economic and cultural collapse.

Similarly, marriage is depicted as a pillar of nationalist stability, a necessary refuge, or an incipient site of violence. "Protection of women," which looms large as the ground of debate, carries a range of valences: protecting women *from* change, protecting women *through* marriage, protecting women against violence *within* marriage, protecting women *from* coerced marriage, or protecting certain women from *other* women's modernizing whims. A prominent anxiety worked out through these frameworks of protection is that of maintaining religious pluralism in a robust democracy, especially negotiating the extent of autonomy in marriage for religious minorities and castes. Social inequalities of class, especially rural poverty represented through symbols of simple naïveté, are another dominant trope of protection. Gendered entitlements in marriage are constituted through these negotiations, with marital dissolution as a site for working out identity, rights, property, and nation.

MODELING DIVORCE FOR WOMEN: THE MUSLIM DISSOLUTION OF MARRIAGE BILL DEBATES (1939)

The pre-independence Muslim Dissolution of Marriage Act (MDM) has long been rhetorically invoked as the gold standard of Indian women's legal reform and "the last progressive legislation pertaining to Muslim women" (Jain 2005, 213). The debate around the bill provides a reminder that in contrast to the potentially regressive economic provisions envisaged in the Muslim Women's (Protection of Rights on Divorce) Act (1986), it led the way on divorce reform for all Indian women. Instituted at a delicate national point of negotiating religious multiculturalism in an emergent plural democratic state, the 1939 bill was the second of two[6] to set uniform national standards for Muslims and move past differences of custom and sect. During the MDM debates, a number of Muslim legislators from a variety of political and religious positions, as well as many Hindu legislators, including a lone woman, primarily discussed religio-legal authority, religious differences within marriage, and age of consent. But while the remediation of women's plight dominated as a trope, women's economic rights in marriage were conspicuously unaddressed, setting an unfortunate precedent.

The MDM bill was repeatedly cast as a modernizing move to benefit Muslim women, and eventually all Indian women. *Modernization* had at least two resonances here: enacting a progressive slate of Indian women's rights and bringing the rights of Indian Muslims in line with those in progressive Muslim nations. The former is best exemplified in a passionate speech by K. Radha Bai Subbarayan, the one woman legislator to speak during these debates:

> I rise with pleasure to support the motion . . . as I feel that this Bill recognises the principle of equality between men and women with regard to marital rights. . . . It was heartening, most heartening, to me, Sir, that to see my Muslim colleagues condemn this state of affairs [Islamic laws being ignored to the disadvantage of women] and advocate that justice should be done to women and that women should have the right to claim divorce on the same terms as men. May I express the hope, Sir, that my Honorable friends on my left will continue to be guided by this sense of fairness and justice with regard to all matters affecting women that may come before this House.[7]

Subbarayan here explicitly recognized this bill as the putative first step of legal reform for Indian women. She foregrounded her gender identity ("a woman who understands women"), praising the bill because it "definitely raises the status of women and recognizes their individuality" (881–82). But she also identified herself as a non-Muslim who hoped to benefit from the momentum of reform, describing it as a "good beginning in the matter of reform of marriage rights" that "recognizes urgency of the need to amend our existing laws to meet modern conditions," making a hopeful pitch for "one common national law for personal affairs"(881–82). Here MDM was hailed in terms of its progressive potential for all Indian women.

Subbarayan's enthusiasm was promptly subverted by a sarcastic response from the law member of the Governor General's Council (the colonial state's representative to the legislature), Sir Nripendra Sircar. He described her as "treading dangerous ground" and framed his retort sardonically as that of "a mere man" identifying a logical assumption "in spite of the equality between man and woman" (882). If reform of Muslim marriage involved going back to the original seventh-century norm, he asked, would Hindu women be willing to return to marriage norms from four thousand years ago?

> I do not know how Mrs. Subbarayan would like it if I took my stand on the Hindu Sastras and said, "Don't move. We were there four thousand years ago, and we must not move. We have only got to find out what was laid down four thousand years ago." That will be the logical conclusion of the argument that has found favor with Mrs. Subbarayan. I think there is a very short way out of the difficulty of Hindu women. Surely, if they become Muslims, they can take advantage of this law [notes indicate "laughter" in the assembly], and in order that there may be an even handed measure and to get the full benefit of this law, I should advise the lady to see that her beloved spouse is also converted. (883)

This was a masterful put-down on multiple levels, signaling simultaneously the foolhardiness of such claims to justice, condescension at backward-looking reform, and mockery of the female legislator. Sircar emphasized the irony that the "modernity" being celebrated was a return to original intent, and hence a conservative move by definition, the implied contrast being with the forward trajectory of colonial governance. Skepticism was directed toward the political claim that optimal Muslim modernity lay in the original Qur'an, which had been corrupted in practice, and the danger in such an argument was exposed by analogy with the specter of a return to Hindu texts.[8] In the context of a law designed to prevent Muslim women's religious conversion, his audacious suggestion that a Hindu woman could convert to Islam just to embrace the "progressive" law offered a barbed reminder both of the abysmal state of Muslim law that brought the matter to legal attention and of the forms of loss inculcated in conversion. The suggestion that her husband convert similarly raised the specter of changing religion (especially of Hindus converting to Islam in a moment of politically charged religiosity), while evoking the figure of the out-of-place woman on the floor of the legislature, in a topsy-turvy world where she could get her husband to change religion at her bidding. The imagined chaos of legal reform and the dire consequences of happy naïveté converge in his sarcasm.

Modernization, as Sircar's jibe correctly identified, was repeatedly defined (almost entirely by Muslim legislators, in line with globally popular renditions of Islamic modernism) through the contradiction of being simultaneously a proper *return* to Qur'anic values and an end to retrograde and diverse local customs corrupting such values. Abdul Qayim referred to MDM and the 1933 Shariat Act as an "outcome of the great awakening that has taken place in the

Mahomedan [Muslim] community in India," claiming that "the more enlightened section of the community believe that a time has come when a serious attempt should be made to restore all the rights which were granted by the Koran to Muslim women so as to put them on terms of absolute equality with men" (621). Similarly, Muhammad Yamin Khan argued for using the Hadis and Qur'an texts to give women a "say in all matters including repudiating marriage by her father" (630). However, he depicted himself as representing the very opposite of Qayim's "enlightened section of the community," in speaking for the many uneducated Muslim women who were not in the assembly but could be present in much greater numbers with improved education. Khan also contended that the bill was a model for other religions and indeed nations—"as much advanced as you will find in any other advanced and progressive country" (886), reiterating that Muslim law would show the way for other Indian religions and be on par with global reforms.

A significant goal of reform was the need to supersede uneven local customs by emphasizing the gender equity of Qur'anic precepts. Muslim personal law was asserted to have primacy over local custom (depicted as regressive), as a way to claim a purer and more progressive Islam at the core of Indian Muslim identity. This bill followed a number of local laws making agricultural property conform to Muslim personal law, prevailing over custom, which completely disinherited women. Momentum built up for comprehensive national reform, with Muslim women's organizations collaborating with community leaders (Suneetha 2012), resulting in the MDM and the Shariat Act (1937), which reformed divorce and inheritance, respectively, for women. But while these laws provided de jure advantages to Muslim women, their reliance on religious texts as a technique of modernization (rather than relying on alternative traditions of argumentation or adaptation to contemporary practices) established a precedent for Qur'anic interpretation (and not considerations of gender equity) as the touchstone of reform. The turmoil around the Muslim Women's Act (1986) most obviously illustrates the troubled legacy of this perspective (Agnes 1999; Basu 2003).

The MDM debates cite the need to protect women both by enabling women's divorce—in contrast to men, who had a broad and almost arbitrary right—and in preventing women from converting out of Islam merely to get out of bad marriages. Williams argues that while specifying divorce provisions was the manifest motivation for the bill, the primary concern lay with the putative threat of conversion (2006, 84–86). Anxieties about the survival of religious minorities and "losing" women to conversion were thus prominent. Other discussions during the debate also demonstrated acute anxiety over waning patriarchal control, such as women's right to "repudiate" marriage upon puberty (that is, to withdraw consent at adulthood and challenge a father's authority) and whether such repudiation could happen after consummation of marriage, as well as the terms of desertion, apostasy, impotence, and "moral turpitude" in divorce claims.

Critically, the act left open the question of financial support for divorcing women. The debate involved long discussions about grounds of divorce and the mechanisms of maintenance payments but nothing on the distribution of marital resources upon divorce. "Ancillary relief" (in line with matrimonial provisions from English law, which the grounds of divorce drew upon) was not specified. Flavia Agnes speculates that this may have been a result of Muslim women's superior rights to property compared to women of other religions at that point (following the Shariat Act of 1937). Muslim women may also bypass formal law to make other arrangements using *Khul* (a form of woman-initiated divorce) in Qazi's courts, but as Vatuk (2008) demonstrates, the move almost invariably weakens women's economic position; it can, however, be useful to elite women and provides a way out in desperate situations. Judges are able to give larger maintenance awards to Muslim women following the *Danial Latifi vs. Union of India* (2001) challenge, but inequalities in provisions still hamper Muslim women compared to women of other Indian religions (Basu 2008; Agnes 2012). Moreover, because Muslim women have a substantial gap in access to resources and education (Hasan and Menon 2004), these legal differences have a socioeconomically disproportionate negative effect.

The MDM debates presaged later legislation on family law on a number of registers: anxieties around family, property, and authority; religious identities at the core of marriage entitlements; expanded grounds of divorce with murky economic resolution; easier divorce as a marker of modernity alongside regret at its ease. These themes resonate with other nations' attempts in the nineteenth and twentieth centuries to institute women's rights in marriage and property while considering their place within religious traditions (Smith 2000). I end here with M.S. Aney's long speech during the debates to provide a sense of the tensions in constructing a "progressive marriage law":

> As far as I understand the progressive marriage law, it should be a law that would make the married life of the couple happier, longer and lasting to the end of the

lives of both. Whenever we find a newly married couple approaching us, at least the Hindu way of giving them blessings is that "May you always live a married life and may you be happy with each other as husband and wife to the end of your life." But it appears now that no marriage can be good or happy unless facilities are given to the couple at the same time to put an end to it in their lives as many times as they choose. So, the creation of opportunities for ending the marriage is a sine qua non for looking upon it as a happy or progressive marriage. These are the ways or the directions to which the ideas of people are moving and judged by that this House must congratulate itself upon having produced a very progressive measure. (888–89)

The inherent contradictions of a "progressive marriage law" are precisely captured here. Calls for greater justice and dignity for women, for clearer adjudication and easier access to law, are grounded in challenges to familial and religious authority. The triumph around women being able to take advantage of more laws therefore means a transformation in harmony and happiness. Because change happens primarily through legislators such as Aney, these regrets are never quite erased from the fabric of "progressive marriage law."

"AN ATOM BOMB ON HINDU SOCIETY": THE HINDU CODE BILL DEBATES (1949)

The extensive reform of Hindu law in the immediate postcolonial moment magnified the anxieties around religion, class, and caste in the new nation, hence around political hegemony, resource distribution, and cultural identity. The Constituent Assembly debates on the Hindu Code Bill (HCB),[9] a deeply foundational project for Prime Minister Nehru and Law Minister Ambedkar (Williams 2006, 105), provide a passionate record of these negotiations.[10] The Constituent Assembly had voted positively on "principles of equality [including gender] and absence of discrimination between the sexes" (Som 1994, 170), and it might have been expected that ensuing legislation would adhere to these principles, but legislators' reactions to the draft Hindu Code Bill demonstrate otherwise. As in debates over the MDM bill, legislators claimed to speak for women during the HCB debates. Again, Hindu women's economic rights in marriage and family were underemphasized,[11] making the legislation ambivalent for gender justice.

Prime Minister Nehru, whom Som describes as deeply committed to women's equality, considered the bill critical but underplayed its radical connotations, portraying it as "a very moderate measure of social reform . . . indeed very largely a codification of the existent law." He depicted it as part of his "larger perspective of all-round national development," as social reform parallel to the five-year plans for economic development (Som 1994, 167, 181). Law Minister Ambedkar primarily emphasized the bill's goal of uniformity: "To codify the rules of Hindu law which are scattered in innumerable decisions" (Som 1994, 171). To Ambedkar, the bill also had an explicit, incendiary goal of social reform as a direct hit at upper-caste Hindu patriarchy: "The codification had a dual purpose: first, to elevate the rights and status of Hindu women; second to do away with disparities and divisions of caste" (Guha 2007, 235). This purpose was consonant with his public stance that the modern state needed to transcend the omnipresence of religion, "in order to reform our social system, which is so full of inequities, so full of inequalities, discriminations and other things, which conflict with our fundamental rights" (234). Liberal political visions of equality across gender, caste, and religion were thus front and center for the principal framers of the bill.

A range of groups rose vociferously against the proposed changes; these included conservative hard-liners and Hindu fundamentalists within Nehru's own Congress Party, other religiously oriented groups such as the Hindu Mahasabha, Sikhs who objected to the homogenization of Sikhism under "Hindu" law, and Muslim legislators who forecast doom in the imminent breakup of the family (Som 1994, 172–73). Hegemonic Hindu groups[12] claimed that marriage law was divinely granted based on the Dharmashastra texts; thus they depicted Hindu law as unchangeable, parallel to other religions based on single sacred originary texts. The Mahasabha found the legal proposals to be "radical departures from the main body of Hindu law" (Guha 2007, 236), asserting that the changes would bring about a godless society and rampant incest, in which "wives would marry sons and sons marry daughters" (Som 1994, 174, 179). Constituent Assembly President Rajendra Prasad complained to Nehru that the changes would "impose the 'progressive ideas' of a 'microscopic minority' on the 'Hindu community as a whole.'" Swami Karpatri implied that Ambedkar's caste did not entitle him to intervene in matters to be decided by priestly authorities among high-caste Brahmins. In a Rashtriya Swayamsevak Sangh (RSS)[13] rally, the bill was compared to an "Atom Bomb on Hindu society," and to the colonial Rowlatt Act, which drastically curtailed freedom of movement (Guha 2007, 238).

Divorce was one of the most explosive points of ideological confrontation.[14] Ambedkar launched the issue with a brilliant rhetorical strategy that preempted predictable outrage about the violation of custom and the longevity of Hindu practices. Well known for his lower-caste identity and his critique of caste hegemony, he placed caste practices squarely at the center of his provocation. He audaciously queried where the norm of the Hindu majority lay: "Coming to the question of divorce, there again I should like to submit to the House that this [divorce] is in no way an innovation. Everybody in this House knows that communities which are called Shudra have customary divorce, and what is the total of what we call Shudra? . . . practically 90 percent of the total population of the Hindus."[15] The comment was both a reminder of and a rebuke to the way Hinduism had been represented in terms of upper-caste interests. Ambedkar propounded that because Shudras (the lowest caste in a fourfold caste scheme, widely seen as a pejorative term) constituted the majority of Hindus, Shudra practice ought to be the norm around which Hindu law was constructed.[16] Ambedkar's social position can be seen at its greatest divergence from (the upper-caste) Nehru here, with Ambedkar stressing "the static quality of Hindu society" and the need for change through law, and Nehru rhetorically emphasizing Hinduism's "dynamism" and capacity for change (Som 1994, 187).

Ambedkar's frame of caste set up a debate where the typical contours of power were reversed. Ambedkar described himself as conservative, a proponent of slow change, of not doing nearly enough. Legislators who argued for preserving the status quo claimed the identities "radical," "revolutionary," and "conservative" in deeply ironic ways, preceding their opposition with lengthy support for women's causes and castigating Ambedkar for being insufficiently radical.[17] Govinda Das turned the challenge back on Ambedkar, alleging that the legislation ought to reflect actual Shudra practices of divorce (though this itself would be vastly diverse), rather than imposing a strange Western form, in effect calling Ambedkar's bluff on "custom." There were objections that practices of divorce prevalent in southern Indian states were being imposed on the northern ones (Som 1994, 180), in a regional riff on the majority/minority argument. Most ironically, conservatives spoke the language of minority rights, as when Maitra objected to the law of the majority being imposed on the 10 percent (of high-caste people) who believed divorce to be repugnant within Hinduism.

With the gauntlet of caste privilege thrown down, justifications of Hindu practice reached creatively beyond the usual rationales that divorce was proscribed for upper castes and that marriage was an indissoluble sacrament

(Subramanian 2010, 790). V.S. Sarvate spoke of Hinduism as prescribing restraint on enjoyment; divorce connoted the pursuit of unfettered enjoyment, and thus a ban on divorce would further the greater good. Preserving tradition was promoted as a mark of postcolonial distinction on behalf of the entire Hindu community, the diversity of caste and gender interests notwithstanding. A dominant protest was that the interests of the many who had agricultural land were being overridden, and the benefits of polygyny or the joint family were being ignored. In counterpoint to "permissive lines and sins of the western society" and "westernized women" as "social butterflies" (Som 1994, 175, 179), Lakshmi Kanta Maitra used the mythological example of Shakuntala,[18] citing her desire to be in her husband's home, even as a maid, as prototypical of the Hindu woman's blind devotion to conjugality. Advocates for divorce, on the other hand, invoked Islam as the progressive alternative that set the standard of fairness for Hindu women, forecasting the threat of conversion if there was no reform, in a remarkable move to bring (high-caste) Hindu women's rights on a par with that of low-caste and Muslim women.

Support of divorce was tenuous, however, even among those who voted for it. H.V. Kamath suggested that "the policy should be that marriage becomes easy and divorce difficult" (Basu 2001, 106). H. Siddaveerappa proposed that divorce be discouraged, and that anyone filing for divorce be asked to live with the spouse for some time first (107). The utopian longing for marriage is vivid in Govinda Das's reluctant support: "I would submit that notwithstanding the fact that no 'Marriage Code' has so far been invented in the world which may be regarded as the panacea for the removal of all ills, still we have got to see that if the husband and wife cannot lead a harmonious life, they should be given the right of divorce."[19] Even strong supporters such as Sucheta Kripalani contrasted the HCB provisions with the specter of unfettered Western divorce: "We have not allowed any divorce on frivolous grounds as it has been in some parts of the Western world" (870). These comments, in their ambivalence toward "good" divorce, mirror Aney's wistful delineation of "progressive marriage law" during the MDM debates.

Legislators across a variety of ideological positions spoke in the name of "protecting women" but constructed very different categories of women in their pleas. A common accusation (exemplified by *Mr. & Mrs. 55*'s contrast between canny feminists and content wives who take violence in stride) was that the bill was championed by elite urban women, and masses of rural and illiterate women had little idea of its existence, let alone found anything in the reforms compatible with their worldviews. Thakur Das Bhargava referred to the legislation as aimed at "people on Marine Drive [an elite suburb of Bombay] and the palaces of Calcutta and Delhi." Lakshmi Kanta Maitra professed that he had "not much of love or liking for the lavender, lipstick and vanity bag variety," thereby identifying himself as representing non-Westernized women, specifically his "humble wife—married according to Hindu shastric rites—a simple, unsophisticated lady bred up and nurtured in the ideas of our Hindu homes."[20] The implications were that urban cosmopolitanism and fashionable femininity, allied with the notion of the rights-seeking subject, were inherently out of step with the solid values of women of the masses who would prefer to have no changes. The fact that many nonelite women's groups, in addition to elite women, were politically mobilized (Kumar 1993; Nair 1996; Sinha 1998; Sreenivas 2008) was ignored in these assertions, while the backgrounds of the elite male legislators were assumed to be neutral (Virdi 2004, 76, 85).

The next position is more complicated: it champions the HCB and supports women having independent economic resources to escape violence or live with dignity, but expresses profound anxiety about women's capacities and proclivities, and hence about ceding ground for change. B. Pattabhi Sitaramayya argued that all women should go on a "love strike" of noncooperation if any one woman was ill treated, but followed this up with an anecdote about a woman who objected to him interrupting her husband while he was beating her up. He joked, "I am in the habit of twitting my lady friends by asking them 'Why do you want a share? You are going to become the queens of another home,' but immediately added 'But that is not enough. It is not enough to be at the mercy of a husband.'"[21] These statements mark a benevolent patriarchal protection, sensitive to violence and destitution but unable to abjure specters of the threat to patriarchy posed by mercenary and contrary women, grasping yet simplistic, unable to determine their own best interests.

Similarly, Sitaramayya advocated for monogamy but promptly bemoaned that young people often did not know enough to respect the boundaries of marriage, with a highly generalized illustration that "educated girls have the habit of picking ready-made husbands who have already got a wife and five or six children." He appended a confusing example that emphasized women's shallow attitude to marriage rather than monogamy, narrating the story of a friend who asked his daughter, "Do you wish to marry so-and-so, who is handsome and good looking, is well educated, passed B.L., or is in the profession, is the son of a rich man and has an upstair house. And she said 'No, father, has he got no motor car and electric lights? If he has got a motor car and electric lights no matter to whom you give me in marriage I am willing to marry him" (360–63). Marriage is material calculation in both the father's and the daughter's visions, an investment in sustaining regimes of property and class. But the daughter's attitude, depicted as foolish preference for consumption goods over more tangible economic and social capital, is presented as dangerous. Yet again, urban fashion stands synecdochally for women's legal rights. Sitaramayya palpably struggles to advocate for legal reform on the grounds that it would mediate women's socioeconomic disadvantages, but is unable to fully convince himself of their ability to take advantage of these rights as citizen-subjects. This doublespeak is noteworthy as a dominant mode that marks women's subsequent engagement with economic entitlements.

Women legislators occupied a complicated position in the debates. Women's widespread involvement in the independence movement had spurred their interest in questions of female status, and many women legislators argued during the debates that the HCB was necessary but did not go far enough (Som 1994, 168, 174). They appended testimonials of their nationalist contributions to underline their worthiness in the postcolonial moment. Sucheta Kripalani, veteran political activist of the Quit India movement, close compatriot to Gandhi and member of the Drafting Committee for the new constitution (and later the first female chief minister of a state), argued that the Hindu Code Bill asked only for some long overdue equalization rather than unfair privilege, in deference to the women who had been men's companions in politics. Equity in citizenship, entailing labor and responsibility, she reminded the assembly, ought to be grounded in equitable distribution of assets: "If men and women are to work equally, if they are to function as equal citizens of the state, if they are to fulfill their obligations towards the state, how can we have such discriminatory rules in the matter of property rights of women?" Yet this claim was modified by drawing careful attention to women's loyalty and lack of greediness: "I want to tell my brothers that we women even when we pressed for our rights have never forgotten the greater good, the larger good. . . . Even in the new Constitution we have never pressed for separate rights for ourselves. We would have pressed for these if we did not think that they go against the benefit of the entire society."[22] Albeit indirectly, this claim too evokes selfish and mercenary "modern" women with foreign values who seek legal change, contrasted with Indian women dedicated to the nation. Women's "separate" rights are held up against "social" benefits, women's best interests depicted as lying in familial harmony. Given that Kripalani is arguing for a slate of economic rights including inheritance and alimony, this argument requires one to imagine that divorce and property division do not entail "separation," but merely an expansion for socially beneficial ends.

The HCB did not pass in the above form, but rather in 1955–56, as four separate bills with substantial modifications (Williams 2006, 104–6).[23] Monmayee Basu argues that the ambivalence around women's access to money and ease of divorce in the debates is reflected in the "peculiar conservatism" and "half-hearted endeavor" of the eventual Hindu Marriage Act, which was almost reactionary in being structured around the fault theory of divorce, the surest basis for high levels of conflict (2001, 118). A significant legacy, related to the nostalgia for marriage, was the emphasis on reconciliation attempts as the first step in divorce currently required by family courts. Another was the widespread opposition to gender-neutral alimony; the discussion of alimony had been treated with "outrage" by women legislators who feared it would be accompanied by tests of chastity. The notion of men claiming alimony had also been deemed insulting by many male legislators, and was alarming to women such as Sucheta Kripalani, who called it a "monstrous kind of equality" blind to women's economic situation (Som 1994, 177). Overall, the economic parameters that undergirded traditional marriages were placed under erasure. Marriage was represented as a fundamental, stable value that kept community and nation together. The slough of economic problems that prove devastating for women in divorce (most notably the lack of matrimonial property and recidivism in maintenance payments) thus remained unaddressed.

Divorce was a relatively small part of the whole HCB debate, which was dominated by anxieties around women inheriting family property. Hindu women's rights to family property remained all but token until 2005,[24] and they still have no rights to matrimonial property (other than *stridhan* or wedding gifts). Yet, as we will see in subsequent chapters, women's inheritance of natal or affinal property and their power to bequeath property—that is, questions of women's economic rights and money management—are of a critical piece with divorce, with the potential to transform Hindu women's dependence on marriage or the accommodation to violence to keep marriage intact.

The predominant anxiety in *Mr. & Mrs. 55* is that a propertied woman will not need to rely on marriage; as Virdi puts it, "The implicit threat that women with money pose is their lack of dependence on men" (2004, 81). The father of the heroine, Anita, is so troubled at this prospect that when he makes her his only heir, it is on condition that she marry before turning twenty-one, failing which the huge estate would go to an orphanage. Thus Anita would receive her inheritance only under the condition of being "protected" through marriage and husband. Casting the penurious hero as a putative recipient of alimony, the film demonizes alimony as an inhumane monetization of intimacy, while deflecting the fear that it will mean "having to pay for institutions men could enter and exit with complete immunity" (Virdi 2004, 77).

Ironically, this specter of the propertied woman was deployed during a period of women's growing disentitlement to gifts of family property. In the modern state, fathers' property gifts to daughters, previously believed to "signal a father's affection and indefinite moral obligation," were deemed legally invalid, and daughters' claims were cut off, marking a paradigmatic shift in "the connectedness between property and personhood" (Sturman 2005, 611, 635–36). Conjugal care, including women's property claims as wives, rose as a popular discourse, insistently invoked to "free" men from circuits of familial obligation into those of mercantile capital (Sreenivas 2008, 48). Conjugal responsibilities were thus depicted as being at the core of "modernity," enhancing men's individual access to property (and wives' access, but only *through* men), while daughters and widows steadily lost property. The question of Hindu divorce aptly indexes these anxieties in introducing the idea of women's access to resources when they are no longer wives, thereby challenging hegemonic Hindu privileges of property, caste, and class.

FEMINIST VOICES: THE *TOWARDS EQUALITY* REPORT (1974)

The impact of women's political activity, including the women's movement, is either barely visible or an object of vilification in the two far-reaching interventions into marriage and family discussed in the previous sections. Mobilization around gender equity became far more prominent in the postindependence decades, especially in the 1970s and 1980s, in no small part due to global feminist networks. *Towards Equality: Report of the Committee on the Status of Women in India* (CSWI 1974) emerged at this time as one of the most powerful and enduring compendia of Indian women's status, with collaboration among academics (including academic feminists), movement organizations, and the mandate and authority of the state. The document may be credited with formulating some of the most significant gender equity policy initiatives. Many of its most radical critiques of marriage and family, however, remain untranslated into policy or practice.

Towards Equality was specifically commissioned as a preparatory step to the UN Decade for Women (1976–85).[25] As the committee saw it, there were three main "dimensions and objectives":

a. To assess the impact of the constitutional, legal and administrative provisions on the social status of women, their education and employment particularly in the rural sector during the last two decades;
b. To examine the status of women in the changing social pattern;
c. To suggest remedial and other measures in the fields of law, education, employment, public policy, etc., which would enable women to play their full and proper role in building up the nation. (CSWI 1974, 1)

The committee combined scrutiny of scholarly material, surveys, reports from issue-centered task forces, regional visits, and interviews with key figures in generating the report. It was presented to both houses of Parliament in 1975 and resulted in a motion "to initiate a comprehensive programme of specific administrative and legislative measures aimed at removing, as far as possible, the economic and social injustices, disabilities and discriminations to which Indian women continued to be subjected" (Gopalan 2001, 2). The 2001 retrospective credits it with having effected a number of significant changes, including establishment of the National Human Rights Commission and the national and state Commissions for Women, the emphasis on women's development in the Sixth Five Year Plan, the proliferation of women's self-help groups, an increase in women's participation in local governance, and the flourishing women's movement (Gopalan 2001, 5).

Towards Equality typifies the political and ideological stances of women's movements of the 1970s and 1980s, in India and elsewhere. It foregrounded a socialist feminist stance (these days we might also say it foregrounds "intersectionality") in the way it paid equal attention to patriarchal structures and "caste, community and class," and to the effects of "modernisation, democratisation, development, urbanisation, industrialisation, etc."(CSWI 1974, 3). Reflecting emergent feminist imperatives to record women's contributions to production and reproduction as the first step to making concrete claims, it urged the creation of a database of information on women's lives, particularly for the most invisible and marginalized groups. It named categories of violence, critiqued the coalescence of family structure and economic policy in fomenting oppression, and recommended changes in law and policy, further typifying feminist analyses of the time.

Towards Equality asked for changes in law and development policy from the state, rather than diminishing the role of government. Its persuasion squarely drew on fundamental rights and freedoms, as well as "Directive Principles" of social welfare guaranteed by Indian constitutional mandates, underlining the *Indian* nature of the claims against putative charges of Western values (CSWI 1974, 1). It began with the guiding principle that "equality of women is necessary, not merely on the grounds of social justice, but as a basic condition for social, economic and political development of the nation." But it moved far beyond the customary liberal scope of claims to the state. It counted women's unpaid labor, promoted their public impact, and argued for shared division of labor. The document insisted that "marriage and motherhood should not become a disability in women's fulfilling their full and proper role in the task of national development," "the contribution made by an active housewife to the running and management of a family should be admitted as economically and socially productive and contributing to national savings and development," saying that "society owes a special responsibility to women because of their child-bearing function; safe bearing and rearing of children is an obligation that has to be shared by the mother, the father and society" (CSWI 1974, 8). *Towards Equality* was thus both an example of working within the state and trying to push against its norms.

Towards Equality identified women's economic dependence and their limited rights to property as significant factors in the matrix of women's subordination. Analysis of matrilineal and patrilineal descent, inheritance, and residence patterns was used to critique the problems generated by preference for sons, including literacy and health discrimination. Consonant with these approaches, the family was identified as the locus of women's subordination: "It is not the fact of patriliny by itself but its association with joint property, and joint household and certain rules and patterns of marriage which lead to greater constraints over women and affect their position in an adverse way" (CSWI 1974, 58). Some nonhegemonic practices (nuclear households among indigenous/"tribal" populations, or the lesser alienation of daughters among Muslim and Hindu groups, who customarily arrange marriages between kin) were presented as positive alternatives, in contrast to the harm caused by

(Hindu) ideologies, which emphasize daughter-in-laws' extreme subservience in patrilocal families.

These comparisons led to a strong recommendation to challenge the cultural sacredness of the extended family. The report recommended the nuclear family as facilitating women's empowerment: "A simple family allows greater scope for a woman to have less restricted roles and greater part in management and policy decisions. . . . Thus situated a woman has much greater initiative to have sustained contacts with her own kin, not only as prescribed by custom (and mainly on formal occasions) but on a basis of equality in which both mother as well as father are equally relevant for reckoning kinship ties" (61). Of note here are the qualifiers to this endorsement, acknowledging systemic problems of power and violence that foretell problems in marriage governance: "*Depending on the personalities of the couple and personal equation,* a woman can truly be the mistress of the house. *If she is educated and enlightened,* she acquires a personality and a dignity of her own" (1974, 61; emphases mine).

Divorce and matrimonial property were not explicitly discussed in the long section on marriage practices but featured significantly in two analytically foundational sections: a discussion on the harms of polygyny and a critique of dowry practices (which enumerated problems such as the accumulation of wealth by married women's affines and the economic devastation of women lacking financial support from husbands). Divorce was discussed primarily in the context of recommendations for parity or uniform provisions between personal laws and the addition of divorce by mutual consent across personal laws.[26] Related recommendations—such as parity in rights to guardianship between fathers and mothers, a uniform secular adoption law with gender parity, allowance for maintenance claims in all personal laws without a maximum, and a requirement that an economically independent woman maintain her dependent husband, children, or parents—represented women as significant actors in the public sphere, with economic entitlements and obligations. Several of these recommendations have found their way into law, including the extensive reform of Christian marriage law in 2001, restrictions on unilateral divorce by Muslim men, the Hindu Succession (Amendment) Act (2005), the Juvenile Justice Act (2000), which allows for adoption regardless of personal law, and the expansion of divorce by mutual consent into various personal laws. Other critical provisions remain unfulfilled, notably uniformity among religious communities, the expansion of wives' economic rights regardless of conduct, and wives' economic obligations.

Despite the relatively scant concern with divorce in *Towards Equality*, a marked departure from the 1950s conversations on marriage was the shift in emphasis from fault-based to mutual-consent divorce, consonant with the notion of women as empowered agents in public and private spheres. In place of the idea that marriage ought to be preserved if at all possible, the report envisaged the possibility that "two adults whose marriage has, in fact, broken down can get it dissolved honorably" (CSWI 1974, 123). Most significant to the scope of this book, family courts were proposed to expedite personal law matters in one consolidated space, based on the principle of conciliation rather than adversarial interaction. Japan, a modern Asian country with long-established mediation courts, and Indian indigenous dispute resolution were cited as precedents. The precedents signaled that family courts were both a continuation of tradition and a functional modern institution (CSWI 1974, 141). However, while *Towards Equality* contained an unambiguous critique of marriage and support for swift and dignified divorce, the word *conciliation*, used in recommending the nature of the courts, has been taken up later with increasing ambivalence to signify "reconciliation" as a goal of divorce courts, as explored in chapter 4.

Towards Equality is definitely an outlier in the trajectory of divorce legislation discussed in this chapter, not just because it is a unified policy document read against a number of legislative debates, or a research-heavy report that contrasts with the rhetorical flourishes of legislators light on evidence. Like the other documents, it claimed to speak for women, indeed was officially authorized to do so. Its "protection for women" was explicitly feminist: it aimed to place women at the center of national development, critiquing the structures of vulnerability that impeded equal participation. "Tradition" was the focus of *critique*, rather than the touchstone of women's sensibilities and practices, involving a reappraisal of women's place in the family, the workforce, and the nation. The report attended to diversity with a call for uniformity in personal laws, in contrast to the usual invocation to preserve religious and ethnic traditions that subordinate women in the name of religious pluralism. Examples of nonhegemonic practices were used to trouble the commonsensical value assigned to the oppressive practices of majority groups. Changes were framed with persistent reference to the reformist modern Indian state (in references to the constitution, UN participation, and development policies), deflecting common charges of foreign, Western imposition in the document. This is not to claim that the document reflected the sensibilities of "real" Indian women across regions, religions, and classes, but rather that it stands as a critical strategic document that embedded some insights of the women's movement within the state.

FINE-TUNING DIVORCE LEGISLATION: THE FAMILY COURTS BILL DEBATE (1984)

It was ten years before *Towards Equality*'s recommendation to institute family courts was debated in Parliament, under a Congress government in 1984. When the Family Courts Bill finally came to the floor, Law Minister Jagannath Kaushal called it a "progressive and in a way revolutionary measure"[27] that had been brought forward on the recommendations of the Joint Committee on the Dowry Prohibition Act and the Law Commission. He acknowledged that the measure was influenced by repeated requests for such courts from women's organizations and welfare organizations, in emulation of "advanced countries" like the United Kingdom, Australia, and Japan. Pressure was mounting to create a venue for "providing quicker settlement to the family disputes where emphasis should be laid on conciliation and achieving socially desirable results" (181). There are echoes of the *Towards Equality* report here in the references to other models and the double entendre of "conciliation." But no explanation is given of "socially desirable results," leaving open the question of whether facilitating or preventing divorce is the desirable social result. The ensuing Family Courts Bill debates demonstrate that notions of families as protective havens and of women as needing protection through marriage had not fallen away with the efflorescence of the women's movement. At best, divorce provisions and the acknowledgment of violence against women had become more acceptable. Debate anxieties focused primarily on modes of delivering optimal justice: on access to courts and their effectiveness.

Unlike previous legislative debates, and possibly because of agitation by the prominent women's movement, no one challenged either the need for legal divorce or the reality of women's economic suffering and vulnerability to violence; indeed, legislators frequently referred to these urgent priorities. Yet, in seeming contradiction, the family was persistently depicted as a utopian space of happiness, shelter, and safety, with courts as the very opposite, as in the following declarations by three women legislators. Jayanti Patnaik declared that "family is an institution that postulates the intimacy of the highest order" (203), and therefore that the philosophy of the family court ought to be "the desire to shield the family from the rough and tumble of ordinary judicial process." Usha Choudhry praised the government for the wondrous ("mahat-vapurn") provision that would protect women and children. Vidya Chennupati argued while there was ("we had") a "man made society" where women were in second place, disputes between husbands and wives were temporary and the "family system was strong," and thus family courts were needed. The confusion in Chennupati's logic might be said to arise from the need to valo-rize the family while acknowledging patriarchal relations, with courts seen to be mending superficial tears in a fundamentally strong fabric. These state-ments cast women as needing protection from both marriage as an institution and the state, and as inseparable from their association with children, with little problematization of power relations within the family. The courts that were to be imagined into being were, correspondingly, seen as a necessary evil.

In a related essentialization of gender, women's "natures" were evoked in terms of superior compassion and understanding. Although G.M. Banat-walla's plea that judges be of the same personal law (that is, of the same religion) as litigants found little support, numerous legislators recommended a prefer-ence for women judges. Women were discussed as being more approachable and more in tune with matters related to the family (their prominent role as perpetrators of violence in the extended family was, of course, absent from such representations). The woman judge could thus be a figure of authority, if relatively less authority, given the lesser judicial weight assigned to family matters in the legal hierarchy. These discussions were related to proposals to engage a broader pool of judges, by allowing social workers or other profes-sionals to function as family court judges.[28] There were also several recom-mendations that family courts become a space where "women's issues" could all be tackled in a consolidated venue, including bigamy, kidnapping, and particularly rape and dowry offenses. Here, *family* and *female* were assigned almost identical connotations, and *women's spheres* was conflated with *family*.

Opposition to the bill (even from supporters) was often organizational, pertaining to location, availability, and funding. Some legislators complained that the clause restricting family courts to cities with over a million in popula-tion deprived people in smaller towns and rural areas of access, suggesting alternative provisions such as mobile courts. Remarkable here is the exclusively urban character of the provision, given that the majority of the population was rural, and no less that the needs of rural women (connoted as simple and con-tent) were a recurrent discursive trope. Easy divorce would thus become the prerogative of the privileged urban woman evoked as the specter of trouble.

The most vocal opposition to the bill came from seemingly unexpected quarters, considering the introductory tribute to women's groups. Female legislators such as Susheela Gopalan and Pramila Dandavate, who were strongly identified with the women's movement and its requests to institute the courts, vehemently protested that the bill did too little too late. They complained that it had been circulated late in the day and the season, so that the ruling party could claim to have enacted the reforms before the elections, while not allowing sufficient time for discussion and ignoring many important recommendations of the Joint Committee. "You have taken women for granted" (99), Pramila Dandavate accused.

These legislators drew on their connections with women's organizations to look beyond families and marriage to the critical issue of violence. Susheela Gopalan cautioned that judges often had the same "feudal" attitudes toward women as the rest of the population, and thus that courts would not necessarily be progressive. She queried the vagueness in the bill's mandate "to preserve the institution of marriage and promote the welfare of children." Presciently pointing to the fuzziness of the word *conciliation*, she reminded people that parents often forced their daughters to continue to live in homes with discord and even violence: "Conciliation is good. You must try it. At the same time, separation is needed. . . . There must be provision for that. The girls who are being sent back to their in-law houses by force are being killed after some days in the in-law houses. . . . This is very dangerous" (192). Similarly, Geeta Mukherjee of the CPI (M)[29] (from a different party but a legislative ally on women's issues) also stringently criticized the belief that broken marriages were the worst sort of problem:

> The point is that our society has not yet come to a situation where the principal problem is that of marriages being torn asunder. . . . The most serious problem is the feudal inheritance. . . . That being the case, there are millions of families where the marriage institution is in the so-called protected condition but the woman is subjected to unsufferable dignity [sic] and thereby the entire institution of marriage is brought to a pass that sometimes it is really a sort of insult to us. . . . [I]n the society as it stands, it is the dignity of woman which is in the most jeopardized condition and thereby I would say really it is subverting the very institution of marriage. (219)

Reminiscent of *Towards Equality*'s critique of patrilocal marriage, this argument is in stark contrast to the ideology that marriage is fundamentally beneficial and divorce is a Band-Aid for the occasional incompatible marriage.

Here the problem is identified as a material one (perhaps consonant with the speaker's Marxist leanings), related to the indignities and disempowerment of brides that structure the dominant ideal of marriage. Marriage is foregrounded as a site of violence. Both legislators argue that courts are an insufficient panacea, if patriarchal control of resources and violence in marriage cannot be mended.

Gopalan and especially Pramila Dandavate also used their time on the floor to extensively discuss the problems of dowry violence, an emerging issue within the women's movement, trying to bring visibility to the recently passed Dowry Prohibition Act.[30] They made some final attempts to include dowry-related crimes under the aegis of the family courts. While their long testimonials about dowry often seem irrelevant, they signaled a critical preoccupation for women's movements of the time, which analyzed dowry-related violence as the graphic coalescence of domestic violence, preference for sons, and marginalization from family property (Basu 2005). Thus courts dealing with family troubles would inevitably have to contend with the money and violence at the heart of the problem.

The Family Courts Bill debates overwhelmingly addressed concerns with the geographical scope of the courts and people's access to them. While it was repeatedly described as a major reform on women's behalf, family was often represented in terms of haven and safety, even as dowry dominated the discourse, with the effect of highlighting women's suffering rather than women's agency in the public sphere. The rural woman was eclipsed entirely as a recipient of this legal innovation. While the influence of women's organizations was much more apparent than in previous debates, the circulated bill did not engage with the analysis of gendered inequities that lay at the root of the claims made by these organizations. The allegations of the legislators that the bill was a placatory and cynical attempt to play the woman card and thereby cast the state as beneficial, reminiscent of colonial maneuvers, seem noteworthy in that context.

CONCLUSION: LIVING LEGACIES

Numerous squabbles erupted toward the end of the long parliamentary session during which the Family Courts Act was passed in 1984, over whether the session should run overtime and whether the senior politician Madhu Dandavate would stay on as chair of the session. The often humorous Dandavate quipped,

"I am not a Judge of the family court." Somnath Chatterjee responded, "Let it be a family house." Domestic connotations of Parliament aside, this interlude captures one of the dominant metaphors through which the family, and by association family law and family courts, were visualized in legislative debates: the inevitability of conflict and commitment, the assumption that this conflict was connected to women's presence and interests, and the belief that law would prove troublesome and was avoidable. In these acts of transference, it was the court and not the family that became the site of conflict, the nostalgia being for the protection of family *from* court even as legislation was driven by the need for protection from *family* and the need *for* courts. The home, in contrast, was seen as informal and intimate, where occasional squabbles were resolved by a wise elder. The irony here is that Indian family courts were imagined to be a homelike space of mediation and conciliation, of divorce with minimal conflict.

The interlude above occurred in the shadow of discourses highlighting the contested nature of divorce: divorce was alternately visualized as a tool of women's empowerment, a panacea for their helpless situations, a revenge mechanism and privilege of elite women, or a measure of bureaucratic effi-ciency. Its contradictory representations included the benefits of saving women from bad marriages and the preservation of marriage as a utopian space. The selfish, manipulative, greedy woman (of the "lavender, lipstick and vanity bag" ilk or its updated variations) was all too often a straw figure, launching the fear of widespread abuse of process, with the potential to destabilize the social order, including the generational distribution of property. The "real woman" was invoked to justify a satisfied status quo, as part of pleas to prevent the vitiation of marriage through law.

Women's "protection" has been one of the critical sites for identity politics around religion since before independence, with interventions sought by Hindu majoritarian groups and (non)intervention by hegemonic cohorts within minority groups, while women's economic rights within marriage were ignored by both. Since the 1930s, even the staunchest defenders of "tradition" were unable to ignore the inevitable association of marriage with desertion, deprivation, and violence. The *Towards Equality* report and the women legis-lators' speeches during the Family Courts Act debates were critical here in drawing the lines between marriage, family structure, economic control, violence, and legal redress.

Yet feminist analyses of these power structures never displaced the sacrosanct status of marriage. Much of the legislative focus fell instead on managing divorce humanely, whether by expanding access or attending to maintenance payments and violence, none of which altered the valences of marriage. The existence of the family courts testifies to the role the women's movement played in determining the form of divorce, but it is the process-related recommendations that have endured rather the feminist critique that underlay them. The silence around distribution of economic assets within marriage and the nature of matrimonial property have proved to be formidable problems resulting from this ambivalence. Meanwhile, legislators' anxiety around the misuse of liberal marriage law, easy divorce as an instrument of wrecking culture, and marriage law as destructive of religious identity continue to resonate beyond the debates in everyday adjudication, as we will observe in the following chapters.

CHAPTER 3

Beyond Equivalence

On Reading and Speaking Law

Mukh khuley bolun, eta apnar mamla, amar noi. [(Open your mouth and) speak up—
this is your case, not mine.]

—Kolkata family court judge to male litigant

If you speak in law, who can hear you? If you don't speak, can you be heard at
all? In this chapter, we explore questions of legibility and method in law by
examining speech, expression, and the translation of categories in courts. Law
may only be one venue of cultural negotiation, but it is a preferred one because
of its regulatory power. Those who come to law are most effective when they
frame issues in terms of available remedies and sanctions and cite authorized
histories of precedent; emotion or life details are met with impatience as being
inefficient (Comaroff and Roberts 1981). Yet people routinely inhabit the law
by challenging these norms. They disrupt courtrooms and prelitigation meetings with emotional breakdowns and seemingly irrelevant histories, forcing
alternate reckonings (even if these are ultimately suppressed). They create
funny and poignant new linguistic registers, which then become part of everyday discourse. They seek to mark their desires and anxieties through law, no
matter how difficult it is to disturb law with unruliness.

This chapter is framed by the assumption that law is not merely about
packaging grievances efficiently, but also serves as a space for negotiations of
identity. In living within the "nomos" that Cover posits—a "normative universe" of "right and wrong, of lawful and unlawful, of valid and void"—people
narrate their lives through the logic of laws even though they rarely encounter
formal cases (Minow, Ryan, et al. 1992, 95–97). Thus legal guidelines become

signs with which to communicate (99). Similarly, Hirsch (relying here on Judith Butler and Michel Foucault) contends that law is a critical site of performance, that "people are constituted and constitute themselves as gendered subjects" through legal discourse (1998, 19). That is, people make themselves heard (within and mostly outside courtrooms) through changes enabled by laws, interacting actively with them in either compliant or resistant ways (see White 1990 for one evocative example). The resilience of norms is tested in these resistances; moments of agency are not impossible, but radical transformations are also unlikely.

It is critical to remember, in this and the following chapters, that performances in court, or in mediation sessions, or indeed in interviews, cannot simply be read off as truths or desires. They are necessarily framed by legal strategy, being ways to ensure optimal advantage structured by a speaker's economic and cultural capital; to echo Kidder, "I make no assumptions about the true state of people's meanings or their true 'voice.' Rather, I assume that their words and actions contain information about what they want the observer to think about them" (2002, 91).[1] However, if law is constitutive, as Hirsch suggests, then these legal encounters also themselves *generate* new subjectivities (Coutin 2002), with claims, identities, and appropriate affect shaped by perceptions of legal/moral being, by the nomos. In seeming violation of the feminist (and anthropological) methodological principle to assume that traumatic utterances are "true," it seems pointless to ask what is "genuine" and more useful to recognize that identity is based on "particular social locations and discursive frames" (Naples 2003, 167). This aligns with the postmodern understanding of culture as performative and of agency as contextually performed (Ramazanoglu and Holland 2002, 90).

In the following sections, we examine these processes of knowledge production and legibility, as well as attempts to exceed the meanings possible within law. These processes pertain to *legal* method, and its contiguity with the metadiscourse of *ethnographic* method in studying law. I track attempts at approximation among culture, language, and law on a number of levels: calibrating words against silence, finding literal equivalents in the multiple languages used in court, seeking ways to bring unsayable signifiers of body and sex into legal reckoning, and trying to translate violence and violation into financial compensation. Such attempts at translation and equivalence, necessarily incomplete, are used to better understand the language of law, and law as language.

I examine forms of reading and speaking in law through reflections on research methodologies, as well as ethnographic observation of two family courts in Kolkata and Dhaka where litigants directly present their cases to judges. These locations help us consider the methodological limits as well the productive possibilities of what can be revealed by ethnographic court observations. The two courts portrayed are both formal and informal legal institutions, with a mandate to use judges and mediators in alternative dispute resolution for more accessible, efficient, and customized disposal of cases, involving clients as active participants. I challenge the foundational claim that speaking in court equates to agency by looking successively at questions of silence, translation, agency, and violence. Mediation by judges, I argue, is not a more accurate or seamless rendering of grievances into law, but rather a form of disciplinary efficiency. In attempting to make sex and violence legible within legal discourse, judges fill the cultural silences around these topics with their own interpretations, often reducing questions of pain or violation to the pinch of the economic bottom line. The inadequacy of these attempts is laid bare by litigants' incomprehension and resistance.

LURKING IN COURT AS METHOD

Like many other women around the Kolkata Family Court, I sat on the hard wooden benches when there was a seat, day after day with little obvious purpose, with a bag full of notebook paper and other sundry fieldwork tools. "I've noticed you've been sitting here all day every day this week," a woman next to me said one day. "Your husband must really be giving you the runaround if you have had to turn up every day to get the maintenance money and he hasn't shown up." This has been my commonest fieldwork incarnation: sitting on the rear court bench, sharing despair and fragile hope, moments of camaraderie, and assorted bureaucratic scoldings with the other litigants.

Courtroom ethnography, a classic methodology of legal anthropology, was at the heart of my formulation of this project. I wanted to see law at work, to notice how people looked and behaved in legal settings, to understand the difference from the summaries of events I read in appellate cases or the case histories given by litigants or lawyers. Later sections of this chapter testify to the unique advantages of this method, such as better capturing the processes of creating a legal record or marking the erasure of affect in legal narrative. But I was also intensely aware of all that eluded this methodological choice, such as the ways that law and culture are fundamentally limited as diagnostic of each other.

Sitting in on a courtroom or a dispute resolution venue makes one feel comfortably proud of inhabiting a well-trodden disciplinary space: the observation of formal and informal legal venues. "Deep and thick ethnography" is seen as one of the best ways of capturing "the complexity of law and legal processes" (Starr and Goodale 2002, 8). "Trouble cases" are thought of as microcosms of legal-cultural systems, where "everyday practices" and disputes illuminate cultural understandings (Sarat, Constable, et al. 1998, 2); in this view, disputes are flash points where we see "a portion of a society's life in which tensions of the culture come into expression, in which the play of variant urges can be felt and seen, in which emergent power-patterns, emergent security-drives, religion, politics and personality, and cross-purposed views of justice tangle in the open" (Llewellyn and Hoebel 1941, 29). However, as this book posits, if we conceptualize law beyond the narrow focus on dispute settings and see it as broadly productive of cultural practices, then the focus on cases is narrow. The methodological challenge is to decide what to designate (or exclude) as legal culture.

Courtroom observations are also fundamentally limited as indexes of demographic information. What can we tell by looking (or hearing)? Class or social status, deduced through clothing or performance, is often adopted deliberately as a legal strategy—both in the sense of looking good for court and looking poor to avoid having to pay maintenance. Occupational and salary data are inconclusive, especially in the Indian context, where people often derive several times their stated income through informal sector remuneration (tutoring, piecework, bribes to government servants, and "black money" portions of business and real estate transactions all fall within this category). Caste is frequently ambiguous, explicit only for particular legal provisions. Reading off ethnicity or religious identity from the names of litigants is flawed, because it assumes that the person "is" Bengali or Gujarati or Nepali, Hindu or Muslim or Christian, based on name alone, ignoring that people may occupy multiple ethnic or religious categories, or belong to a less well-known religious or ethnic group.[2] The only way the issue comes up is when religion, caste, or ethnicity is deliberately evoked in court, or where specific personal laws are at issue.[3] Perhaps most importantly, demographic categories are problematic because they rely on a simplistic notion of identity derived from race or class or religion or gender, a form of tokenism that misses crosscutting identifications and conflicts across these categories, as well as people's own purposeful and strategic identifications (Ramazanoglu and Holland 2002, 111; Weston 2004, 201).

The richness of ethnographic participation as method, however, lies in the possibility of noticing the role of emotion, behavior, and cultural capital, of investigating nuances that may be invisible in more "managed" formats like interviews or written responses (Kritzer 2002, 153). Arguably, these are ineffable, subjective signals, posing difficulties for interpretation. As an observer, one is reading off legal strategies *from* performance rather than reporting what people say their motivations are or how their lawyers frame their cases (although these too are not the "truth" of a case in any superior way). The trade-off is that it is uniquely possible to mark the ways performative dimensions play a role in legal processes: we attend not just to what people say they are doing, but to how they present themselves and what that might mean in cultural context. The method is optimal for reading the legal "case" as a diagnostic of social conflicts and values, providing a sense of prevailing legal strategies as well as the impact of economic factors, media discourses, and evocations of custom (Friedman 2002, 189). The focus is not on the teleology of judgment but rather on the dynamics of the hearing.

Sitting on the hard court bench among litigants is a pretty comfortable role for the legal anthropologist cum feminist scholar, evoking illusions of "passing," listening in, participating affectively, all in the name of good method. As one of the most romantic fieldwork images, it elides dissonances of identity and location. The predominant dissonance is that of being the researcher, one from a foreign space at that, which often interrupted my illusions of having become one with court space. In one such disconcerting episode, I was "outed" as exemplar and stranger in an in-camera hearing, with the judge frustratedly breaking into the divorcing couple's heated squabble and pointing to me: "Is this behavior what you want her to take back to America? Do you know that everything you say is in her notes?" These two moments, of fading in and being singled out, are the poles of relative invisibility and marked overdetermination between which I moved while working in a "public" space.

Though I disclosed my role to those with whom I talked at any length and word spread to many others, many people assumed from my waiting presence that I was in court on business or that I was a journalist. More commonly, because they saw me talk to the counselors and judges, they thought I had something to do with the counselors and was present in official capacity; this posed a greater problem for both comfort and disclosure. In private hearings, when the judge or counselor sought permission for my presence, a lawyer or litigant would often explicitly ask for further details, usually provided along the lines of "she is doing research on the courts." Most uncomfortable were moments when I was too closely identified with the mediators based on my constant presence around them, such as when a father negotiating a maintenance settlement for his daughter suddenly turned to me at the far end of the table and sought my intervention in reasoning with the counselor. Unlike the bits of daily assistance I could easily render, by reading things out to people or pointing them to places, or even explaining court procedure and process, here I had to hastily demur by foregrounding my nonofficial status and my role as observer, sounding a discordant note in the delicate process.

During my previous fieldwork in Delhi, I had been keenly aware of the complexity of intersectional categories that confuse the question of whether one is an "insider" or "outsider" in the field (Behar 1993; Narayan 1993; Naples 2003).[4] In that case, being Indian was only a small piece of possible identities; language, ethnicity, class, age, marital/childbearing status, and studenthood forged varying levels of identification and disidentification with participants (Basu 1999, 17–20). In Kolkata, it could be argued that I was even less of an "outsider": I was a native speaker of Bangla, I had been raised primarily in the city and gone to school and college there, and I thought I knew my way around.

However, the very question of how "native" a "native anthropologist" must be (Narayan 1993), or what putative advantage this might provide, is an impossible determination (Visweswaran 1994; Wolf 1996, 15–18). Feminist analyses, critical in thinking through these myths of identity, have emphasized the methodological complications in being "skinfolk" but not necessarily "kinfolk," to use Brackette Williams's trenchant distinction (1996), while reminding us also of the value of researchers who may be kinfolk in their depth of connection and commitment even if they are not skinfolk (Narayan 1993). Scholars working in communities with which they have mixed cultural and demographic alliances, and particularly their strategic negotiations of identity depending on context,[5] have problematized the notion of a standpoint. The very notion of "insider" and "outsider" locations, Naples argues, is a false polarization because neither is a static identity; rather, "these are ever-shifting and permeable social locations that are differentially experienced and expressed by community members" (2003, 49).

In my case, there was a distinct ease to familiarity: some contacts were much easier to make using educational and familial kinship grids, and linguistic subtleties could be deliciously parsed with much greater skill. On the other hand, categories of identity like religion, sexuality, class, or nationality (NRI, or nonresident Indian, being always somewhat pejorative) were all too transparent, or rather, read off from homes, schools, friends, family. That is, anonymity and invisibility were categorically impossible; people I worked with allied themselves in relation to those identities, depending on their own positionalities. The double-edged nature of intimate access was well demonstrated here. I was also reminded daily, in court but especially on site visits when I accompanied the counselors, that when we say we feel at home in a city, we are often comfortable only with spaces and people congruent to our experiences. Fieldwork was an excellent mode of learning anew about homes and offices, neighborhoods and politics, in "my" city. Ananya Roy's comments on her fieldwork, also in Calcutta, resonate strongly with my sense that our presences are "a seemingly paradoxical combination of embodiment and 'deterritorialization.' Here, Calcutta becomes a territory from which I am displaced but which I also negotiate, dismantle and imagine as a site of return" (2003, 22).

These questions of method for studying law highlight the uncertainties that go into producing "knowledge." They emphasize that research is produced through absences and nuances as much as through recordable events. They remind us that we learn from bodily and linguistic performances, and cast doubt on the truth-value of self-reports or the homogenization of demographic categories. They trouble identity as a stable category of knowledge, perspective, or connection. In the next few sections, we track knowledge production in courtrooms using similar rubrics—deducing identity from apparent demographics, characterizing silence and withdrawal, and reading the body against the grain.

THE POWER OF SILENCE: CAUTIONS

The invitation to speak in court fetishizes speech as *the* mark of legal empowerment. Alternative dispute resolution (ADR) venues, including family courts, are reflexively obsessed with speaking, speaking properly, and speaking enough but not too much. As the judge's rebuke in the epigraph to this chapter indicates—"this is your case, not mine"—clients are frequently asked to be the ultimate arbiter of their own cases by speaking up. As a foundational marker of democratic participation, speech "is regarded as a right, and the suppression of speech as a denial of that right in a democratic polity"—that is, access to speech serves as a cornerstone of social legibility and its absence as a sign of "subalternity" (Rajan 1993, 84). These injunctions also echo feminist critiques that women are vulnerable to being silenced through legal categories of speech and need informal, nonstructured spaces to have their voices be heard. The judge's admonition in the epigraph is a reminder of these histories.

At the same time, litigants are asked to conform to legal process by precisely recreating in *words* their *written* witness depositions. As I describe at greater length in chapter 4, in clients' attempts to "be" lawyers, they are constantly reprimanded if they speak outside the script of the petition. Moreover, equating speech with empowerment and silence with aporia can be inadequate in legal processes. Bhattacharya demonstrates that even a woman's dying declaration (that her husband tried to kill her), a form of utterance with sacrosanct evidentiary value in Indian case law on "dowry" murders, can be deemed invalid and incoherent by police and medical authorities (2009, 363–64). Women testifying to sexual harassment may be sexualized, their speech taken as a form of sexual agency (Seuffert 1999, 238). Thus, as Rajan reminds us, not only are "silence and speech . . . never absolutely distinct categories," but "speech is never transparent, and . . . silence is not always an imposition" (1993, 84).

Silence may emphasize or gesture to forms of abjection that lie beyond representation; precisely because we cannot turn to content for interpretation, we have to look for meanings of silence in "its space, its temporality and its facticity" (Rajan 1993, 86). It may be purposefully partial, interlaced with intimacy, laughter, and gossip, at the "confounding yet tactical junction of disclosure and exposure" (Visweswaran 1994, 50). It may be deployed in the face of violence as a form of disaffection and revenge, or it may counter legal silencing with a refusal to be emotionally or psychically silent (Bhattacharya 2009). It may be a way to refuse to remember political and sexual trauma, just as testifying to trauma may also be a mode of eventually forgetting it (Roy 2010, 35).

Watching an elderly woman in shabby clothes in the Kolkata judge's chamber one day, I was struck by the presence of one such poignant silence. She cried soundlessly and said nothing, despite the judge's kind treatment and the question addressed to her in Hindi: "Apka kya mana hai?" (What are you asking [the court] for?). The woman just held out her lawyer's petition to the judge and the counselors, which stated that she was applying for maintenance from her son under S125 of the Criminal Procedure Code (an antipenury provision under which parents and children, in addition to spouses, may seek maintenance costs). In a court whose modus operandi promotes speaking on one's own, without lawyers, for supposedly better justice, it was deeply ironic that here only the lawyer's letter could speak, while the litigant herself was beyond words. Yet one could take her silence as communicating discomfort and grief,[6] in the shame of having to publicly seek living expenses and the failure of the customary filial expectation of a son's financial support.

The following case exemplifies a more punitive consequence of silence: Shobha, a litigant, would not speak at all, possibly for reasons of mental disability, further enhanced by fear of public interrogation in court (see chapter 5 for more on her case). She would not even say out loud that her lawyer was absent and her witness deposition needed to be deferred for that reason. When Shobha's father mentioned the lawyer's absence, the judge said, "Who is going to talk, she or the lawyer? Is the lawyer going to produce words out of her mouth? She *must* speak—or else why is she in this court?" (*Taholey bolbey ke, o na holey ukil, ukil ki mukher thekey katha bar korey debey? Oke boltey hobey, naholey e court-c keno*). Initially, the judge threatened to give an ex parte ruling, usually a measure signifying that one of the parties is not present, which implies prejudice to the absent party (not least because they are not there to make their case). That is, here Shobha's presence was not sufficient to count as *presence* if her voice was not heard, *or* if her lawyer did not speak on her behalf. Finally, the judge entered into the record with some prejudice (in English), "The respondent does not speak out a single word and we do not know whether she in a position to contest the case when asked," and granted her a temporary reprieve with dire warnings. We do not know whether the no-show by the lawyer was a deliberate delaying tactic, but the case provides an extreme example of how a litigant's privilege to speak can be regarded as a *compulsion* to speak. Silence proved dangerous, even if speech may provide only minimal enabling rather than empowerment.

Thus speech, silence, and action all require strict scrutiny. The above examples, as well as the sections (and chapters) that follow, demonstrate that questions of agency in litigation are complicated. They are heightened in the family courts by the equation of "plain language" with authentic voice, intent, and truth. Reasons for choosing litigation over mediation, or adopting particular legal strategies, or choosing certain rhetorical or affective paths in court are inscrutable. Nor is it possible to separate stated emotions from culturally popular "structures of feeling"[7] and to ever know whether an utterance is authentic to the self (or what that means), a mimicry of culturally popular emotional repertoires, or strategically appropriate for its context.

The notion of affect is useful here, in the sense of embodied feeling (contrasted to emotion and intent in the realm of conscious articulation, within language).[8] In emphasizing the unsayable and the contingent, affect helps conceptualize subjectivity as "embodied, located and relational" (Koivunen 2010, 8). However, problems arise when trying to interpret agency: we might be able to mark the traces of affective moments and deem that the "corporeality of affect" is a tangible cultural force (Ring 2006, 107–8), but such moments are also, by definition, beyond representation, and we can only speculate about the content of an affective gesture. Abu-Lughod's reclamation of "emotions" as "tokens in the construction of our subjectivity" that vary by social context is a rather more effective tool; she recommends tracking the discursive contexts in which particular emotions are expressed in order to understand that "language and culture are understood pragmatically and not referentially" (2009, 129). As Sara Ahmed suggests, if we ask not "What are emotions?" but rather "What do emotions do?" we can study emotions as units of circulation and communication (2004, 4, 191). In the following sections, we will see the ambivalence both of speech and of nonverbal expression, of saying *and* simultaneously not saying. These are produced in contexts where legal argument is privileged and rhetorical or affective excess are considered irrelevant nuisance. The insistent disruption caused by such excess, however, indicates that multiple expectations are worked out in law, and we attend to their effects.

MISSED TRANSLATIONS: "HOW TO WRITE A LIFE LIVED BETWEEN LANGUAGES"

My previous research methodology of conducting interviews and reading texts of appellate cases had not prepared me for the dizzying linguistic intricacies of the Kolkata Family Court, for "living life between languages," in Ingram's words.[9] The work of the court involved constant translation and paraphrasing, modulated by (perceived) ethnicity, religion, class, and gender, the process strongly triangulated through the judge. Judges spoke to litigants in Bangla or Hindi or (more rarely) English,[10] depending on their perception of the litigants' ethnicity and language skills. For example, there was a tendency to address Christian litigants in English, as if religion was associated with primary language use, or to address Gujaratis or Marwaris—people not of Bengali ethnicity—in Hindi (not their native language either), even if they were lifelong Kolkata residents and might be familiar with Bangla. The judge listened to their response, usually in the same language, then translated, transformed, and summarized this "into the record" *in English*, thereby generating the formal text that lawyers, judges, and scholars subsequently peruse. The judges I observed were native speakers of Bangla, less adept speakers of Hindi (with some exceptions), and used awkward legal English for documents. The process thus has fundamental gaps between languages of colloquial expression, technical inquiry, and legal documentation, related to the problem of eliciting information in a multilingual state while purportedly preserving efficiency by maintaining records in English (one of the two national languages).[11]

This dynamic leads to some interesting translations between colloquial registers of asking and legal categories of information.[12] In trying to establish whether a marriage existed (as information for starting a case file), a judge asked, "Apnader ki emni . . . maney shombondho kore biye hoyechhilo?" (Were you married in the regular way, through a family-arranged marriage?). He translated the affirmative response into the record thus: "Our wedding was performed according to Hindu rites," conflating modes of setting up marriage ("family-arranged") with religious ceremonies ("rites") instituting legal marriage. A female petitioner's negative response to a question about her occupation, "Apni ki kichu koren?" (literally, "Do you do anything?"—perhaps more colloquially, "Do you work anywhere?"), was translated as "housewife," thereby defined as the absence of a job. The next example demonstrates the slippage between legal and common-sense meanings particularly well. The judge's question asking a petitioner to restate his plea, "Ki chaichchen?" (literally, "What do you want? What do you need?" but legally and technically, "What are you applying for?"), clearly escaped the man, who said, "Kichu na" ("Nothing," perhaps indicating that he was not seeking either maintenance or custody). He was promptly reprimanded—"Chaicchen na ki, court e ki beratey eshechen?" (What do you mean you don't want anything, are you in court for a vacation?)—and stammered, "Mutual divorce." In these cases, judges bridge legal and colloquial registers, creating equivalence between approximate and sometimes fairly distant terms, while fashioning a new text for further legal interventions, such that "an event or act is named or forged through the idiom of judgment" (Arondekar 2009, 68).

Linguistic slippages are particularly marked as sites of unease when it comes to taboo or intimate topics. One critical area is that of proving consummation of marriage, a legal standard upon which rests the validity of marriage and the economic and custodial rights that flow from it, but one in which direct evidence is elusive. Judges need to ask about consummation—that is, about having sex within marriage—but find themselves resorting to numerous sleights of phrase. These include asking, "Biye ki consume hoyechchilo?" (literally, was the wedding "consumed?"—likely a malapropism meaning "consummated"); translating the answer to "Apnader ki kono shantan achche?" (Do you have any children?) as "Our marriage was consummated"; and the particularly confusing "Apnara ki shami-stri hishebey ekshonge thekechchen?" (Have you lived together as husband and wife?), the affirmative reply also translated as "the marriage was consummated." Because this last phrase conflates sexual "consummation" with cohabitation or living in the same house, I observed an instance of miscommunication where a woman replied in the negative to having "lived together" as husband and wife—she had never been taken to live in the husband's house after a registered marriage—and then went on to describe her pregnancy. One of the court helpers or "counselors" suggested here that perhaps "shami-strir shomporko" (the relationship of husband and wife) might be the most appropriate approximation, but this assumes the sexual as the defining register of a conjugal relationship and might not be perceived as such by clients.[13]

These examples are amusing and horrifying in showing the challenges of fitting individual experience into legal categories, but their significance lies not so much in being *mis*translations as in indexing certain methodologies critical to family courts. Indian family courts, imagined as lawyer-free courts, are deemed to offer gender equity and legal innovativeness because litigants pursue their own cases in their own words, speaking to the judge without the "alienating" mediation of lawyers. Judges' transformation of litigants' assertions in the legal record is thus the *only* mode of transferring information. However, this is not a simple process of writing out oral claims. Litigants write petitions, often with the help of counselors, which then become documents that the litigant must confirm and validate through oral deposition in the courtroom.[14] Litigants are, for example, constantly scolded by judges because they answer questions in ways that do not exactly correspond to written plaints. Because this alternative-style courtroom is after all a lower-level court, the legal record created by judges then becomes the formal document that is the basis of subsequent appeals or claims.[15]

In these "plain-language" courts, therefore, legal language is anything but direct and unmediated. Ironically, the desire to see people bring their stories directly to court is rendered through "correct" answers to judges' questions. Acts of translation are erased other than in the ethnographic moment. Voices have to be made appropriate, often forcefully. Litigants are reminded that a deposition or witness testimony is a form of iteration, not a speech act in itself. Sexual matters that litigants would rather elide have to become explicit. The process trains litigants to live in (and speak in) the sociolegal world they approach, rather than working *from* their narratives, though it is frequently interrupted by litigants' noncompliance, confusion, humor, and anger. Discourses of conjugality are constituted through these disciplinary processes, as questions about bodies, residence, and desire generate legal interpretations of marriage and sexuality.

While translation is only one mode through which these gaps in testimonial processes are produced, some insights from translation studies are useful for thinking through these processes. A translator or interpreter is not an invisible medium but rather someone who plays an active role in constructing the legal subject, as an extensive body of anthropological research has demonstrated. Interpretation in bilingual courtrooms brings in a new set of meanings, in excess of what litigants depose: there are additions and alterations by court translators, affecting the pragmatics of both source and target languages (Berk-Seligson 2002; Hale 2002). "Powerless speech" features (Conley and O'Barr 1990) may be removed and a more assertive presence depicted, or hesitations may be added by the translator that do not reflect the speaker's pauses. The cases in this chapter deal with legal translation by *judges* in multilingual courtrooms, rather than interpreters or paralegals or lawyers, but they similarly reveal an active construction of legal meanings in the process of translation. The significant difference here is that judges have the dual authority to create the legal record through translation, and then pronounce judgment on the basis of that record.

Other slippages occur when life histories and clients' perceptions of grievance are turned into legal reports, involving the transformation of "experiences" into strategic legal categories. One telling contrast comes in a study of protective order hearings at a district attorney's office, regarding the difference between women's accounts of abuse framed through narratives, or "stories," and the paralegals' attempts to elicit facts from them to best structure their "reports" in official forms (Trinch and Berk-Seligson 2002), a reminder of the superior legibility of "rules" over "relationships" in law (Conley and O'Barr 1990). Similarly, the "documentary requirements" of forensic examination protocols for sexual assault erase rape survivors' experiences and replicate rape myths in producing data (Mulla 2011, 2). Transplanting international legal norms into "vernacularized" local discourses often makes for a poor fit with existent laws and practices (Merry 2006b, 39). As Clark Cunningham suggests, translation and mediation into legal registers is both necessary and constraining, helpful and insufficient: "No sentence can be perfectly translated from one language to another. If one feels a sense of loss in speaking to a translator, there is also something to be gained. By speaking through a translator, one can be heard and understood in places where otherwise one is mute"(1991–92). Judges' translations and other maneuvers to fit narratives into law in the Kolkata courtroom are also, in this way, fundamental to legal legibility despite the slippages through which they are constituted.

Unlike legal anthropologists' concern for full, smooth rendition of narratives within law, other social theorists of translation studies,[16] often relying on deconstructionist readings, depict smooth and seamless translation as a form of erasure. They call for keeping translation jagged, for preserving the mark of transfer to a different currency or medium. Benjamin visualizes optimal translation as a transfer that "does not cover the original, does not block its light": "Translation, instead of resembling the meaning of the original, must lovingly and in detail incorporate the original's mark of signification, thus making both the original and the translation recognizable as fragments of a greater language" (2000, 21). Similarly, appending broken, fractured translations that invoke the original, Spivak argues that "the task of the translator is to facilitate the love between the original and its shadow, a love that permits fraying" (1993, 181). These perspectives seek to deliberately incorporate dual or multiple linguistic worlds, as well as to dwell in the space between languages; as James Mcguire puts it, "The question really is not 'what language to write,' but rather 'how to write two languages simultaneously, how to write a life lived between languages'" (quoted in Ingram 1997, 215).

Litigants exemplify inhabiting life between languages not only in legal testimony but also in framing their experiences through awkward jokes and dramatic declamations from popular culture. The following moment of performative excess, portraying new imaginaries launched by legal change, cannot be represented without convoluted, jagged translation. A male divorce litigant said in desperate jest to counselors in 2005, "Dhananjoy theke Mrityunjoy na hoye jai" (I hope [she] doesn't turn me from Dhananjoy to Mrityunjoy). He was angry and frustrated that his wife had filed a rape charge in a criminal court on top of the divorce case. To follow his meaning, we would have to know that in 2004, Dhananjoy Chatterjee was hanged for the gruesome rape-murder of fourteen-year-old Hetal Parikh. Both these proper nouns are male names: he anoints himself Dhananjoy as a shortcut to the popular image of "rapist," and puns on the word *mrityu* or "death" to express his anxiety and disdain. A smooth translation of his words that deleted context and wordplay would be, "She's filed a rape charge against me—what's next? Is she going to have me hanged?"

While calls for jagged *literary* translation pertain to modes of practice very different from law, they allow us to think about legal translation in critical ways. The legal record is constituted through an instantaneous filtering and interpretation of litigants' accounts. Because the emphasis is on efficient and coherent outcomes, narratives pursued by litigants and narratives elicited from them are erased, their sense of injury or harm rendered invisible in legal documentation. Fractures in negotiation are removed, as legal legibility is paramount. Ethnographic moments discussed throughout this chapter are, however, among the few traces that preserve the jaggedness of translation and thereby point to performances and desires usually invisible in formal records.

SEX TALK: READING BODIES AND HABITS

Nowhere is the elision between legal meaning and culturally acceptable modes of speaking more prominent than in attempts to read bodily signs for determining sexual behavior, consent, and desire, against the grain of silences and ambiguities. This most corporeal of inquiries ironically has to be discerned through language. As Butler contends, ways of (not) talking about sex are forms of regulation, producing notions of the legal body: "'Sex' not only functions as a norm, but is part of a regulatory practice that produces the bodies it governs" (1993, 1). The law's "enunciatory," or naming/creating function, *produces* categories of licit and illicit sex, and reads bodily surfaces as evidence of mental states, exemplifying Foucault's contention that "power is that which dictates law to sex" (Das 1996, 2412).[17]

Enunciations of sexuality are explored in this section through cases pertaining to valid (consummated) marriages, particularly relating to sexual knowledge. The case law here enunciates norms of heterosexual conjugality, defining eroticism, romance, marriage, and the heterosexual body through "the institutions that undergird the cultural mandate of reproductive sexuality—in particular, the family, the couple, childhood, and ideals of eroticism premised upon romance and domesticity"(Bernstein and Schaffner 2005, xv). The legal medicalization of the body in terms of (hetero)sexual practices also supports such definitions (Schaffner 2005; Baxi 2014). We move from appellate cases that define legal understandings of the sexual body to an ethnographic example that mirrors this appellate record while revealing excesses of performance typically invisible in appellate accounts.

Two of the grounds on which Hindu marriages[18] may be rendered invalid or void ("voidable or annulled by a decree of nullity") are impotence and fraud. One may get an annulment if "the marriage has not been consummated owing to the impotence of the respondent." Fraud is relevant in this context because parties to a marriage could have been deliberately kept in the dark about known sexual problems.[19] Impotence is legally classified into three categories: physical and psychological, both described as "organic," and "impotence qua a particular person," described as "atonic."

> Physical potency implies, in the male, ability to achieve erection and penetration (*vera copula*), though not necessarily ejaculation; and in the female, the physical capacity to be penetrated, naturally or as a result of surgery, and regardless of whether or not she has functioning female organs. Mental incapacity implies an emotional, psychological or moral repugnance to the sexual act, which may be only *qua* the petitioner and not *per se*, and which is to be distinguished from "wilful refusal" to submit to sexual intercourse, which amounts to desertion or, arguably, to cruelty (Uberoi 1996, 335).

Desertion and cruelty are two related grounds for divorce (rather than annulment), centering around a conscious lack of willingness to have sex rather than an incapacity to do so. "Three days and three nights in the same room" has constituted the judicial standard for "ample opportunity to consummate the marriage" (Uberoi 1996, 335).

One immediately notices here that the standard of potency for both sexes is penetrability alone, with no reference to sexual satisfaction or even to reproduction. Heterosexual penetration is thus the standard that legitimizes marriage. Mental incapacity for sex is seen as a form of impotence, as bodily constraint, a failure of physical or mental functions. Lack of willful consent, however, constitutes desertion, a different ground of divorce. Brook's analysis of same-sex marriage legislation in the Australian Capital Territory points

out that such criteria serve to consolidate heterosexual conjugality as fundamental to the state, with "consummation" as the "corporeal yoke linking law
and marriage," to be invariably instantiated through "vera copula" or "true
consummation of bodies" in heterosexual penetration (2000, 140). Consummation occupies a sanctified space because of this symbolic yoking, standing
"as 'sex' as such, or as *all* sex" (148), memorable in U.S. president Bill Clinton's
testimonial that he "did not have sex with that woman" (because there was no
penile penetration). Similarly, in the Indian cases, *vera copula* (with some
leeway for mental states) or the heterosex imperative is asserted to be foundational to marriage.

The Indian appellate record on impotence is consistently murky. Patricia
Uberoi (1996, 323) argues that Indian judges have waffled between marriage
as a legal contract with well-defined rights for parties[20] and a set of supposedly
sacramental commitments, such as for women to become fully identified with
their affinal families, or for marriage to be indissoluble except in extreme cases.
Penetration, defined in terms of men's erection and women's "penetrability,"
continues to be the standard of potency, but judges show some ambivalence
as to whether impotence or sterility should be the most significant issue in
dissolving a marriage, depending on whether sexual desire or the desire for
children is seen to be the primary characteristic of marriage (Uberoi 1996).
The intersections of sexual and contractual agency and consent further highlight judicial ambivalence.

Cases involving women's legal "impotence" and "sexual fraud" have often
deemphasized the body in favor of contextual decision making. *Ruby Roy vs.
Sudarshan Roy*[21] entirely erases questions of desire and ability to stress questions of contractual validity: the husband alleged fraud because his wife was
"devoid of female organs and incapable of cohabitation" (note the jump to the
residential), with burn marks and no right breast and only a nipple as left
breast. The case rested on whether the husband's father's knowledge of these
marks was shared by the son. The judge's decision that it was and that the
husband therefore was bound to a surrogate contract placed questions of
consent outside the realm of the conjugal couple. The judgment in the *Godinho*
case,[22] however, measured impotence in terms of behavior, invoking neither
contract nor penetrability; it was held that the wife was impotent "qua" her
husband despite having had a child by him, because though he had forcibly
had sex with her, she had always remained "sexually averse" to him (perhaps
the marital rape may have had some connection to her aversion?).

Women's preference for sex in pleasant circumstances was highlighted in *Sadanand Rawool vs. Sulochana Rawool*.[23] The husband alleged that the wife had abnormal sexual organs and a strong aversion to sex, while the wife countered that she had normal organs but their few episodes of sex "were not happy occasions," "on account of the shortcoming of premature ejaculation on the part of the husband." In determining that there was little to prove the husband's allegation, the court declared that "the wife is a poor illiterate lady, determined to maintain the marital tie, come what may," lacking "the guile and intelligence necessary" to fake normalcy in a medical exam. The court also pointed to their living arrangements with the extended family in a small room as lacking the privacy that "was the primary requirement for a couple to have pleasant sexual intercourse." Nonconsummation could not be considered proof of a woman's impotence, and the burden of proof lay with the man to prove it, the court declared in *Mangho Dasani vs. Smt. Mohani*,[24] in one of many cases of "relative impotency." In this case, the judge declared that "it is now established law of medical phenomenon that the wife [can be] potent yet mentally impotent" depending on "some psychological reasons." Both women's economic necessity to have sex to stay married and the standard of pleasant circumstances as a reasonable expectation—that is, married women's choice to refuse sex in certain circumstances—were invoked in these cases to counter allegations of women's impotency. Contrary to Uberoi's contention and legal definition, penetrability was not the necessary standard for women's impotence in these cases; especially in the Dasani case, sexual activity was viewed in terms of reasonable consent.

Men, on the other hand, have been held to more rigid standards of bodily potency. In *L.B. vs. A.B.*,[25] the wife contended that her husband was impotent qua her because they had only had sex once, on their "disastrous honeymoon," when she had "lured" him much to his disgust, but the judge pointed out that impotence could not be claimed if he had managed to have sex once, seduced against his will or not. Impotency is here judged in terms of the singular, any one time, rather than the habitual. Manjula Deshmukh's husband[26] was deemed impotent despite her pregnancy following the standard that potency was the ability to have "ordinary and complete intercourse"; here he "could not achieve any penetration for lack of erection," but masturbated and rubbed the penis "smeared with semen" against her vagina without penetrating, and "she became pregnant by this act of rubbing." Male "potency" was thus defined not in terms of fertility but rather erection and penetrability, the standard being either concern for the woman's presumed sexual satisfaction (equated with penile penetration) or a failure of full physical functionality. There is greater absoluteness, and questions of consent or mood are not invoked as they were for women.

These characterizations of sex, of body and mind, set up by appellate decisions are not strictly followed as precedents in family court, though they do seem to influence the terms of interrogation. The following case from the Kolkata court demonstrates similar modes of reading the body to produce legally determinative categories, but also allows us to examine processes of investigation ethnographically, thus mapping the trail of bodily evidence. This divorce case involved charges of insanity and impotence alleged by the husband, Prasun, and a countersuit for maintenance from his wife, Rima. Prasun, smartly dressed in court in a white striped shirt and brown pants, worked for a Tata affiliate at about Rs. 6,000 a month (low-middle to middle income). Rima looked plainer in an unironed black cotton sari, wearing a few gold and red *shankha* bracelets and *sindoor* (vermillion) in her hair (signifiers of marital status). She had long, oily hair and plump, rounded lips. Her mother sat on the bench close to me, partially blind, in a limp white sari. The court counselor Shilpa whispered to me that they were very poor and that Rima's mother had put most of her money into the daughter's wedding; Shilpa seemed overtly sympathetic to Rima's narrative though representing both parties.

Prasun alleged that Rima's insanity had emerged in their months of marriage, and moreover that she had a physical problem having sex, thereby thwarting his desire for children. The judge took him through a detailed deposition of events, during which he admitted that they had "spent the night in the same room" during the *phulshojja* ceremony (the flower-laden ceremony marking the conjugal night) of the wedding and once at her parents' house. As he seemed hesitant to answer what exactly happened on those conjugal occasions, she cleared the courtroom (I managed to stay because I was associated with the counselors), creating a space that was confessional and therapeutic even as it was interrogatory.

When only about ten people were left in the courtroom, Prasun said that they talked a bit on those occasions and fell asleep. Judge K asked if he tried to kiss her, and he said, "Yes, but she said no." Judge K: "What Bengali woman from a good family is going to say, 'Esho amay bhog koro'?" ("Come, consume/ enjoy me now," is my very inadequate translation). The judge told him his wife was shy and inquired whether he persisted in trying to have sex with her. He said he did, upon which she asked if he had sought advice from his friends or read anything about having sex. He said he hadn't, at which time Judge K dictated into the record *in his voice*, "I had no idea and concept of how to consummate a married life" (another remarkable example of legal translation). At that point, he muttered that he had talked to his friends a bit.

Asked about her insanity, Prasun said he saw Rima briefly before marriage and didn't sense problems but later thought something was "abnormal" and stayed away. He described her as speaking roughly sometimes. The judge reminded him that rough behavior is not tantamount to insanity and that he should have had her examined by a doctor if he was going to make that claim. Judge K told him that he could talk about "bad adjustment and lack of understanding, but this is a different matter."[27]

In Rima's cross-examination, Judge K asked her about the details of the *phulshojja* (conjugal night) and whether anyone played customary pranks such as hiding in the room. Rima said there were no such events, that her husband shut the door and she didn't object to that, and that they had "physical relations" that night. When Judge K asked if she had the usual "obstruction *jeta meyeder thake*" ("the 'obstruction' that women customarily have," referring to an unbroken hymen), Rima said she didn't notice anything like that. (According to Shilpa, Prasun had alleged that Rima had been pregnant before marriage because he found stretch marks on her breasts. They were related to her weight, Shilpa reported, but questioned, "And how can he make that allegation if he hasn't seen her breasts?"). Rima claimed she didn't get pregnant because Prasun told her he didn't want to have children yet. When Judge K asked about their use of birth control and she claimed they had used none, the judge commented in inimitably bad Hindi in an attempt at humor: "Nirodh nahi tha to phir birodh kaise hua?" (My translation, "How did you create a barrier if you had no condoms?" does little to capture her pun on *Nirodh*, a once-ubiquitous—but old-style at the time of the hearing—brand name for condoms, and its assonance with *birodh* as an alternate word for obstruction). This then had to be explained to Rima in Bangla, who didn't have an answer for the lack of pregnancy.

This account highlights the complex narratives through which sexuality is talked about in court, as opposed to points of law authorized in appellate cases. Prominent here are techniques of reading the body (the hymen, the breasts) as a juridical system of signs. The body is deemed to speak through lacks or absences that are ambivalent as evidence: Are stretch marks on breasts about a fat body or a once-pregnant body? Can the lack of a visibly ruptured hymen say anything definitive about successfully executed sex? Is it penile penetration or shattered hymen that determines consummation? Is the lack of pregnancy without contraception (in one or two sex acts) to be interpreted as a physical defect, thereby conflating intercourse with instant fertility and signaling fertility as a standard of (female) potency contrary to legal precedent? Imputations that Rima was not a virgin hover at the edges of this conversation, despite its irrelevance as a legal standard in divorce. These readings of bodily signs as evidence aptly illustrate Veena Das's claim that judicial readings of sexual embodiment often put the woman's "body and speech . . . at war with each other," with bodily "surfaces" substituting for her sense of "bodily integrity," while the surface of the male body is not similarly read (1996, 2418).[28] Prasun's body was invisible in interrogation, while Rima's hymen, breasts, and womb were scrutinized through conversational hearsay.

There is closeness and even conflation between grounds for impotency, insanity and cruelty (further explored in chapter 5). Prasun's testimony cited his wife's occasional rough behavior and refusal to go out with him, alongside her sexual behavior and failure to be pregnant, as insanity. Is asexual affect necessarily pathological? How do consent, compatibility, and atmosphere count? The judge's questions indicated she would not grant that Rima's reticence toward sexual activity constituted impotence. She introduced the notion of creating preparedness, even seduction, as a criterion that put the onus upon the husband, turning the issue back to his putative lack of skill. Significantly, these criteria are different from the legal standards of "impotence qua a particular person" or "refusal to have sex," which may be held to be tantamount to the legal ground of cruelty. Her behavior here echoed the appellate record of judges' concern with "first-night etiquette," "'a want of elementary courtship' on the part of husbands," in Derrett's phrase, specifically that "brides may be revulsed from sex and therefore marriage too early, and thereby the entire edifice of marriage may be in jeopardy" (Uberoi 1996, 337–38). In this formulation, gendered norms of sexuality are used both to exempt and limit women's sexual agency; while the wife is not expected to be sexually assertive to be deemed "potent," she is also contained by that characterization, inscribed as hesitant and shy, the recipient of sexual knowledge to be gathered by her husband from his friends.

Such sexed bodies, read as sign and symptom, are produced through legal discourse, based on dominant as well as negotiated discourses of sexuality.

On the one hand, expert knowledge is constructed through interrogative processes that read the person's body against his or her speech. The "two-finger test" central to medical evidence in rape trials purports to determine "the difference between 'physical' and 'true' virginity," and the difference between consent and "habituation" to sex, a refusal to take it "interpreted as evidence of a false complaint": in this use of manual penetration to test virginity, "the relationship . . . between the clinical test and the erect penis is one of mimesis" (Baxi 2005, 275, 282–84). Similar to this process of "law recreat[ing] rape in order to know it has happened and society has been harmed" (301), in Rima's case the loss of virginity on the conjugal night was recreated in the courtroom by interrogation in the face of resistance. On the other hand, sexuality was not defined in court or case law by physical pathologies or reproductive capacities; rather, questions of desire and pleasure, mood, even women's consent to sex as payback for their dependence on marriage were acknowledged. These more expansive considerations were, however, located within essentialized gendered norms of female reticence, silence, and ignorance, toward which the law could be benevolently protective.

FEARING THE SUIT COW: ERASING VIOLENCE THROUGH MEDIATION

Mediation is posed as a methodological alternative to law—simple, cheap, and customized, equal if not better at delivering solutions. But its focus on efficiency, on economic settlement and backlog clearing, is often achieved by silencing emotional conflicts or unspeakable violence, by pronouncing closure in offering (monetary) legal remedies for cultural violations. "Settling" a case, the driving force behind courts, is always ambivalent, suggesting simultaneously closing out and giving up. Criminal sanctions are secondary when economic settlements can be negotiated. Yet this language of effective equivalence can come up against litigants for whom the logic of economic efficiency leaves the violence of marriage unaddressed. These negotiations are also quite prevalent in the Kolkata Family Court (chapter 4), but here I draw on my brief fieldwork in 2001 in Dhaka (Bangladesh) to demonstrate how monetary solutions fall short as translations of harm and anger.

A group of young Dhaka judges, discussing the disposal of litigation, regaled me with metaphors of legal burden, as the horrific Other of "settlement." A commonly circulated cartoon, "the suit cow," visualized the lawsuit as a fertile cow providing an endless supply of nourishment to lawyers. Another saying they loved, "Mokkel hoitechche ukiler baganer pholoban brikhkho" (The client is like an abundant fruit-bearing tree in the lawyer's orchard), also referred to images of endless financial delivery, of clients being juicily consumed. Mediation was seen as breaking this cycle of impoverishment from litigation.

In Dhaka, the Family Court Act passed in 1985, establishing courts for handling divorce, maintenance, custody, and guardianship (with no mandate for mediation). Under Muslim Family Law in Bangladesh,[29] women cannot claim lifelong alimony but can get a three-month payment following divorce, corresponding to *idda* (child support payments), and deferred dower (*mahr*, often *denmohar* in Bangla) as specified in the marriage contract, plus other fines levied by judges.[30] Judges therefore have leeway to make substantive lump-sum economic awards in divorce, as opposed to granting long-term alimony or maintenance.

Since 2000, three of the Dhaka family courts have been designated mediation courts[31] by the Law Ministry (Monsoor 2008, 142–43), to which fifteen civil courts in the city can send cases.[32] Consultants to the project recommended the technique of directive mediation, in which judges were asked to guide *actively*, contrary to a previous theory that guidance would encourage judges to intervene too much (Hasan 2001). This intervention appears to have jump-started a program touted as a symbol of immensely successful legal intervention; monetary recovery and associated well-being, as well as caseload reduction, are the primary indices.[33] Seventy percent of cases brought under these courts in Dhaka were resolved outside the trial docket. There was an over threefold increase in money granted through the courts between the first six months of 2000 and the last six months.[34]

Judge E, from whose courtroom I draw these cases, widely deemed to be the most successful of the mediation court judges, expressed great satisfaction that he had been able to close cases and make provision for women. One morning, Judge E inquired about the well-being of a woman in her thirties in a plain burka as he wrote out her monthly alimony check. He told me later, "She had to wait twelve years before I resolved her case through mediation. This is what pleases me, when I begin to see her clothes get less tattered, that there is more flesh on her bones." He claimed he had awarded 5,000,000 taka through his courtroom alone since he started, more than is given out in commercial courts in a given year. In his view, mediation had been particularly successful at breaking down the intransigence of legal process and achieving this transformation of bodies and lives.

Persuasions or threats to clients were most often translated in terms of economic consequences by the judge: "Shali-ke niye ghurchhen, kapor khuley court-e ghurtey hobey" (You're trying to go around with your wife's sister [now], [but soon] you'll lose all your clothes from having to be in court), he threatened one client. In another case, he said to a man who appeared to be lying about bigamy, "Your wife looks like there's nothing in her body and she has no money. But she is here with Legal Aid and can keep her case going, it won't cost her anything, whereas you will end up spending lakhs."[35] Moral admonitions were thus commonly framed in terms of the consequences of destitution.

This Dhaka court exemplifies the widespread excitement around mediation as the optimal solution to legal distress. But remembering Nader's cautionary appellation of mediation as "coercive harmony" (1997) and the need to attend to questions of power and silence, I want to trouble the fetishization of the economic bottom line as the ultimate objective of ADR. It is in the nature of these proceedings that grievances are translated into monetary terms, with a range of violations, not necessarily translatable, having to be metonymically resolved through the language of settlement and gain. I focus here on a case where the bargains and limitations of mediation are particularly marked, with the logic of economic efficiency failing to provide a remedy to gendered violation.

This in-camera hearing for postdivorce maintenance had been brought back for renegotiation after the initial session was unsuccessful. They were a youngish couple, Farid smartly dressed in trousers and a light shirt, and Feroza, very fair and pretty in a faded *salwar kameez*, accompanied by her father, who looked old, clad in a lungi, with a goatee and skull cap (connoting simple, pious Muslim attire). Their children came in at first, then were sent out to a waiting female relative. Farid tried to grab the elder girl, about nine years old, asking her to sit with him. This was the first I sensed Judge E was angry with him, as he said to Farid, "Lojja korey na?" (Aren't you ashamed of yourself?), chiding him for not having treated his family well. Farid had earlier offered 300 taka for each of the three children and was now upping it to 500 taka per child (1,500 taka total), plus 30,000 toward his wife's dower. As an alternative, he offered to raise them himself, saying her family wasn't serious about education. The counterproposal from Feroza's side was for him to pay a dower of 60,000 and 2,000 taka total per month for the children, with previous cases of dowry recovery being withdrawn in exchange. Farid's side did not seem agreeable to this, and the judge sent them away while he talked privately with Feroza and her father.

Judge E spoke to Feroza's father first, addressing him respectfully as *Baba* ("father") in tribute to his age and religiosity, advising him that it was in their best interest to have the case go away. If he could get them to compromise on an amount, he assured them that he would exert his judicial authority to ensure that Farid did not default on payments, by imposing a 150,000-taka penalty upon default or else a jail sentence. In addressing himself to her father, he followed the customary norms of patriarchal authority, in a perfect example of deferring to community norms of gender despite the state's objective of increasing women's presence and voice in formal legal spaces.

Indeed, Feroza did not wait for a resolution according to these norms of authority. She broke in with a long testimonial to the judge about her husband raping an eleven-year-old girl, their servant. At the time she testified for him against the girl, her family paid much of the legal expenses, and he got off. Farid had often beaten her over the years and was suspicious of her relationships, she insisted. Her father had helped Farid's business in all sorts of ways. She said, "I want him to acknowledge all the things he has done—the money is not the important thing."

Judge E explained the deal again, emphasizing the equation: "This way you can get the money from him right away, get him where it hurts. If you persist with the trial, you will lose a lot of money in the process and will have to endure that, and who knows what the result will be? If you persist with the criminal charges as well, this will last ten years and he may not be convicted. Or if he is convicted, he will appeal, which may take as long again, and you will not be getting any money, only spending it." After a long pause, Feroza said heavily, "If I take the money he's offering, Allah will say I have forgiven him on the day of *Qayamat* [judgment day]." She then described the last night when Farid had been violent toward her, implying sexual violence, saying there was not a part of her body that was not left bitten and bloodied. To this, the judge responded, "Allah visualizes judgment day as a court," implying that court is a hellish place where one doesn't want to stay. He offered that the greatest peace might lie in taking the money. Feroza said in a reluctant voice, "Apni ja bolen" (Whatever you want), but simultaneously refused to accept the 30,000 taka. The mediation session was held to be unsuccessful, and a date was set for trial.

The case illustrated the moral currency of maintenance payments in the transformation of injury into financial reparation. The judge, deservedly known as a skillful negotiator, moved smoothly between pragmatics and theology,[36] responding to Feroza in her own terms, turning the metaphor of Judgment Day on its head to evoke trials as a living hell and punning on judgment in the legal and religious sense. But while he could match these discursive registers, as a mediator he stressed convenience and peace through financial restitution and overcoming anger (Nader 1997, 714). Even in this space of supposedly alternative speech, where personal negotiations are seen as more significant than legal formalities, "relational" or "storytelling" accounts got less favorable judicial attention than "rule-oriented" formulas (Conley and O'Barr 1990).

What about Feroza's motivations? Clearly in economic distress, she turned down a stable source of funds while potentially committing herself to years of expense with little hope of a final payoff. Her gesture may be read as that of a tough negotiator holding out for more in the mediation process. But her detailed, emotional account of numerous betrayals and violations disrupted the discourse of economic reparation. Sexual violence had to be made visible, whether through testimony, trial, or an acknowledgment of guilt through payment of the higher sum. Can we understand her testimonial as affective excess beyond conscious calculation, or was it rather an appropriate display of emotion for legal leverage? Was her reference to Judgment Day an attempt to "really" evoke a religious dilemma or a moving strategic point? While these determinations are irresolvable, it is clear that, in contrast to the streamlined efficiency of mediation, a trial in all its messiness may serve as a public testimonial of violation while financial satisfaction erases the context.

CONCLUSION: TRANSLATION BEYOND EQUIVALENCE

Negotiating within the law involves inhabiting it through language and action, folding one's needs and desires into legal categories, converting body, sex, and violence into discursive signs. The translation involved in these processes is imagined as a tool of optimal transfer. Similarly, settlements are intended to establish equivalence between grievance and solution. However, such equivalence can be seen as seamless only if the unruly moments are invisible. Disciplinary processes of legal knowledge gathering and economic reparation exist alongside litigants' attempts to conform to performative expectations as well as their confusions and struggles. Judges' admonitions to be faithful to written depositions, the awkwardness of verifying sex within marriage, judges' insistence on eliminating grievance through money, and the failure of economic settlements to address violence all participate in this smoothing process. Ethnographic methods to capture law can track performative legal maneuvers, revealing the partiality of identity and knowledge gathering.

Questions of the body are central to such considerations because formal language tends to fail in explicit discussions of sexual behavior and sexual violence, obfuscating the ties linking heterosexual marriage, reproduction, and property. Consummation establishes a particular kind of sex as normative, providing prime access to economic and cultural resources through regimes of conjugality. Economic protections of marriage minimize the violence often present within it. These linkages, typically invisible within law, can be revealed through failed translations.

CHAPTER 4

Justice without Lawyers?

Living the Family Court Experiment

Sukhendu [the husband]: Instead of [play]-acting like husband and wife, we should . . .

> Archana [the wife]: A "mutual separation"—that will be better.
> Sukhendu: But . . . that . . .
> Archana: Just as it should be, according to the law [*Thik ain-e jebhabey hobey, sheibhabey*].
> Sukhendu: Oh, without making a scene.
> [My translated textual rendering of a cinematic moment completely fails to capture the devastated yet defiantly implacable expressions of the two actors.]

—*Saat Pakey Bandha* (Tied in seven circles [of marriage]), dir. Ajay Kar (1963)

This scene from the 1963 film *Saat Pakey Bandha*, redolent with regret and grief, conveys with deep visual irony that there is really nothing final or simple about taking marital dissolution to court. Marriage is knotty, it suggests, through a close shot of a needlepoint sampler customarily given at weddings. The sampler wishes, "Saat pakey bandha miloner raat; shoto pakey thak joriye jiban" (The seven circles around the sacred fire [in a Hindu wedding ceremony] help bind the night of meeting/union; may your lives be entangled in a hundred binds/circles). It puns on *paak* as both twist and knot; what ties also complicates, what holds fast gets entangled. Or, if you can slip the knot so easily, it wasn't well attached in the first place. In this scene, the educated, modern couple turns to new legal provisions for an easy remedy that allows them to move on with their lives, but divorce does not ameliorate the fundamental conflict. Law seems enabling but insufficient.

FIGURE 1. Life outside court: a row of typists with manual typewriters can help with petitions and forms.

In contrast, the court portrayed in this chapter, deemed exemplary for providing informal legal access, is ebulliently described as a new way of improving both marriage and law despite having divorce as its raison d'être. It is premised on a series of apparent contradictions: justice without lawyers, efficiency in a legal bureaucracy, divorce through conciliation. In giving form to these aspirations, however, it never quite sheds the specter of law as insufficient, as regret.

The Bankshall Courts Complex in Kolkata, housed in an old building believed to belong to Nawab Siraj-ud-dallah in the eighteenth century, is part of an extended law complex in the heart of the city, minutes from the High Court building and the modern City Civil Court. A vibrant legal culture thrives here on weekdays. One hears the clatter of manual typewriters from petition writers in tables and chairs set on the pavement and the calls of touts following those

FIGURE 2. Walking into the busy court premises, one is invariably approached by a variety of touts offering help with petitions, lawyers, forms.

who look like potential litigants, promising everything from stamps and petitions to lawyers. Low-slung blue plastic sheets hung over benches serve as lawyers' al fresco offices. Clusters of black and white signify the presence of lawyers, interspersed with the more colorful garb of clients. There are sputtering food carts with noodles and fried orbs of *luchi*s jostling alongside roadside barbers and cobblers, Hindu shrines to assorted gods and saints, and a mosque inside the court perimeter.

One wing of three rooms on the second floor in the courts complex, the Family Court or Parivarik Adalat, is imagined to incorporate a different form of legal process than the rest: a lawyer-free (or lawyer-avoidant) space where divorce and maintenance cases proceed through a direct relationship between the judge and the litigants. The wide corridor in front of the courts is often occupied by couples who steal furtive glances at each other while trying to put space between themselves, occasionally loudly reenacting domestic quarrels in public as mediation sessions revisit touchy ground. Women litigants often appear wearing customary signs of marriage, like vermillion on the forehead and conch bangles (there is no telling whether these have been strategically

FIGURE 3. Wooden sign announcing the "Family Court" or Parivarik Adalat.

donned for court). Litigants carry folders where bright red-and-gold wedding cards (which serve as standard evidence) stand out against a fat pile of court papers. A large number are almost permanent visitors, returning day after day to recover maintenance money or begin criminal recovery procedures for habitual nonpayers. Noncustodial parents, often fathers, stand clutching bundles of brightly wrapped presents for their children, in anticipation of a short visit at the back of the courtroom, the parent striving for moments of connection while the child stands shy or awkward or petrified, the encounter monitored by court counselors, police, grandparents, with other litigants not far away. Paralegal helpers ("counselors"), black-and-white-clad lawyers, and assorted family members and neighbors frequently join the fray with advice, admonition, and occasional physical intervention.

Amid the terror of public spectacle that palpably haunts the court corridors, it is sometimes hard to remember the court's conception as a utopian site of new meanings for marriage. As a lower-level civil court, this is a quotidian space in which marriage, alimony, and custody are negotiated, petitions accepted, and evidence heard. But family courts are also an exceptional space touted as a legacy of feminist activism, a triumph of the Indian women's movement's demands. In reading the feminist policy documents and legislative

FIGURE 4. Corridor (marked by askew sign) leading to the two
Family Courts and associated offices, typically very crowded.

debates on family courts from the 1980s, I was struck by the energy and optimism of this experiment, particularly the sense that this would be a radical
measure to destabilize the patriarchal nature of legal discourse.[1] However,
newspaper reports began to show that it was not easy to transform modes of
power or create alternate legal structures; they described the ease of access in
the courts but also pointed out that women were often dependent on judges'
mercies there, that these courts were not necessarily a supportive atmosphere
free from expectations of conventional gendered behavior.[2] This court illustrates some problems with institutionalizing feminist legal reform: the intransigence of gendered norms, the ambivalence of forgoing lawyers, and the
problems of adjudicating violence alongside divorce and maintenance.

The utopian vision suggests that family court is easy and facilitative, a harbinger of new possibilities for judges, lawyers, counselors, and litigants. But it is always simultaneously represented as a site of loss, shame, and failure, of bringing down one's family. It is a new public space for negotiating gender, class, and religious norms, yet limited by structural and cultural constraints. Akhil Gupta argues that reform measures of the postcolonial state are often met with enthusiasm rather than rejection but incorporated through "new meanings," which may "reinforce and redouble existing forms of domination" even as they "open up new possibilities for the empowerment and enfranchise-ment of the poor" (2012, 135). The following two linked cases lead us vividly to these ambivalences, generated by the family court's associations with easy solutions, interminable conflict, and blatant fraud, and the law as a necessary but embarrassing solution.

In July 2010, in the longest single hearing I have ever attended, Judge A appeared to be steadily losing his legendary cool as the case for a custodial visit kept going around in circles, with the upper-middle-class litigants con-stantly renegotiating details and amending claims. The mother, Sheila, herself a lawyer, argued aggressively that she did not want the father, Sujoy, to have any visitation rights because her marriage had been traumatic and Sujoy had not sought contact with his son for six years. Her son would be scarred by this intrusion, she contended, because his mother and maternal grandparents had been his whole world.

The judge had been using one of the most common registers of mediation in this court, appealing to the notion that it was better for children's health and well-being to wrap things up as quickly and efficiently as possible. "Alle-gations and counterallegations waste the court's time, and the child cannot be healthy in the midst of all that [shontan er modhye kokhono shustho hoi na]," he warned, adding in English for emphasis, "The child is spoilt when the parents' relationship is bitter." Spoilt seemed valid in both senses here, both the rottenness brought about by festering in conflict and the archetypal spoiled child who is overindulged and underdisciplined. Using the specter of court routines—too many dates and hearings—he tried to convince Sujoy to back off from the plea for monthly visitations and instead opt for occasional visits. He sardonically said to the seemingly unstoppable Sheila, "Don't use up all your words in this one case; there are still lots of cases to come" (Shob kotha ek mamlay shesh korben na, aro onek mamla hobey). Retorting to her argument that the visit would ruin her son's future by saying, "Your son's future is already bad, and the case is also bad for parents and society," he underlined that visitation on a birthday only arose because the parents were persisting with litigation rather than settling. Law, in these assertions, was tedious, pointless, and indeed harmful, and the judge, ironically, argued for dispensing with it.

Pressing her claim that visitation should be cut off to protect her son and that her family had been through enough already, Sheila invoked class privilege as the ultimate insurance, saying she was from a "conservative, *shombhranto* [respectable, elite] family." The judge immediately contradicted her: "No, you are not. Maybe you were once, but now you are from an 'ultramodern' [said in English] family." He then added, "The more educated you [all] are, the less sense you have; a degree doesn't mean you have learnt anything" (*Apnara joto shikhkhito toto jnanbodh kom; degree thaklei shikkha hoi na*). Modernity was invoked pejoratively here as consonant with law, specifically to deny any privileges of protection that appealed to customary hierarchies.

Two women litigants sitting on either side of me gasped audibly at the judge's comments on modernity. A large woman on my left, in a sleeveless gray *salwar kameez*, with short, bright red, henna-colored hair and wearing about six rings and gold earrings on each ear and hand, reached across me to a slight woman with long braided hair in a beige *salwar kameez*. "I didn't like his remark," she whispered fiercely. "Our troubles have brought us here [*ekhaney ghatey dhakka kheye eshechchi*]; that doesn't mean we are ultramodern." I describe her appearance in detail because she precisely fit the cultural specter of the ultramodern woman undoing social values—"more rings than fingers," the opposing side's lawyer derided her.

The specter of a topsy-turvy world enabled by the court was enhanced by this woman's presence on the stand shortly thereafter, across from a short, plump, bearded man in a faded *kurta-pajama* and skull cap marking him as likely a Muslim. She testified, in what was probably the most surreal hearing I have attended, to being Hena Singh and having met and married and been deserted by Azhar Khan. However, questions from the opposing lawyer and then the judge elicited a life of multiple identities: she had a number of aliases, including Archana Hazra (usually a Hindu name). The lawyer alleged that she had been married to Amit Hazra, had lived with his family and their two sons, and when Amit left her, had filed a maintenance claim against him in this very family court about five years ago. Her discomfiture at the questions and her responses—mostly "I don't remember"—indicated a sinister plot. Azhar Khan was transformed in these interrogations from a neglectful, greedy man to an entrapped, clueless one, from the popular specter of a Muslim predator to a poor mark. The anxiety that family courts might create a legal apparatus empowering unscrupulous women to prey upon men's vulnerability, seducing and impoverishing men through marriage, was validated in this entirely atypical case.

But Hena/Archana was, after all, justified in her original outrage. Neither "ultramodernity" nor being in court should be contemptible in the state's framework, where legal access exists for negotiating a range of travails and subjectivities. This chapter depicts the everyday life of the court as a space where discourses of class, taste, religion, and health are worked out, in judges' pronouncements and litigants' claims and assessments from audience benches. Like other urban spaces that are "both a product as well as a process ... [r]elate[d] to the procedures of the state, the maneuvers of the market, the anxieties of urban life, and, the positioning of the family within these contexts" (Srivastava 2009, 345), the court and its daily routines reflect the economic, political, and social matrix in which they are located. Fraudulent plots indicate, in fact, that the court has been incorporated into everyday practices of testing and shaping cultural norms.

This chapter follows the bureaucratic and political difficulties of materializing a new kind of court: How could judges, counselors, and litigants speak and behave differently while being part of a formal legalistic apparatus of appeal and evidence? Would the absence of lawyers really be useful? Women's movement organizations are split around the usefulness of mediation versus the empowering presence of lawyers (or the return to law as solution), particularly in the context of violence. While portraying the enthusiasm for these new modes of governance, including new subjectivities of litigants, counselors, and judges, I argue that seeming innovations continue to be embedded in deeply gendered conceptions of conjugality, allowing for limited negotiation. New ways of speaking and listening are not necessarily transformative without altering legal process or the inscription of marriage. These cases demonstrate the law's collusion in enforcing gendered vulnerabilities while ostensibly acting in women's best interests: marriage serves as women's refuge but thereby entraps them within cycles of violence and impoverishment.

FAMILY COURTS: HISTORY AND BACKGROUND

Globally, for at least the past half century, there have been attempts to create alternatives to trial courts. Following the CEDAW (Convention on the

Elimination of Discrimination against Women) recommendation that nations take steps to make access to the legal system easier for women, several nations instituted family courts based on the model of "unmediated" access to the law. Another critical influence was the rise of alternative dispute resolution (ADR) methods in the 1970s, which focused on decreasing the volume of cases and reducing delays by creating set-aside courts, as well as on achieving outcomes better tailored to both parties (Nader 1997, 7). These courts fall into two primary categories: those that focus on legal matters related to family and children, sometimes supplemented by pretrial mediation programs (United States, Australia, Hong Kong), and those that not only deal with particular "family" matters but are also cast as informal, comfortable spaces where litigants frame their own issues and conciliatory rather than adversarial practices are emphasized (Japan, India).

The primary rationale for establishing family courts of the latter kind has been, seemingly contradictorily, to provide a refuge from law. The argument goes that women and other marginalized social groups who have historically had less access to the law often describe formal legal proceedings in courtrooms as alienating and incomprehensible. Their claims for justice have to be translated into specific legal provisions and mediated through lawyers, and they feel little connection to the issues that brought them to court. Peter Smith narrates British litigants' "sense of unreality, the invasion of privacy, followed by distress and finally humiliation" and the recurrence of the words *frightening* and *terrifying* in describing court experiences (1988, 153, 157). To mitigate this alienation (particularly in family law, where women are present in large numbers), some legal theorists have suggested a more holistic and direct approach: to create family courts where parties would express their grievances and rebuttals in their own words, without lawyers, making legal decisions more meaningful and the law less intimidating. For example, a (failed) California legislative initiative suggested family court as the best option to eliminate fault in divorce because adversarial scenarios would not need to be artificially created (Kay 1987, 35). Smith argues that "the introduction of family courts [in the United Kingdom] would be the most effective and sustainable means" of addressing litigants' problems and ensuring "greater sensitivity" from "court officials," "less intimidating" courtrooms, and procedures that would "facilitate participation and communication"(1988, 159).

Studies indicate that these alternative-style courts have cut down on the length of proceedings, simplified logistical procedures, and involved the parties more directly through everyday language (Mir-Hosseini 1993, 31). But family courts have also created new forms of control. The Family Court of Australia, planned as a "helping court," is beset with problems pertaining to legal authority, administration, finances, and mediation procedures (Star 1996). In Iranian family courts, women are constrained by religio-legal provisions, economic priorities, and ideologies of gender (Mir-Hosseini 1993). The Japanese Kaji Chotei, an institutionalized form of customary dispute resolution, functions as "a deeply conservative institution," trying to balance the contradictory goals of "harmoniz[ing] the emotional and social relationship with a view to reconciliation" on the one hand, and relegating marital disputes to private realms where familialist ideologies prevail on the other (Minakimata 1988, 123, 126). In Canadian, Australian, and English courts (Buddin 1978; Eaton 1986; Sangster 1996; Star 1996), ideological understandings of gendered behavior don't change simply because the format and even the content of laws change.

An important corollary is the growing feminist skepticism about protection of women's legal rights provided through mediation-based divorce programs. Laura Nader, who describes alternative dispute resolution systems as "covert power mechanisms" that deny conflict and anger (1993, 2), argues that mediation sets aside questions of equality and justice for a controlled environment where definitions and speech are monitored (Grillo 1990–91). These scholars recommend instead that the public legal system be improved or that alternative dispute resolution, which can better attend to issues of power, safety, and accountability, be implemented (Edwards 1997; Mathis and Tanner 1998; Presser and Gaarder 2000).

The Indian approach to ADR veers between being aligned with traditional/indigenous dispute resolution systems and engaging optimal modern efficiency to cut down on legal backlog. Postcolonial proposals to develop indigenous systems of justice grounded in rural decentralization had been thoroughly unpopular, with only one group of Gandhians showing enthusiasm.[3] Lawyers strenuously argued against indigenous systems, in favor of "Anglo-Indian law as a most beneficent result of the British connection" (Galanter 1972, 57). It was not possible to simply revert to a notion of the precolonial past, Galanter argues, because colonial law had become "indigenous" and "thoroughly domesticated," and people were "bi-legal" in accessing formal and informal forums (63–64). The Constituent Assembly raised concerns that drawing on ancient Hindu texts would be inappropriate for a secular republic committed to social equity, an obstacle to "national unity," and that indigenous systems of dispute resolution had negative effects on socially marginal groups (61–62). ADR in India is thus deeply rooted in the postcolonial modernity of formal legal structures even though it is strategically claimed as a form of vernacularization.

The growing popularity of ADR in India reflects the good fit between global trends and India's particular difficulties with backlog and uneven justice. Civil litigation rates are very low, but there is immense court congestion, which may be explained by the nature of the lower courts: "India has only one-tenth to one-sixth the number of judges per capita found in the developing part of the common law world. Indian courts tend to be poorly equipped and inefficient. . . . [O]utmoded procedural laws provide abundant opportunity for delaying tactics, especially interlocutory appeals and stay orders. Judges, fearful of the bar, lack leverage to discipline lawyers or even to use the available tools to expedite proceedings" (Galanter and Krishnan 2003, 100). Courts vary in quality, a popular argument being that "the higher reaches of the Indian legal system have proved extraordinarily responsive and resilient, [while] its lower reaches seem to be trapped in a spiral of ineffectiveness" (96). Galanter and Krishnan deduce that people try to avoid courts if they can, aware that lawyers have limited effectiveness, and that the process favors those hoping for delay; alternatives to litigation therefore seem attractive. Family courts find favor here as parallels to other new Indian legal ventures, such as consumer courts, traffic courts, and Lok Adalat ("People's Court," specifically focused on a one-sitting resolution of cases).

The establishment of family courts in India was championed by numerous women's organizations and social work organizations "to ensure that crucial rights of survival of women are not subsumed beneath technicalities and legal jargon" (Agnes 2011, 271). The Family Courts Act (1984) provided the basis for courts dealing with divorce, maintenance, adoption, and custody cases, where litigants would express their concerns to judges in "plain language." Lawyers were discouraged, appearing only as an amicus curiae (friend of the court) by petition. "Counselors" (paralegals or social workers, not lawyers) were the navigators of this "plain language," helping clients negotiate settlements, trying to bring couples back together, and advising on legal issues. Jaipur got the first court in 1987, followed by Bengaluru, Pune, and Mumbai. There were ninety-one courts in sixty-eight districts by 2005 (Agnes 2011, 275), despite sustained opposition from lawyers' groups (Vanka and Kumari 2008, 116).

PARIVARIK ADALAT (FAMILY COURT), KOLKATA: A SKETCH

To find "the law" in India, we must look beyond the records of the legislatures and the higher courts to the workings of the lawyers and the police, to the proceedings in the lower courts, to the operations of informal tribunals and to popular notions of legality.

—Marc Galanter, "Use of Law"

The contemporary Indian legal system, as Galanter describes it, exhibits thriving legal pluralism through a variety of formal and informal, rural and urban, large and intimate options, including village compounds and clerks' quarters and office rooms and grand court buildings, verbal pronouncements and handwritten lower court files and appellate cases found in law reports. The court at the center of this chapter spans several of these levels: a lower level civil court as well as an ADR venue, a locus of formal authority and an official site of informal bargaining, encompassing a warren of administrative offices and a citywide sphere of unofficial investigation.

Each court under the Family Courts Act (1984) is governed by rules enacted at the state level. The Kolkata court, brought into being under a long-standing left coalition led by the CPI(M) (Communist Party of India [Marxist]), was a joint project of the Kolkata High Court administration and the West Bengal Ministry of Law. It drew judges from the judicial service,[4] hired administrative staff, and recruited volunteer "counselors" primarily from leaders of the ruling party's women's wing. The first Kolkata court came into being on 12 September 1994 under Judge S. N. Ganguly. Lawyers stormed the court and charged at the judge on the first day, but it has continued to function since then,[5] with the addition of a second court in 2000. The jurisdiction of the family courts covers about 20 percent of Kolkata's population (a specific urban quadrant between Park Street and Sonagachchi), and the court handles 4 percent of the matrimonial litigation of the state of West Bengal (Agnes 2004b, 25).[6] The court has a relatively small caseload compared to other courts in India (Agnes 2004b), but so far the government has been unresponsive to calls to expand its scope and size as originally announced.

The "alternative" courtroom, significantly, looks exactly like every other civil and criminal courtroom in the complex. About half the room is occupied by a raised platform for the black-robed judge, the front taken up by the judge's clerk, stenographer, and bailiff. While most litigants and their lawyers stand at on the lower level and speak across the platform, witnesses have to step up to a wooden box with bars at the judge's side. One of the courtrooms

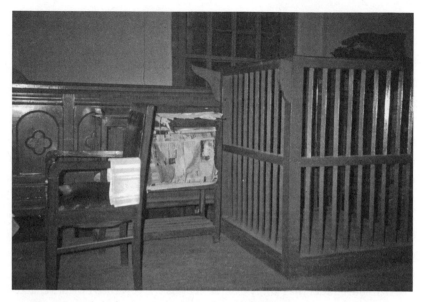

FIGURE 5. Raised platform in Courtroom I, featuring the judge's chair in the background, and the court clerk's chair and witness box in the foreground. Litigants stand in front of the platform at ground level and are deposed in the witness box.

has a wire-covered rickety "cell" (very seldom used) to house any prisoners who might be in court. A few fragile wooden benches, grossly inadequate to accommodate waiting family members and allies, and a separate bench to the side for counselors are at the back of the room; the bailiff perennially shushes the audience (both conversation and mobile phones) and scolds them into sitting with both feet on the ground. Next door, in the counselors' room, a jumble of extraordinarily rickety furniture is scattered into four or five groups, and anger or laughter from a counseling session easily drowns the adjacent one.

A quantitative summary culled from Flavia Agnes's report on the Kolkata Family Court (commissioned by the West Bengal Women's Commission) provides an equally telling portrait (2004b, 26–31).[7] Far more women than men file for divorce (71 percent), annulment (75 percent), judicial separation (78 percent), and restitution of conjugal rights (91 percent). Maintenance claims constitute 43 percent of the court's cases, filed overwhelmingly by women. Restitution cases are often filed by men in counterpoint to maintenance cases from women, petitioning for women to return to the marital household in lieu of seeking maintenance, or else to forfeit the marriage through divorce.[8] The

FIGURE 6. Enclosed temporary holding space for litigants in custody or jail, Courtroom 1.

demographic makeup of litigants reflects the quadrant of the city served by the courts; it is common to see a range of social classes from the elite to the poor, and a majority of Hindu law cases with a regular smattering of Muslim and Christian law cases (no such figures are maintained).

Claims of "speedy disposition" are generally merited in these courts: 20 percent of cases are dismissed at the preliminary stage for want of prosecution, and 75 percent of the cases that continue are cleared within the first year of filing, with another 13 percent by the second year. Only 3 percent of cases take more than three years, unlike district courts where matrimonial cases are part of a much larger pool.[9] The annual figures provided by the family court (table 5) give a similar portrait of fairly smooth passage through the courts.[10]

However, it is important to submit these figures to some methodological skepticism (which several of the judges share). These numbers record "closed files"—decisions from specific petitions (sometimes several related petitions are rolled into one). There is no way to account for the numerous cases that come back to family court after being bounced back from higher court appeals or to track the many criminal law maneuvers that get attached to these cases

TABLE 5 CASE CLEARANCE STATISTICS, KOLKATA FAMILY COURT

Year	Mat Suits Filed	Mat Suits Disposed	Misc Suits Filed	Misc Suits Disposed	Mat Exec Filed	Mat Exec Disposed
1994	56	15	112	20		
1995	231	369	165	56		
1996	271	490	166	116	17	4
1997	233	222	99	109	6	4
1998	257	212	155	175	7	7
1999	236	268	185	140	7	3
2000	226	296	201	209	9	8
2003	271	211	231	200		
2005	204	147	137	91	4	4
2006	277	285	227	227	9	4
2007	268	191	214	120	12	10
2008	293	241	210	196	11	13

NOTE: The figures reflect the categories of data collection by the Family Court. "Mat (Matrimonial) Suits" pertain to divorce-related matters. "Misc (Miscellaneous) Suits" deal with requests for maintenance under Sections 125 and 127 of the Criminal Procedure Code, and "Mat Exec (Matrimonial, Execution)" with maintenance questions under the various personal laws, including issuing execution orders for recovery of funds in cases where judgment has already been passed. Data is unavailable for 2004.

because of frequent recidivism related to maintenance. That is, these numbers do not reflect how quickly legal issues get resolved for any given individual. I have met litigants who started appeals five years after a decision or opened up a new aspect of the case years later. Nor do these numbers bear any traces of other criminal or civil litigation between the parties; hence they fail to measure people's total legal involvement.

Claims to minimize the adversarial nature of divorces in this court seem valid to some extent: 9.5 percent of cases are deemed to be "reconciled, settled or withdrawn," 13.4 percent are granted an ex parte decree, and in 33.6 percent cases there is a matrimonial decree. Almost half the cases where decrees are granted (48 percent) are mutual consent divorces, and in another 17 percent, contested matrimonial cases (on fault grounds) are converted to mutual consent divorces.[11] Settlements and mutual consent divorces signal the new horizon of nonadversarial divorce: often the agreement comes at the end of numerous highly contested legal showdowns, with a monetary agreement struck at the end for resolution (though attempts to recover money and negotiate custody can be ongoing).

Modes of legal representation notwithstanding, family courts are fundamentally lower-level civil courts.[12] This means litigants must respond to a summons and are subject to fines and imprisonment if they fail to fulfill legal orders, including ex-parte orders. Maintenance cases (including alimony and child support both during and after divorce), which constitute a full 43 percent of the cases in this court and are mostly filed by women, exemplify this puni-tive dynamic. Every day, a large number of women come to court, often repeat-edly, to find husbands defaulting on payments. This begins a retaliatory, potentially criminal hearing against the husbands, who typically show up at the hearing, make a variety of excuses and pay what is minimally necessary, then often begin defaulting on payments once again. Fifty-eight percent of maintenance cases here are filed under Section 125 of the Criminal Procedure Code, which is meant to provide support in penurious circumstances, and 30 percent deal with "recovery" of funds—that is, failure to pay according to the judgment. The economic difficulties of divorce for women are perfectly illus-trated here by the large number of women in penury outside marriage and the routines of male recidivism and women's humiliation and harassment. Agnes argues for streamlining maintenance by attaching salaries directly (2004b, 27), but that elegant solution does not account for the ways end-runs around maintenance orders express women's disentitlement.

THE TRIUMPH OF (RE)CONCILIATION

Family courts function with a profoundly ambivalent view of divorce, and thus of power, resources, and violence in marriage. Nowhere is this ambivalence better reflected than in the language of the legislation. According to the 1984 act, family courts are set up "with a view to promote conciliation in, and secure speedy settlement of disputes related to marriage and family affairs."[13] Con-ciliation is a slippery concept here; while some family court practitioners deem it to be a mode of conflict resolution, an antonym of "adversarial process,"[14] it is commonly interpreted in the Kolkata court as "re-conciliation," or doing the utmost to patch up a marriage. The slippage between the two terms reflects a long-standing legal elision.[15] The language of the act (Section 9) and the parliamentary introduction of the bill both ambiguously refer to "conciliation in marriage," and the latter frames it in terms of "preserv[ing] the institution of marriage and promot[ing] the welfare of children" (Family Courts Act [1984], 192). Legislator Susheela Gopalan's objection to the bill on the grounds that "conciliation might expose some women to further violence" presciently indicates that "reconciliation" is very much signified by *conciliation* (192).

Not only are preserving marriage and serving women's best interests potentially contradictory goals, but the two stated purposes of the act—efficiency and preservation of marriage—are also fundamentally at odds. It may be economically pragmatic for women to remain married in the absence of a radical transformation of labor markets, but the legal push often places women back in superficially changed domestic conditions. Rekha Mirchandani portrays a domestic violence court in Utah that is part of the "technocratic state," which emphasizes efficiency and coordination, though meant to incorporate "substantive justice" (2005, 384–85), arguing that this court bridges these seemingly incompatible identities. But in the Kolkata court, the goals of efficiency and substantive justice often clashed, not least because the drive toward "reunions" lengthened cases despite the directive to clear the caseload speedily.

The contradictions and potential harm of the "conciliation" standard is best exemplified by the enthusiasm for "reconciliations" seen in the Kolkata courts. At a 2001 hearing for a case filed initially in 1995, the judge privately called a couple into his chambers and deliberately asked their lawyers to stay outside, saying to them, "I know this has been going on for a while, but as long as your case is in the family court I'm going to try to see if I can get you back together." Even at the end of a long and bitter session involving lawyers, with a fragile détente at the end of the meeting, he ended by asking them to make up, saying, "Because we are in the family court, I want to stress the humane [manobik] aspects one last time." Neither the passage of time nor the mounting complications seemed to faze his conviction.

When I told counselors about my research, the first piece of evidence they triumphantly cited to proclaim the success of the family courts involved the number and kinds of "reunions" each had brought about. Resolved cases, however, often seemed packed with potential danger. Shopna, a counselor at the Kolkata courts, proudly described a case where the daughter-in-law was being physically tortured by her parents-in-law in the extended family home. Having received several frantic calls from the daughter-in-law, she had roused the municipal councilor, arrived at the home with him and some police officers, and brought out the woman in a grand rescue scene. But then, according to Shopna, "the next day we sat down with the parents and also her husband— we all talked, I did some counseling for two or three days, and then I sent her back home. Her husband is a good person—it's the parents-in-law who are violent, but he is economically totally dependent on the family business and they cannot move away. I will try to check up on her, see if she and her husband can have some separate space in the house."

In another case, she described bringing together a couple where the husband was extremely paranoid and jealous, routinely violent, and finally slashed his wife with an axe, causing her to lose three buckets of blood.[16] The client reportedly told the police that she accidentally fell on the blade, because otherwise her husband would have lost his good government job and she wouldn't be able to get maintenance for herself and their two children. Shopna described to me how she persuaded the man to see a psychiatrist for his paranoia and to allow his wife a little freedom ("Let her go to your daughter's school at least. There'll be another five parents sitting there and she can converse with them"). The couple reunited, and they stay in touch with Shopna, reporting that they are ecstatically happy.

These two accounts exemplify a narrative genre among counselors, who often describe complicated negotiations with prominent and difficult people, involving similar conversion tales of axe-wielding husbands, with happy endings whose veracity is impossible to ascertain. Reconciliation is always the optimal outcome, the triumph lying in being able to secure greater mobility or independence for the woman within the patched-up marriage. It is useful to notice that the focus of these dramatic parables is counselors' sense of accomplishment at their new jobs and the skillful negotiating tactics showcased by the reconciliation arrangements. They highlight the counselors' role in ensuring a better deal for women clients and leaving them with a sense of having a vigilant ally. Rather than assuming an absolute antiviolence stance, the counselors view ensuring strategic survival within an existing marriage as their most valuable service.

If this solution seems regressive given the enormous energy Indian women's movements have directed to antiviolence campaigns, compare Brazilian police stations for women, also a product of feminist demands. Everyday management was in the hands of women police officers who did not identify with feminist analyses of marriage, such that "it was not surprising to hear statements from policewomen that clearly undermined the original goals of the women's police stations" (Santos 2004, 43). In the Kolkata courts, too, counselors enacted broader social norms, inscribing the reconciled family as an optimal economic, emotional, and spatial solution, and violence as a bad habit (maybe this much was a legacy from the women's movement) to be eradicated by appropriate counsel.

TRANSFORMATION OF JUDICIAL AUTHORITY:
IN A DIFFERENT VOICE?

The family court is meant to be largely free of lawyerly interjections: judges directly speak with litigants, conduct most depositions and cross-examinations, and dictate (while simultaneously translating) cases to create the legal record (see chapter 3). New modes of speaking are self-consciously seen as (positively) transformative: judges and counselors frequently speak of themselves as being involved in a satisfying new experiment with more meaningful access to the legal system and as facilitating law and culture in important ways. As one Kolkata judge said, "I am very pleased with working in the family court, because I like to talk with people, and here I am very patient, though not otherwise in life." Justice S. N. Ganguly, the first judge of the family court, repeatedly described his work in the court as "lively" and "interesting." He described his charge to be that of presiding over the proceedings rather than guiding their content:

> The judge was there for facts of law, to see whether the law was being followed. But parties . . . [would] be at liberty to, and competent to, assess their cases. . . . Actually, the object of the act was this: that the parties will come direct to the court, they will put their grievances directly before the court, the judge will examine their cases, then after completing all these proceedings, the judge will come to a decision. We had to follow the Evidence Act, but the Central Act provides that the Evidence Act will not be so elaborate in the matter of family court.[17]

Beyond mere sociability, judges see themselves as optimally setting right matters of marriage and family with minimal guidance. But as we will see, their protection and patronage is often double-edged in mediating questions of gender.

The quality of judges' authority has supposedly changed: they are able, indeed encouraged, to get into the work of family reconciliation. As a female Kolkata judge said to a male client, "This is not like other courts—here I will talk to you in my chamber like a member of your family. This is what your elder sister should have been saying to you if she was thinking about what was best for you." The statement invokes the signature informality and ease of access of the family courts, in deliberate contrast to the impersonality of other courts, suggesting that informality equals greater comfort. Remarkably, the court is signaled as a better space of kinship than the family, the judge a better voice of family harmony than embroiled or indifferent family members.

While male judges had their own ways of establishing connections, this judge repeatedly invoked her gender (and her identity as mother, former teacher, judge) to justify essentialized feminine empathy and nurturance, deemed critical to this new legal process. Performances of kinship such as gift exchange, birthday celebrations, and meals, as described below, were critical to creating the spaces enabling such authority.

However, the family advice analogy also defines the court as a space where familial gender expectations may prevail. A more extensive look at the judge's rhetoric reveals the authority exercised by the female judge over the male respondent, mediating his husbandly authority. The husband, Babu, had come to court to meet his child as part of a formal visitation on her birthday. Judge K began by attempting to transform this occasion into a potential reconciliation: in her chambers, she asked Babu and Mila about getting back together, commenting on how happy they seemed in each other's presence. She advised them to make up, telling Babu he would have to change his ways a bit. "Why not her ways?" he asked. "I'll tell her too on my own," she said, "but you're the only child of your parents, and you have to realize it can't always go your way in the husband-and-wife relationship." Judge K told him he was a good person because he didn't drink or do drugs ("You don't, do you?" she asked after a moment) or smoke. "I don't even have an addiction to tea," he said. Judge: "So then, why do you say in your complaint that she refuses to make tea for guests, when she isn't used to it because her husband doesn't drink tea?" "But *she* drinks tea," he protested. The crux of the problem was that Babu had behaved badly when some of his demands were thwarted. One major issue was his refusal to allow Mila to work outside the home, although she had a good job at the Titan watch showroom and he only made about Rs. 3,000 a month (far from enough to adequately support the three of them). The judge told him, "I can't ask her to quit a good job when things are so unsettled."

The case echoed the dominant theme that "marital reconciliation" is optimal not just for the child's well-being but also for the couple, that the goal was getting past the conflict. Here Judge K appeared to be chastising the husband fondly and speaking in the wife's interest. She was enacting the perception that legal recourse is beneficial for women, that judges are favorably biased toward women's needs. But she scolded him *while* deferring to his expectations of the wife's responsibility for domestic service and his right to control her occupation and mobility. When the judge sought to modify his opposition to his wife's paid work, she did so by emphasizing the instability in Mila's life, for which Babu was at least partially culpable (because of both the unsettle-ment of the separation and his meager income), citing his failed role as bread-winner and head of household to bargain for his wife's claim. Wendy Brown's contention that "the heavy dual price of institutionalized protection is always a measure of dependence and agreement to abide by the protector's rules" (1992, 8) applies here as much to the protection extended by judicial authority as to the matrix of heterosexual conjugality.

Even though women's options within marriage appear to be negotiable, their access to the workplace and hence to income relies upon a normative patriarchal contract around men's control of labor and movement. To invoke Molyneux's useful formulation (1985), Mila's "strategic gender interests" had to be undermined to attain the benefits of "practical gender interests": because ensuring that she kept her job was critical, practical intervention was most effective, while symbolic challenges to gender might have been more threaten-ing and rhetorically less useful. This judge told me in a candid moment, "It was a good thing to have the courts, but their purpose is not being imple-mented, because the gender bias is still there." Like her negotiation, this statement might indicate that using the kinship model is a strategic move to help women, echoing the rationales of counselors' conversion narratives. But gendered subordination within marriage is not destabilized through such strategies.

OWNING THE NEW SUBJECTIVITY: AUTHORITY TO SPEAK

Chope! Ye court hai, mohalla nahi hai. [Shut up! This is a court, not your neighborhood.]
—Judge to female defendant (who was shouting over the judge, two
    counselors, and her husband's lawyer)

In this court, litigants are theoretically persons with voice and presence who are in charge of their lives. They are to conduct their own cases, put together their petitions, gather court documents, organize and maintain their files, show up at hearings, cross-examine witnesses, and manage appeals. In prac-tice, few people are able to negotiate these steps without the help of lawyers and relatives, regardless of their level of education. Still, the experience does transform women's engagement with the public sphere: many women, accus-tomed primarily to the home, now have to learn about public transportation and important court offices, cultivate a relationship with court personnel so they can ask for occasional favors, and train themselves to make their point in front of the judge. Even interactions with other litigants, such as daily prolonged conversations on the court benches, open them up to other narratives of conflict and corruption.

Social privileges strongly influence litigants' power and comfort within the courtroom. Litigants' new powers of engagement in the family courts are best utilized by those who have some educational and cultural power. As an older woman whose daughter was a litigant said to me poignantly when there was a burst of laughter in the courtroom, "What's going on? You can laugh at what the judge said because you can follow English." The proceedings in this case were occasionally but not mostly in English; however, the cross-examination being conducted largely in Bangla sounded just as foreign to her.

Those with minimal literacy skills often suffered frequent rebukes or ridicule for the way they spoke. More tangible consequences included the dire effect of ignoring court summons that read like gibberish. In one case, a barely literate woman had been given an ex parte divorce without getting the chance to oppose or apply for maintenance. Another man faced a criminal sentence for nonpayment of maintenance granted through an ex parte order, because he had simply ignored the registered court summons. When the counselors (and I) visited him in a small town three hours by train from Kolkata, we found that he had tucked away the papers in a trunk full of discarded stuff, assuming it was a summons for recovery of dowry. It seemed he mostly feared prosecution under the criminal sanctions of the Dowry Prohibition Act (1961) and believed he was in no danger from that law, having cleverly received his cash dowry through a circuitous route that could not be traced back to him. Because criminal sanctions of maintenance are not part of public apprehension in the same way that dowry crimes now are, his minimal literacy and a larger cultural legal illiteracy had blinded him (and his family) to punitive legal deadlines. Even though they could have enlisted legal aid or counselors, they did not know enough to approach the court to ask for it.

Among the educated, I observed several women who took to the court process with gusto, reading up on details of the law, gathering thorough evidence, and filing a range of complaints in civil and criminal venues. Often these were women who experienced litigation as a chance to finally make grievances public. Court functioned as a space to expose financial and moral hypocrisies and bear witness to violence or neglect, with the triumph of evidence and the backing of legal sanction. Even this potential empowerment, however, was limited by expectations of judicial control.

A case in point involved Rupak, a youngish man who had a high-end job at a reputable bank, and Ratna, who occasionally earned money by tutoring. Most litigants, when invited by the judge to cross-examine, were at a complete loss; typically, they would repeat the complaints they had against the opposing party, and the judge would try to translate this into questions for the witness. But Ratna was meticulously prepared on the day of Rupak's testimony, using a style of questioning that mimicked lawyers. She asked him about his hidden bank accounts, his recent attempts to obtain an expedited passport, his drunkenness and violence, and his irregular maintenance payments (calling him a "habitual offender" at this, using those English words). Her relentless questioning continued: "Did you have money in that bank or not, Mr. Roychoudhury?—you must answer" and "Do you regularly pay maintenance?—you must answer." He was usually nonresponsive, at which she would turn to the judge and tell him to direct the witness to answer.

However, *formally* Ratna was only allowed to ask questions as interjections to the judge's own process.[18] He was ready to cross-examine on her behalf and had been going through the plaint asking Rupak to confirm or deny allegations, becoming increasingly irritated by the active role she enthusiastically assumed whenever he turned to nominally seek her assent. When she smirked in directing a question to her husband, he scolded, "Don't laugh, this is a courtroom." He finally silenced her by saying, "So do you want to do all the asking? Then I can just let you do this job and not say anything." Such active roles assumed by clients are perceived as disruptive and inappropriate. In other cases, judges publicly reprimanded those who sought to negotiate with them personally. When a client plaintively asked, "But can't I appeal to you? Whom else can I appeal to?" (*Apnar kachchey appeal korbo na?*), the judge angrily yelled, "Is this a vegetable market that you think you can bargain here?" (*Eta ki alu potol beguner dokan je dam komaben?*). Clients' activities have to fit a specific legal script that demarcates a judge's power, where docility may be critical for currying favor.

"SEEING WITH BOTH EYES": COUNSELORS AND LAWYERS

The ideal of family courts imagines that the technicality and expense, the "waste," of lawyers is surmounted through the work of counselors. However, to others, including many feminist groups, lawyers bring optimal efficient strategy and protect clients from judicial coercion, while counselors act in line with authoritative power.[19] In the Kolkata Family Court, lawyers and coun-selors each saw themselves as best representing clients. They passionately accused each other of hindering and impoverishing clients; the political and logistical structures of their work fomented mutual animosity. Who better served the gender justice goals of legal access and economic provision is a more complicated question.

Counselors work to fashion a petition after talking to litigants and their families (even visiting them at home), taking them through the whole legal process. They often describe themselves as being involved in an important social experiment and emphasize the court's unique method, citing the special parajudicial powers given them by the act to investigate and craft mutual-consent divorce petitions. They depict themselves as providing a superior impartial perspective and solutions untainted by family dynamics, as experts skilled in kinship work and in making the beneficence of the state legible. They are a critical piece in the alternative dispute resolution process through their personal interaction and help with legal framing.

Kolkata Family Court counselors represent their voluntary labor as highly honorable, an apt extension of their skills in negotiation and their network of contacts. As Monisha said:

> The thing about family courts is that people's idea of what a court is does not mesh with what we have here, because the self-interest of lawyers doesn't work here. The government appointed women like us as counselors here: we were sent by women's organizations as representatives, because we've had a long experience of doing this kind of work, and we have a responsibility to our organizations and to society. . . . Unlike lawyers, we don't support one side, we want the best interests of both sides to be served. This is very hard work, takes a lot of time. You also need the person-ality to get along with all the people. But when we can see the work has gone well, when we see the couples become one again, then that is such a huge mental peace, you can't compensate for that with a lakh of rupees. And that is the meaning of family courts—both counselors and also judges work toward this.

Another counselor, Shilpa, used the metaphor of stereoscopic vision: "Our biggest difference with lawyers [is] that we are appointed by the court and don't represent any one side. I see both sides and also the court's interest, for example to curb delays, all of that. What do lawyers do? They look out of one eye only, not both eyes." They underline their social work as pivotal, pointing to the complex set of skills they claim is needed to be successful. However, because they see the fundamental purpose of the job as marital reconciliation and negotiating with families, their work may serve to reinforce gender and class hierarchies, as described in a previous section.

The conditions of the Kolkata Family Court counselors' labor are important in further explicating their passionate attachments. Mumbai and Delhi Family Court counselors are professional appointees (with either the equivalent of a master's in social work or a law degree), deemed to be government servants of fairly high rank, with their own private offices and investigative staff. In contrast, the Kolkata counselors basically perform honorary service, with no salary and only a small honorarium and expense budget, charged per visit and session. And for expenses, they are constantly harassed by the court administration and frequently paid partially, rebuffed by the citation of some subtle new bureaucratic rule for reimbursement. A comparison of the quiet private offices of the Mumbai counselors and their sunny group conference room with the broken and rickety furniture in the Kolkata Family Court counselors' public room provides further proof of the state's low acknowledgment for their work. Little wonder that their number has dwindled from fifteen in 2001, when I first started working there, to about four regular counselors at present.

Unlike family courts in other Indian cities, where elite women dominate as counselors (Vatuk 2006), most Kolkata counselors and judges are from lower-middle to middle-class backgrounds, and the lack of pay poses a serious hardship, as well as subjecting them to routine harassment from the accounts office.[20] The frustration in turn foments corruption;[21] clients and women's organizations allege that some counselors ask clients for informal payments for transportation or food, which not only violates the law but sets up the potential for a favorable outcome for the litigant most able or willing to treat counselors. Some judges respond to this by denying counselors an active role, failing to appoint counselors to cases (in possible violation of the law) and taking on the negotiations themselves. This creates further economic vulnerability for counselors, makes the role of the judge even greater, and increases the adversarial process, as lawyers are likely to get more involved. As the example of the Mumbai courts suggests, a well-paid salary and a clear structure of compensation would go a long way toward enhancing both the dignity and the livelihood of these counselors.

It is important to note that thus far, most Kolkata counselors had been appointed because of their experience in "women's wings" of the ruling party's community organizations (including the CPI(M) but other left auxiliaries as well) and continued to be active party workers. They often referred to the

FIGURE 7. The counselors' room with grouped chairs and tables. An enclosed holding space for litigants in custody has been used in the last fifteen years to hold old files and papers.

counseling structure as a powerful social intervention instituted by a progressive government. Being appointed counselors validated their status within the party as well as their political and cultural capital; they saw themselves as helping the party succeed by managing the sphere of "family." But the gendered nature of their unpaid labor is significant, even (or especially) within a party that foregrounds equity (but primarily of class rather than gender [Ray 1999]). The counselors were in a singularly weak negotiating position for improving the conditions of their labor; while their work reflected positively on the party, their complaints could also only go so far, since they were encouraged not to make the Left Front look bad. In the years since I have begun studying these courts, there was an annual pilgrimage to important personages at the Law Ministry and the West Bengal Women's Commission,[22] always resulting in platitudes and promises, the only visible improvements so far being a wooden locker partially assigned for the counselors' personal possessions. While they were always highly praised for their service, their rights to compensation were not seen as a significant claim in the list of government priorities.

Judges and lawyers express unhappiness with the system of counselors, but ironically the strongest objections have come from local feminist organizations that deal with violence against women. These groups not only allege bribery and corruption in the courts but also find the counselors' focus on reconciliation and marriage and the lack of attention to addressing violence deeply problematic. Krishna Roy of Swayam said in a 2001 interview, "The idea of a speedy trial is okay, but counseling doesn't seem very valuable. Counselors should get training in how women can become independent, not in how to patch up marriage." For organizations such as Swayam and Nari Nirjaton Pratirodh Mancha (Forum against torture of women), the criticism of the counselors is consonant with their wariness toward the methodologies of the family court, and they strongly oppose lawyerless courts. Similarly, Maitreyi Chatterji of Mancha listed a series of grave problems her organization has with the family court: validation of patriarchal attitudes, a problematic emphasis on reconciliation, and the heightened vulnerability of clients who have no lawyers protecting their interests.[23]

What could be bad about diminishing the footprint of lawyers? The innovation of being lawyer-free, meant to enhance litigants' legal agency, does not take account of the average (or even the well-educated and powerful) litigant's discomfort and disorientation with representing herself/himself, such as having to fit problems to legal provisions, negotiate remedies, or depose and cross-examine witnesses, including the spouse. Many feminist organizations advocate for legal representation despite the extra economic burden, identifying the lack of lawyers and the disproportionate reliance on judges and counselors as being the core of the problem with redressing violence. As Krishna Roy of Swayam pointed out, "Laws and procedures stay the same, but women fight their own cases: that's the theory. This doesn't strengthen women's position in itself—only if a judge really tries. A judge will ask women to file petitions, but women don't know what it means. They need a lawyer behind them—for example, Swayam lawyers have drafted cases. Lawyers have to be paid, but judges are also afraid of lawyers watching, can't do illegal things."[24]

According to the Family Courts Act (1984), a lawyer was to be present in the courtroom only as amicus curiae, as *court-bandhob* or friend of court, present merely in a civilian advisory capacity: "Leave your black robe out in the corridor and come in your regular clothes," as one of the judges referred to it. Lawyers saw the amicus curiae provision as harmful to their business, also claiming that it created greater vulnerability for clients and enabled corruption of court staff and judges. These were the ostensible reasons for lawyers' angry

FIGURE 8. Lawyers' temporary offices on court premises.

protests when the Kolkata Family Court first opened, and these courts have stalled in other Indian cities because of similar agitation.

In practice, lawyers have steadily claimed the court as their territory. I observed in the Mumbai (2004–6) and Pune (2004) courts that only clients accompanied by their lawyers were allowed to enter the space of the family court. According to some lawyers in the Mumbai court, this was an interpretation of the act's provision for "in-camera" hearings (except that judges still held in-camera hearings in their own chambers). Remarkably, this turns on its head the logic of allowing only amicus lawyers for the family court, by implying that the absence of the usual "public" in a courtroom turns it into a "private" space for the litigating couple; lawyers are depicted as neutral and without any interests, equivalent to empty space. I have sat in on many courtroom sessions, increasingly since 2004, where a flock of four or eight lawyers would swoop in wearing their black robes, the clients following inconspicuously behind, sometimes even absent. In one hearing in Mumbai in 2004, there were four lawyers in the courtroom, two for each side, while the clients were in Dubai and London.

In the Kolkata court, too, the spatial arrangements signify the reception of lawyers. In 2001, when I started working there, there were three scant chairs that the counselors occupied, and counselors would shoo away lawyers (and litigants) if they sat in them, often to lawyers' great umbrage. Lawyers' protests were feeble: "This must be the lawyers' bench, every court has one," one outraged lawyer demurred. "It must say so on the back of the bench." Now there are three rows of chairs in that space, and lawyers and counselors share seats. Similarly, the picture of legal representation is very different. In 2001, clients were occasionally (in exceptional circumstances) allowed to petition the judge to have lawyers by their side to work with judges and court officers, though most people tried to represent themselves. In 2003, these occasional petitions gained more formal status in the wake of an appellate decision affirming a litigant's right to be represented in court,[25] it becoming practically pro forma for litigants to have lawyers.

The dilemma of allowing litigants to work out their own issues in the spirit of the court as opposed to honoring the legal right to be represented is well illustrated in a case from 2001. Parul, a young, slim Gujarati woman in a green *salwar kameez*, was in court, along with her father and some male relatives. Her absent husband had filed a motion asking for an adjournment, with the rationale that it was a time of year for fasting in honor of ancestors. Parul contended that everyone fasted, and he should not get time off for it, alleging that he had tried various delaying tactics. She told Judge K, "Don't let him ask for any more adjournments, Your Honor." The judge agreed to go ahead with the framing of issues that were the order of the day, and they moved on to Parul's two motions, the first of which asked that the husband not be allowed a lawyer. Parul pled, "I don't want a lawyer and I don't want him to have one either. I will do this myself, Your Honor. I want to see to my own case. He is afraid of me and doesn't want to speak in front of me, and so he has a lawyer. Let us work out our issues directly," adding, "You don't interfere also, Your Honor!" The judge tried to explain to her at length that she had no right to deny anyone a lawyer if they requested one, and therefore she was advising Parul also to get a lawyer. She tried to convince Parul that the lawyer would only be helping as an amicus curiae, and that the litigant would be in charge of speaking and cross-examining, "because this is family court, after all." Here, Parul verbalized almost a perfect rendition of the way the family court was envisioned: an unmediated reckoning between the two litigants, with minimal interference from legal authorities. As the judge's well-meaning attempts make clear, though, in the emerging climate it was to Parul's disadvantage to be the only one without a lawyer because it rendered her strategically weaker.

In the decade and a half of the court's existence, Kolkata Family Court judges' attitudes to legal representation have varied widely. Some judges assiduously followed the directive and expelled lawyers from the courtroom unless they were specifically the lawyer of record. One judge in 2005 was in the habit of saying, "I'm from a family of lawyers; how can I cut down on their business?" According to the counselors, they had to make use of political connections to get him to call upon counselors. A recent judge is seen by the counselors to be exemplary in routinely denying lawyers and supporting the counselors' work. In July 2010, as I saw him reject several petitions for amicus curiae where he considered the litigants capable of representing themselves, I realized that the family court avoidance of lawyers was not necessarily over. In Parul's case, however, the judge illustrated a common contradiction: emphasizing the empowerment of litigants through direct participation, while also warning a litigant that being unilaterally without representation might not be in her best interest.

Having observed the diligent and creative work provided by feminist legal organizations in India, such as Majlis (in Mumbai) and Anveshi (in Hyderabad), and by women's organizations that turn to ally lawyers, such as Suraha and Mancha in Kolkata (some of which is profiled in chapter 7), I have been witness to the vigilance that can be exercised by lawyers attentive to gender disparities. On the other hand, I also realize that many (or most) lawyers do not come to family court with that level of vigilance, or keep their clients well informed of their options, or keep costs as low as possible. My fieldwork diary was frequently filled with accounts (and expletives) regarding lawyers who presented the flimsiest of excuses for delays or were reprimanded for basic errors: a woman whose hearing was delayed at the end of a long day because her husband had arrived in court but his lawyer, who allegedly had all the papers, had not; a lawyer who wanted a deferral because he had left his papers at home (and proved to be completely unprepared to argue when the judge went on nonetheless); as well as numerous examples of failing to complete the most basic tasks in this court, such as the correct steps to get an ex parte order or an arrest warrant for recidivism in maintenance.

Because the choice of counselor or lawyer was such an acute and divisive one in the women's movement, I was frequently asked which side of the argument I supported. I came to believe that my answer was contingent on the nature of counseling and lawyering, and that both could be deployed advantageously. Legal experts have suggested other alternatives (Agnes 2011, 312–16).

Justice Konar, who moved on from being a Kolkata Family Court judge to designing legal clinics, strongly argued that people with some legal training would be preferable to counselors, though the interface could be informal.[26] One of the lawyers preparing the report for the West Bengal Women's Commission predictably recommended improved and precise legal expertise: a legal cell to sort and advise, specialized and extensive legal training for counselors, and help from skilled arbitrators and mediators. For feminist organizations like Swayam, the critical point was greater efficiency in the things women most urgently needed, not necessarily more law. Krishna Roy said, "The solution would be implementing maintenance efficiently in all courts. Women at all levels need empowerment, education, health, skills development."[27]

We see here two drastically opposed perspectives to institutionalizing feminist reform, reflected in the larger divisiveness over family courts: do-it-yourself mediation mainstreamed through state-directed ADR or reliance on (literal) advocates. The irony is that both sides see themselves as helping women by redressing gendered poverty and curbing violence through law. From Swayam and Mancha's perspective, trusting solely in state judicial entities is foolhardy when laws are complicated and legal strategy vital. The personal advocacy of one's lawyer is critical when normative gender ideologies minimize the impact of violence and emphasize women's "adjustment" within marriage. Arguably, counselors represent a different form of agency; they see themselves as helping women concretely on a daily basis by using their skills in community work and devote a great deal of time and mostly unpaid labor to the effort. They are limited by the alternative economic and cultural spaces that can be imagined for women and, moreover, may themselves not be entirely in disagreement with ideologies of gender and class. As with women's police stations, these negotiations may be characterized as struggles between scripts of feminism and femininity (Hautzinger 1997).

CONCLUSION: INNOVATION WITHIN LIMITS

In profiling the family court as a space of new forms of legal subjectivity and cultural encounters, I have highlighted some contradictions that emerge from feminist visions of working through state institutions: the use of mediation for reconciliation, the ambivalent discourses of protection and familialism, and the emergence of unruly subjects. However, such contradictions are an expected counterforce to the shifts in public discourse sought by feminist legal reform. Wendy Brown suggests provocatively that "given a choice between rationalized, procedural unfreedom on one hand, and arbitrary deprivation, discrimination, and violence, on the other, some, perhaps even most, women might opt to inhabit a bureaucratized domain over a 'state of nature' suffused with male dominance" (1992, 10). That is, spaces such as the family court are useful in leveraging the state, no matter the limited effects, in preference to nonregulated cultural spheres of patriarchy.

Law *or* marriage cannot of course be changed through one site alone, or through one recommendation. In these courts, while lip service is paid to alternative methods, following legal format is essential for the legibility of cases. Litigants are subjected to judge-directed techniques and counselors' evaluations, and they are expected to be best represented through the mediation of these personages. In fact, it could be argued that this format has vastly increased judges' unilateral power in exchange for lawyers', with fewer checks and balances. Those with few educational and financial resources are at a further disadvantage, unable either to perform satisfactorily in court or to hire lawyers for a potentially better outcome. Nor are lawyers a guarantee of efficient, cost-effective, judicious results.

Women could carve out a space in family courts to directly confront husbands about private grievances with the backing of the law, especially if they were wealthy or educated. But the broader cultural and legal matrix of women's economic dependence on marriage for food and shelter, and the issue of control of women's decisions and movements, limited any potential empowerment. Domestic violence was primarily treated as a personality-related aberration, and wifehood and motherhood were associated with tolerance and sacrifice, such that "successful" economic and social outcomes for women were usually achieved within these ideologies. In game theory terms, where "the mutuality or asymmetry of a relationship can be measured by the relative capacities of the parties to withdraw from it" (Okin 1989, 137), the negotiations demonstrated women's relative disadvantage: while legal provisions surrounding divorce were conceptually equitable, partners were vastly different with regard to economic capacities and cultural expectations. Altering the mode of litigation was thus not a sufficient condition either for overcoming the alienation of legal process or for transforming the differential privileges of marriage.

CHAPTER 5

In Sanity and in Wealth

Diagnosing Conjugality and Kinship

Rapid growth in population has led to a proportionate increase in the number of divorce cases. Many social factors are responsible for the spurt in their numbers. The most important reason is that women have started asserting their legitimate equal status in the family, refusing to be subjugated by their husbands for life as their grandmothers used to be.

—D. Mahapatra, "Is Hindu Marriage Law Breaking Homes?"

The widespread lament that divorce is becoming more popular and arbitrary diagnoses "modern marriage" as the culprit, based on its association with the progression of individuality and the corresponding loss of the beneficent extended family. The epigraph locates this anxiety in the mainstreaming of gender equity discourses. Similarly, the Chairman of the Legal Aid Services of West Bengal is quoted as attributing rising divorce "to the two 'E's: education (among women) and ego": "The ego clash between husbands and wives in middle-class families is increasing with the rise in educational rate among women."[1]

"You should see how much they care about each other," Kolkata Family Court counselor Shilpa complained to her fellow counselors and me over lunch. The divorcing couple she had worked with that morning seemed much too affectionate to her: they used the familiar *tui* form of address with each other;[2] they were sharing a plate of food as they talked to her; the woman broke her pencil in half to share with her soon-to-be ex-husband. But they wanted a divorce, telling her that while they were in love and had known each other for a while before marriage, they had found they had no physical attraction toward each other upon consummating the relationship after the wedding. In this room, where daily battles were waged to mend marriages against all odds, Shilpa felt baffled by this rationale. Unable to accept sexual incompatibility as a valid reason to end marriage, she contended that they were simply using a convenient legal ground. Using the powers given to counselors for mutual consent petitions, she rendered a formal decision that she saw no justification for divorce upon observation. Quickly, both partners said that the other was now involved with someone else, meaning they could file for divorce on grounds of adultery.

I have a cache of similar stories, often brought up by the counselors as worst-case scenarios, apocalyptic visions of the end of marriage. Sraboni recounted a case in which a Marwari woman had divorced her Bengali husband because as a lifelong vegetarian she was unable to deal with the nonvegetarian smells of her affinal household (including onion and garlic). Her parents refused to set foot in such nonvegetarian space, while her husband was unable to move out, being an only son and close to his parents. As in the previous case, the counselors were puzzled by the couple's affection for each other throughout the process. Similarly, Manoshi had clients who had studied together through college and postgraduate work, but when the husband continued advanced studies in nuclear physics, his wife filed for divorce, saying that "I liked you when we were both students, but now you're so engrossed in studying that there's no life for us." Sushila described a woman who sought a divorce because "I didn't know he would be transferred to Nagaland" (in the northeast corner of India). One of Champa's favorite examples centered around ground turmeric: the husband came from an old-fashioned family, expected his wife to grind turmeric by hand, and refused through long months of reconciliation attempts to compromise on turmeric powder.

Such narratives come to constitute the counselors' archives for diagnosing marriage problems brought to court. As diagnoses, they inevitably involve a teleological reading of symptoms, used for technical knowledge production. The narratives are best read not as "true" renditions of problems so much as litigants' strategic framing and counselors' illustrations of skill at their new jobs, like the accounts of reconciliation in chapter 4. However, their accounts allow us to examine the symptoms of "good" and "bad" marriages to diagnose the nature of the putative "illness."

Media accounts list similarly outrageous reasons. A typical example, connoting falsity and callousness, is implied in the headline "Cook Up a Story and Offload Your Spouse." The article describes some "yarns that husbands and wives weave to convince judges": "I don't like the way he wears his clothes and hair; She applies coconut oil and turmeric every day; He does not eat non-veg at all, wants only vegetarian cooking at home; She has eloped 22 times since we got married 15 years ago, I am not keen to take her back; He always runs around half-naked in the house."[3] Urban women's changing sexual expectations are illustrated by the case of "a 32-year-old software professional who had filed for divorce because her husband did not indulge in foreplay,"[4] their attitude to religion in another's complaint that her "religious minded husband wanted to offer prayers with her at least thrice a day," to which she responded, "Being religious is one thing, but how can I come home during lunch and spend an hour in puja?"[5] Like the counselors' archive, these news stories depict changing subjectivities as cause for alarm, contrasting quotidian trivialities with the capacious tolerance imagined to exist within "traditional" marriage. Women's articulation of desires, domestic, sexual, and material, are signaled as the core of trouble. Significantly, this dominant discourse on divorce elides the raw and difficult questions that emerge in working out marital dissolution: women's economic survival outside marriage, men's responsibilities simultaneously toward wives and natal kin, the generational distribution of immoveable and other property, and living with violence as a condition of marriage.

This chapter is a portrait of marriage constituted through legal disputes and their cultural propagation, focusing on the opposition between the conjugal and the familial. When litigants frame their marital troubles, either through ideologies of custom and tradition or through legal grounds of divorce, such as cruelty, neglect, or insanity, they marshal evidence to fit their arguments or resist them with alternative ideologies. A primary tension in these accounts is that between the couple imagined in marriage law and the extended family, depicted as the normative location of conjugal life. Negotiations typically involve marital assets and alimony, but questions of gendered provision and dependency, as well as intergenerational distribution of property, are fundamentally at stake. Class and religious hegemonies are also reproduced. I trace the embodiment of these tensions in two nodes that illuminate the social-sexual contract of marriage: allegations of (women's) insanity as a ground of divorce speak to the exchange of sex, companionship, and monetary support in marriage, while requests for maintenance reveal performances of masculinity through class, as well as gendered entitlements to labor, income, and property.

KINSHIP IN THE COURT

"Family" or "kin" relationships involve the transmission and exchange of rights and responsibilities, such as usufructuary (use) rights to land or calls upon labor. Kinship constituted the basis of the "legal" long before the advent of the contemporary nation-state, in precolonial attempts to categorize family and kin for purposes of justifying asset distribution or lines of succession (Chatterjee 2004), or in the colonial state's interventions in matrilineal communities (Saradamoni 1999; Arunima 2003) and levirate marriages (Chowdhry 1994). In many of these interventions, "custom" was reinterpreted to establish patrilineal kinship as normative, erasing alternative regional practices and transforming sexuality and entitlement.

The intergenerational patrilineal joint family, attached to a common core of (landed) property, a shared household, and a web of choreographed relationships, is depicted as the iconic family form in India, despite its innumerable variations by region, caste, and ethnicity (Kolenda 1984; Gough 1994). It is often represented by anthropologists as an exemplar of cohesion and mutual dependence. Posited as the most significant economic unit for agrarian families, it is believed to have adapted flexibly to industrialization and urbanization, with "joint family property" being the primary route for intergenerational property transfers, and a benevolent, altruistic head of household as arbitrator of the distribution of resources (Vatuk 1972; Madan 1994; Wadley 2002). Important here is its status not only as a prime vehicle for consolidating economic resources (Agarwal 1994; Basu 1999) but as an overdetermined signifier of self and community, "an oppositional space of affect, memory and wholeness called the Indian family" in the anxious "postcolonial modernity of an urban middle class" (Cohen 1998, 105). As this chapter shows, it is a dense site of signification whether or not common property or cohesion is in play.

Yet the joint family evokes social inequalities and forms of alienation and oppression. The classic 1988 film *Dadi's Family*, about a farming family in Haryana (Camerini, Gill, et al. 1988), attempts to recuperate the theory that everyone benefits by pooling resources and living together. But its careful documentary work cannot miss the fracture points, such as the educated urban son who is starting a nuclear household or the alienation of daughters-in-law. More volubly, feminist visions of social change, such as the *Towards Equality* report (see chapter 2), have targeted this joint family as central to gendered hierarchy and oppression. Feminist accounts emphasize that women, especially younger daughters-in-law, have little or no property interests and live under ideologies of subordination, vulnerable to violence; daughters too rarely get a share of the family's property fund (Basu 1999), and widows are routinely destitute (Banerjee and Mukherjee 2005).

The idealization of this family form is, significantly, an act of moral assertion rather than a statistical fact. While the "ideal" joint family is represented as rural, with expansive space and abundant resources, only 53 percent of rural households (50.3 percent of total households, according to the 2011 census) have more than four members; only two-thirds of households in India are rural (22.1 of 33.1 core households). "Joint families" (often counted by proxy as "households with more than one married couple") constitute 18 percent of households nationally and 15.5 percent of West Bengal households.[6] Much of the rural population is landless or owns a small and unproductive portion of land, especially among lower castes and scheduled tribes (Agarwal 1994). More joint families are emerging in urban areas, likely because of high living costs and property prices.[7] Nonetheless, T. N. Madan argues, "The sentiment for joint family living has remained generally undiminished irrespective of the kinds of household the respondents themselves lived in" (1994, 433), recalling Cohen's emphasis on the affective trope. Such representations idealize not just a patriarchal system but also normative caste and class ideals. Common crises in urban residence and property, the focus of this chapter, include the difficulties of finding affordable residential space (rented or owned), dividing urban property assets, and managing eldercare, romance, and domestic violence. The ideal joint family is rare in the past or future of these litigants but carries force as a form of identity and belonging.

The Kolkata Family Court mirrored these fractures, asserting hegemonic norms of kinship even as it routinely mediated kin conflicts. Court personages self-consciously saw themselves as creating new forms of kinship and using law to enforce kin and conjugal responsibilities. They often did this through the language of fictive kinship, using relational categories to soften the contours of state legal authority. Manavi took along a friend to the house of a male litigant's brother, in a case where they needed the litigant's home address to serve court papers. They went in saying they were (maternal) aunts (*mashis*) of the bride and wanted to meet the new groom. Lest we read this claim as outright deception, it should be remembered that *mashi* is a common relational form of address, both an intimate and a broad kinship term, through which one might customarily hail neighbors, mothers' friends, or friends' mothers, in addition to relatives. Manavi reported that the litigant's brother and his wife treated them very well and promised to produce an address for their brother, who was not living there then.

In the next phase, after she had indeed been given an address, I accompanied Manavi and another counselor to the man's rural home a few hours from Kolkata. Upon meeting the young man, to whom she was to deliver a notice to appear in court (with possible criminal sanctions if he didn't appear), she greeted him warmly, saying how much she liked his face when she first saw his picture, how handsome and gentle he seemed. She established an easy familiarity with him and his mother, talked about his brother's hospitality, and told his mother that her (estranged) daughter-in-law spoke of her fondly. We drank tea with them and met their extended family and neighbors, then toured the neighborhood. After a while, Manavi suggested "as an aunt" (*mashi*) that it would be good if he came to court on the assigned date and talked to the judge himself, her approach softening the nonnegotiability of the legal summons. The family responded cordially and brought all their documents out from a high shelf for us to peruse, responsive to the empathy. The counselors were able to explain the urgency of the summons and the nature of the appearance, making clear to the young man that it was not a summons under the Dowry Prohibition Act, as he feared. The success of informal channels for conveying a summons, as a deliberately alternative form of legal access, is well demonstrated here. Discourses of kinship were deployed both instrumentally and strategically to signal ease and approachability, through familiar registers of emotional response. Counselors performed as well-meaning "aunts" rather than intrusive officers of the law.

In another case that demonstrates counselors working through kinship ties, Manavi recounted recognizing a litigant, the wife of the principal of a renowned college, as a former classmate. She was in court for a divorce and had received the paltry sum of Rs. 500 as maintenance despite her husband's income. When Manavi introduced herself, her classmate delightedly took her home to meet her acutely ill ninety-five-year-old mother. The mother, Manavi narrated, recognized her and held on to her hands and pleaded with her (and the other counselor who was with her) for a better outcome, saying she would not die in peace until the case was resolved, and that she was counting on them ("Tomra koriye dao" [You can make it happen]). When the maintenance order was tripled in a subsequent court hearing (not necessarily through the counselors' intervention), her classmate's mother asked one of her other daughters for some cash and put it in two envelopes, sending them to the counselors, and died the next day. It was not the amount but the thanks that touched Manavi, she claimed. While this connection was serendipitous, it was typical of ties sought by litigants, where they approached court officials by citing networks of relatives or neighbors or friends. The court was thus enmeshed in the simultaneous disentangling and entangling of kinship ties: court officials consciously placed themselves within familial positions even as they were involved in undoing or refashioning family ties in the course of their work. They thereby cast themselves as embodying, and modeling, "better" families.

If the affective complexity of relationships in the joint family is the pre-eminent basis for its claim to superiority, its primary negative associations are with stark inequalities of power. Significantly, the weight of relationality and care falls disproportionately or even entirely on women: the harmony of the household, the viability of the joint family, and hence the sustainability of the marriage are typically linked to daughters-in-law smoothly executing domestic tasks and building appropriate relationships. The following 2004 hearing presents, in Alok's allegation of "desertion" and "cruelty," just such a script for daughters-in-laws' labor and liability for maintaining domestic harmony. Alok testified that his wife, Putul, threw utensils (at someone?), that she refused to do domestic work ("Barir kajkormo korey na"), and that she left and began living with her parents, agreeing to return only on condition that her husband get a separate residence. Complaints articulated in his legal petition (in English)—"I did not want to separate my parents and therefore did not agree to the proposal," "She did not behave properly with the inmates [sic] of my house," that she made his mother ill, and that the household members were in tension—were framed by a discourse in which harmonious life in the extended family was the only possible location of conjugality and separation was a threat to social cohesion. Putul's response echoed a set of strategic positions that complied with her role in the extended family. She submitted that she wanted to stay but could not and that her in-laws' behavior had changed after they did not get the Rs. 50,000 they wanted. These were the most common representations of conjugal roles: being a good wife depended upon a willing, self-effacing harmony with the extended patrilineal household and a severed connection with the wife's natal family, an equilibrium upset only by violence in the former.

The negative valence of women's closeness with their natal families is illustrated by the case of a young woman crying in the corridor, pointed out by

Shilpa. Paromita had been sent back from the joint family home, the in-laws' main allegation being that her father visited her every day for several hours. There may have been unexpressed issues of mental disability in Shilpa's rendition that Paromita's "nerves" and "brain" were "weak" (using those English words), that she often dropped things or miscalculated the number of cups of tea she was making; her father was nervous about these tasks and hung around to help. Shilpa advised him not to interfere in Paromita's new life, but instead to pay for a domestic servant to take care of the chores. Here, the daily presence of the daughter-in-law's natal family was seen as deeply threatening to her assimilation with her affines and their prerogative to control her mobility, labor, and affect, reminiscent of the critique in *Towards Equality* (CSWI 1974) that the isolation of the daughter-in-law in the patrilineal extended family is the optimal locus of control and violence. As discussed in a later section on mental health, it is also significant that her inability to satisfactorily perform domestic chores could cause the marriage to fail, whether or not the rest of the extended family could undertake this labor.

Claims for separate residence indicated women's failure to "adjust" skillfully to family "tensions" and assume the appropriate burden of kinship, thereby introducing the heavy-handed mark of law in the family. Manavi, the counselor skilled in kin negotiations described earlier, described her intervention with Priya, a young woman in her neighborhood who had suddenly gone back to her parents' home while her husband was out of town. This was a neighborhood dispute, as yet informal, in which Manavi had been invited to intervene based on her professional experience. Priya complained that her mother-in-law fussed at her about household work, such as whether the potatoes had been cut properly, and had once said midargument (ostensibly rhetorically), "One day I'll burn you to death" (*Ekdin puraiya marum*). She also implied that the father-in-law had made sexual overtures.

Her complaints fell within the common script of extended family tensions, and Manavi's reported advice about adjustment and eventual empowerment also reflected this ideology: "I told her that her mother-in-law had a lot of health problems like high blood pressure and blood sugar and had been laid up, and that a lot of problems crop up in the domestic realm. When I would leave for my master's courses, my own mother-in-law would say about me, 'Off dancing again' [*Oi je nachtey berochchey*]. I told her [Priya], 'In five months, you haven't put down deep roots in this family's soil yet' [*E poribar-e tomar shikor mati obdhi-i pounchoyni*]—you'll have to make space here, establish your influence [adhipotyo sthapon]." The counselor emphasized the value of living with extended family and of establishing a long-term presence within the family, awaiting a transformation in the balance of power. Gendered hierarchies were minimized and normalized by the reference to Manavi's own (triumphant) life history.

The corresponding burden of kinship on husbands (as sons and brothers) was a heavy financial commitment to their extended families. Husbands often claimed financial responsibilities to the extended family as a strategy to counter claims of neglect, cruelty, and maintenance, arguing that family obligations mitigated those to the conjugal unit. In a child support case, for example, the father proffered that about a quarter of his take-home pay as a professor was going to repay a loan for his sister's wedding. Here, familial obligations for brothers contributing to the family resource pool for sisters' weddings were cited as normative, such contributions being not unusual but also not ubiquitous. In the claim, however, they were equated to a father's child support obligations; when framed that way, the judge would need to either reduce the funds available for child support or challenge the validity of the contribution. Hence kinship obligations had a direct effect on the nuclear family's share.

The extended family was evoked as moral currency even when it was quite evidently in shambles, as illustrated in the judicial reification of "Indian family" norms and the demonization of "the West" in the following admonition to facilitate visits for a noncustodial father and the paternal family. In response to the wife Jaya's attempt to include as a condition for custody that there be no contact with her mother-in-law, the judge scolded, "Indian Hindu family means connection with family. After marriage, the primary family is the husband's family, the wife's family is secondary after that. In a Western country, children move far away from their parents [Chchelemeye boro holey baba ma'r thekey durey jan]. Where on earth have you learned these things—don't you have parents? [Kothay e shikkha peyechchen, baba ma nei?]." In response to this assault, Jaya just mumbled in a low voice, "I had parents" (Baba ma chchilo), while the judge continued, "A mother can't keep her kids away from their grandparents." The husband, Mohan, chimed in that he had an objection to being in his in-laws' home when he visited his kids, but the judge sternly reminded Mohan he could only "have a 'problem,' not an 'objection,'" when they were trying to get back together (milmish)

These comments exemplify the ironic terrain family court judges must negotiate. The very fact of legal dispute over visitation and separate residence destabilizes notions of patrilocal family cohesion and seamless affective bonds: Mohan and Jaya each sought severance from the other's family and exclusive closeness with their own. Yet ideologies of patrilineality, including the role of a woman's natal family in training her to sever the connection with them and a husband's corresponding reluctance to maintain any connection with his in-laws' home, were asserted as self-evident cultural practices. The judge's exasperated Occidentalism touted the exceptional value of the joint family precisely in the face of its threatened status.

THE EMERGENCE OF THE CONJUGAL COUPLE

The most significant resistance to the ideological solidity of the joint family is posed by the discourse of conjugality, which occupies a parallel trajectory in postcolonial law. Marriage law since the 1930s erased the variety of marital and household structures in India (Agnes 1999), positing a heterosexual couple at its center, with contractual obligations: alimony, child support, household and reproductive labor, monogamy as favored norm (even implicitly for Muslims, who can be legally polygynous), and (since the 1980s) the right to be free of violence. The right to maintenance exists whether or not spouses (most often husbands) are employed, and defaulting on maintenance may be criminally punished. The juxtaposition of marriage and extended family responsibilities results in a disjointed map of entitlements: succession and inheritance rely substantially on joint family property, whereas marriage (and divorce) law posits an autonomous conjugal unit grounded in notions of romance and nuclear intimacy. Courts find themselves negotiating these critical contradictions, caught between the economic and emotional pulls of the joint family as the inevitable backdrop to marriage and, contrarily, conjugality as the prime expectation of modern marriage law.

Historians have argued (Majumdar 2004; Sturman 2005; Sreenivas 2008) that postcolonial marriage law evolved in a milieu strongly affected by nationalist discourses highlighting the rise of the individual legal subject in response to market forces and the intimacy of the nuclear family. Nineteenth-century social reform movements to reshape marriage and women's role within the polity and civil society recommended a combination of "Western ideas of domestic management" and "Indian ideals of hierarchy and devotion to produce the dyadic couple form" (Majumdar 2007, 437). In the middle-class *bhadralok* culture in Bengal, men's status began to depend on "participation in public life and civil society" rather than caste (Majumdar 2004, 912, 924), and women's education, characterized in terms of graceful, caste-appropriate homemaker skills, became a form of social capital in the marriage market (926). However, these new conjugal subjectivities were located within the affinal family and enhanced its value. In Tamil Nadu, nationalist resistance was exemplified in "self-respect marriages" that upended Brahmanical hegemony while furthering "contractual conjugality" grounded in "compatibility, equality and companionship in marriage," as cornerstones of the modernized national self (Sreenivas 2008 , 86). Thus the (urban middle-class) couple was central to the constitution of the modernized nation-state.

A related line of argument foregrounds economic transformation in the nineteenth century as a driving force in the emergence of notions of the individual subject and conjugal responsibility, and in loosening the bonds of the joint family. Legislative measures to separate men's professional earnings from their families' joint property associated individual property ownership with national modernity, conjugal commitments, and economic enterprise, and coparcenary joint property with tradition (Sreenivas 2004, 944). Ideologies of individual earnings being earmarked for the conjugal rather than the natal family began to permeate matrilineal communities as indexes of modernity (Nongbri 2010). Colonial adjudications needed to straddle both sets of capital funds for their own economic imperatives, "attempting simultaneously to secure the jointness of the joint family in order to protect the security of creditors and debtors, *and* to increase the independence of family members in relation to each other in order to promote market transactions" (Sturman 2005, 623). These accounts highlight the male legal subject's emerging responsibilities, with wives' economic entitlement justifying separation from their responsibilities to the joint family.

Ethnographers also point to hidden scripts of conjugal emotion within the joint family. "Love" might have to be reconciled, even concealed, within the extended family, and "love-marriages"[8] recast as community-appropriate marriages through convoluted moves (Puri 1999, 140; Mody 2006, 344; Gopal 2012). But conjugal affect may also be strategically asserted, such as in rural Uttar Pradeshi women's songs, which signal resistance to the norm that men's primary loyalties are to their natal families (Raheja and Gold 1994, 124–36) or among urban middle-class women who want "mutual, companionate and egalitarian marriages" despite tension in the extended household (Puri 1999, 147, 151, 153). While practices such as "love-marriage" may have to be reframed, discourses of conjugal intimacy may be used to negotiate the "traditional" space of the daughter-in-law in an extended family.

In the Kolkata Family Court, where a husband's failure to meet the affective standards of the nuclear family could be deemed legal grounds for cruelty, conjugality was often emphasized in similar ways. Such expectations are evident in the case of Romen, who had filed for restitution of conjugal rights, asking his wife, Purba (and their children), to resume living together (in lieu of having to pay maintenance for separate accommodations). Purba alleged that Romen got rid of her because she had two daughters, he did not want to pay for the medical attention she needed, he never took her out anywhere or spent time with her, and he neglected the children. In his response, Romen countered with evidence of doctor's prescriptions, 1,200 pictures of vacations in Mumbai and southern India, and pictures of birthday parties held each year for each child. To make a good "restitution" case, he had to legally efface his joint family ties and construct his final responsibilities as lying with the nuclear unit, a commitment symbolized by the vacations and birthday parties. Critically, the long-term alimony he might have to pay rested on the judicial determination of his good-faith effort. Previously ordered by the judge to find housing away from the extended family (where there appeared to be problems with interference and violence), the couple had come to court because the deal fell through when Purba objected to the size of the dwelling he proposed. This kind of case featured prominently in counselors' moral narratives, as an illustration of husbands' compliance and wives' lack of commitment to marriage; here it highlights husbands' economic responsibility to maintain marriage.

Unable to dismiss the expectation of joint family living, women often invoked troubles in the extended family in framing a demand for separate residence, as in Priya and Purba's cases. Because violence against daughters-in-law is a well-known crisis in the media,[9] this was a strategically strong space from which to open negotiations. Other women articulated desires for romance and conjugal space as a normative expectation of marriage (similar to Puri's findings), asking not for separation but for economic rights and intimacy within a subsisting marriage. However, these could be taken as double-edged moves and often brought suspicion and ridicule upon them. The risks are illustrated in the following account, held at the offices of an organization that mediated marital conflicts, where the mediators were asking both partners to manage and balance their roles, hoping to effect a reconciliation. Shoma had complained of feeling harassed by her mother-in-law about domestic tasks and help with childcare, and by her husband's maternal uncle's wife, whom she suspected of having an affair with her husband, Pratik. She was perturbed that everything the couple talked about among themselves was repeated back to her sarcastically: when she told him she felt like eating an egg roll that evening, when she said on the telephone that she missed him. Pratik demurred feebly that the family members just heard things because they lived close by.

Counselors reprimanded Shoma for her expectation that Pratik should understand what she wanted without her saying it; they told her she should not expect her husband to read her mind but should be explicit, that she needed to learn not to hear a lot of things, and that she ought to help her mother-in-law as she much as she could. This advice mirrored that of Manavi to Priya— that adjusting within the extended family while sublimating conjugal expectations represented the most mature adaptation. However, Pratik was also admonished to keep his marital life private, to not run to relatives with everything, and to negotiate with his mother to get domestic help for his wife; the conjugal sphere and his obligation to speak in support of his wife's well-being were thus validated.

In response, Pratik claimed that he usually told his wife she needed to deal with her own affairs and ignore what others said (which allowed him to avoid addressing her treatment). He emphasized, however, that he could not agree to a separate new residence, leaving his old mother to live by herself. These conditions related to finding affordable urban residential space but also to sons' social and economic responsibilities of eldercare. The counselor immediately agreed: "Of course not, we would never ask that," and made arrangements to meet with his mother (without the couple) to clarify matters. Pratik's framing of the issues here perfectly underlines the contradictory positions straddled by sons, who are held to account for healthy marriages as well as healthy extended family relations and expected to be simultaneously good husbands and good sons with limited economic and spatial resources.

Proposing a separate residence to keep the marriage going matched well with the family court's focus on reconciliation, but support for such proposals was often laced with regret at the crumbling of extended family entitlements, as the following admonition indicates. Here the judge, wrapping up a successful reconciliation hearing, declared (to the husband, with an implicit lecture for the wife as well): "You can't abandon your mother and father and have a family/household. You have to have a *sansar* along with your parents. If you had a lame or disabled sister, how could you abandon her? It so happens that your sister is independent and has a job." Translating *sansar* as "family/household" does little to capture the sense of stability and auspiciousness connoted by the term. The moral imperatives of joint family residence identified by the judge included broad financial and caregiving responsibilities for both men and women, canceled only by possibilities such as single women's financial survival outside the extended family. The conjugal unit was granted preferential legal sanction, while simultaneously seen as a form of abandonment.

I observed mediation sessions with a variety of organizations where complicated arrangements had to be made so that separate nuclear and extended households could be established—often within the same space, because separate rental space (let alone ownership) was unaffordable and unsatisfactory. Given the legal statutes governing domestic abuse, judges often recommended nuclear households if violence was alleged—otherwise, why would a woman not live with her in-laws? However, extended-family living was seen as necessary in other cases, especially when caregiving or financial obligations were an issue. These legal interventions marked the disarticulation between marital obligations and generationally grounded entitlements, and between marriage law and property law.

THE UNSOUND MIND: MENTAL HEALTH AND VALID MARRIAGE

Bujhtey parey na, uttor diley parey na, court e eshchey keno? [If she can't understand anything, if she can't answer, why has she come to court?]

—Kolkata Family Court judge, exasperated at the silence of a litigant whose mental state was in question

The legal category "of unsound mind" refers to allegations of mental illness as grounds for divorce or annulment. A threshold of ability is at issue: What behavior is sufficiently "unsound" to cast a person outside of marriage? What other systems of entitlement do they thereby lose? In what forms can disability subsist within marriage?[10] The conflict between the autonomous contractual subject at the center of marriage law and intergenerational kin obligations has some additional twists here: while people deemed mentally ill might previously have received usufructuary (use rights) maintenance in a larger family, the technical apparatus of divorce in the postcolonial state requires them to be independent legal subjects capable of comprehending contractual obligations.[11] Legal evocations of mental states are particularly effective in illustrating two of the predominant trajectories explored in the previous sections: the contradiction between discourses of kinship obligation and satisfying conjugal lives, relating to responsibility, pleasure, and liability; and the gendered vulnerabilities of marriage grounded in wives' economic dependency and "adjustment" to the domestic realm.

"Insanity" is one ground for annulment and divorce in Hindu, Muslim, Christian, and Parsi law and the Special Marriage Act.[12] Under the Hindu Marriage Act (under which the following cases fall), a marriage is deemed invalid (able to be *annulled*) "if at the time of the marriage, either party, (a) is incapable of giving a valid consent of it in consequence of unsoundness of mind; (b) though capable of giving a valid consent has been suffering from mental disorder of such a kind or to such an extent as to be unfit for marriage and the procreation of children; (c) has been subject to recurrent attacks of insanity or epilepsy." Being "incurably of unsound mind, or suffering continuously or intermittently from mental disorder of such a kind and to such an extent that the petitioner cannot reasonably be expected to live with the respondent" is also a ground for *divorce*. "Validity" pertains to a marriage being "void ab initio" (annulled), either on the grounds of fraud or bad-faith information inducing someone into a false contract or because of one's lack of contractual capacity to enter marriage; maintenance cannot be granted, since no marriage exists. However, where mental illness emerges later in the marriage, spouses may be entitled to maintenance even though the mental illness is a justifiable ground of divorce.[13] False allegations of insanity can constitute "cruelty" for purposes of divorce and maintenance.[14]

Legal definitions of "mental disorder" include "mental illness, arrested or incomplete development of mind, and psychopathic disorder," the latter defined in terms of long-term persistence of "abnormally aggressive or seriously irresponsible conduct." A "liberalization" of this ground of divorce in the mid-1970s for the Hindu Marriage Act and the Special Marriage Act led to broader categories, associated with regular use of the psychiatric disease classificatory system: rather than "incurable and continuous" illness as the standard, "intermittent" mental illness began to suffice, and even being diagnosed once with a mental illness has been deemed a sufficient legal ground for divorce (Dhanda 1995, 360–61). However, more recent rulings have focused on the severity and scope of the illness,[15] the criterion of dysfunction being that the spouse could not "reasonably be expected to" live with the alleger, with the burden of proof on them;[16] treatment and abatement are taken into account, rather than the mere existence of illness.

Kolkata Family Court judges dealt with allegations of insanity on an almost daily basis and were adept at steering litigants to questions of legal validity. Judge BB's admonition in 2001 was typical: "You say she's insane, but have you taken her to a doctor? Is it right to call somebody insane without having them be examined by a doctor?" (*Pagol je bolchhen, daktar dekhiyechen? Daktar na dekhiye ki kauke pagol bola uchit?*). Joy alleged that his wife had been "of unsound mind" before marriage and that this had been concealed from him. They had lived together for only four or five months, and she had been living with her parents since 1988, about fourteen years. "You'll know when you see her in court," Joy retorted, but the offer of plainly evident corporeal proof was not acceptable as a legal standard. The judge explained that Joy needed medical proof of insanity prior to marriage for annulment, which was difficult after fourteen years; were she to be deemed insane, moreover, a guardian would have to be appointed because she would not be considered fit to be a legal agent.

I witnessed a variety of insanity claims in the Kolkata court that showed similar latitude but also pointed to the difficulty of definitively establishing a threshold. A man claimed that his wife had been diagnosed with epilepsy and that this should constitute grounds for divorce based on insanity. A woman alleged that the prescription her husband was using as evidence of her insanity was forged or illegally obtained because she had never been taken to a doctor. She sought to have the doctor examined in court or by court personnel but had had little success with the case in over a decade. In a seven-year-old case, the judge was unwilling to use the doctor's original determination of the wife's mental illness. He wanted a fresh evaluation, refused to take the husband at his word that his wife had fits and had attempted suicide, and was loath to accept that their lack of an active sexual relationship (to be proved) was a manifestation of that medical finding. A telling mark of the judge's skepticism was his insistence that the young son be brought to court by his father: "You're trying to throw her out by calling her crazy, but what effect is that going to have? It would be good if your son was here, because he will ask, 'Why did you drive my mother away?'"

The courtroom thus relies heavily on medical evidence (sometimes patients may be sent to a doctor of the judge's choice as a "cross-check"), consonant with the modernity the family courts are cast as representing.[17] Amita Dhanda argues that the "expertise-deferent" attitude of Indian judges (1995, 349) is often so focused on diagnostic validation that differences in standards between legal and medical insanity are elided. Given widespread corruption, it seems likely that some people (with the right resources or connections) could conveniently find doctors to provide fake diagnoses and prescriptions. Dhanda also describes a variety of strategies used to create evidence of mental illness, including arranging for commitment (1995, 362). However, as indicated by the last set of negotiations from the judge, the indeterminacy of medical validation can also be useful in doubting allegations, here casting doubt on what the judge sees as a set of excuses that might adversely affect not just the wife but also the child.

Women's failure to perform everyday gendered social roles featured as prominent symptoms of mental unsoundness; more severe symptoms, such as suicide attempts, were rare. Typically at issue were ineffable social contracts of daughter-in-laws' responsibility for precise domestic tasks, want of proper frugality, surrender of their mobility, and expectations of appropriate affect. Dhanda's survey of appellate cases from 1933 to 1992 tabulates a telling roster of such "deviations" from gender roles cited as "manifestations of mental disorder," in which fifty-two of fifty-four petitions were filed against women. Complaints included "a. did not know how to do housework; b. failed to consummate marriage on the first night; c. acted familiar with strangers despite being warned; d. cried in front of guests at bride reception [bowbath] ceremony [brides are supposed to be tearful and sad, but apparently this was not quite the right tone]; e. received gifts with her left hand; f. despite being a Brahmin, did not bathe daily [a failure to shore up caste as well as gender norms]; g. put too much salt and pepper in the food; h. made paranthas when asked to make chappatis [these are both breads, the former fried, the latter roasted on a flame]; i. boiled two packets of milk when only one was required; j. gave a rude reception to relatives of the husband" (Dhanda 1995, 361–62). Other "behavioral deviances mentioned by the trial court in granting the husband relief were a. wife wastes soap while washing clothes; and b. wife wastes whatever is paid to her"(362). Lower-level courts had provided the legal relief sought in some cases featuring such allegations.

Women typically responded in two ways, either claiming there was an "ulterior motive" for making up the allegation or that the aberrant behavior had been "precipitated by the conduct" of the husband and his relatives (363)— that is, tensions in the joint family. James Mills argues that colonial and postcolonial psychiatric regimes sought to use work to transform patients "into useful and productive individuals [by] learning the virtues of obedience, regularity, forbearance etc." (2003, 91). These "unsound mind" cases might similarly be interpreted as foregrounding work, with wives alleged to be mentally unsound for their failure to fulfill domestic and kin labor responsibilities, in contrast to ideally docile and productive women. However, gender differences were most marked in thresholds of tolerance to violent mental illness: Dhanda's survey of 215 criminal appellate decisions (between 1860 and 1992) based on the defense of insanity found that women often stayed in marriages with obviously violent, mentally disturbed men (1995, 364–65),[18] whereas men, as indicated above, found even small domestic failures to be intolerable.

The strategic choice of insanity as a ground of divorce or annulment is significant. Many of these behaviors could alternatively constitute mental cruelty or neglect, also heavily coded in terms of female domestic prescriptions, as described in previous sections, and many are indeed simultaneously filed under those categories. Mental unsoundness is thus used to suggest greater severity. These fluidities and elisions were illustrated for me in the following case, where the female litigant's demeanor and aggression indicated the strong possibility of a disturbed mental state, but the "unsound mind" standard was never formally raised. Rather, her pathology was framed in terms of lack of enthusiasm for domestic tasks and inappropriate social roles in the extended family—that is, as quotidian rather than "abnormal." Haresh sought to divorce his wife, Madhu, and move away with his twenty-one-year-old son. The mild-mannered Haresh said in his deposition that the problem was that Madhu did not do household work properly or listen to him ("Ghorer kaj kore na, katha shone na"), that when she did cook, she threw the food at him if he said there was no salt in it. The erratic behavior included in the report included refusing to turn down the volume on the TV when her son was studying in their one room and not giving her son enough food, such that Haresh and his son made their own tea and ate at his sister's home. His lawyer added that the son was deemed to have a bright academic future, so his father wanted to move away to focus on the son's exams; he was willing to let Madhu stay on in the house and to pay her expenses after divorce. Madhu maintained that there were no problems other than people trying to turn her husband and son against her, and screamed at the judge, the counselors, and her lawyer in court. As the judge worked out a maintenance and residence plan with lawyers despite her irritation at Madhu, she asked about Madhu's mental state: whether there were police reports of her behavior (there were not), and whether she was a danger to herself or others. I was struck by how the legal framing of the case, here from an atypically mild and financially responsible husband, can elide the question of insanity despite some behavioral manifestations. The court record merely reflected common gendered allegations of bad cooking and bad mothering.

Does marriage involve passing financial responsibility to the affinal family of a married woman deemed to be of "unsound mind," such that her natal family is free of the "burden" of care? Or does a husband's claim to conjugal life trump the multigenerational contract into which his family may have entered with the marriage? Where do women's desire, labor, and consent fit within these transactions? The following two cases, dealing with sexual, social, and economic life around long-term care and mental health, underline these murky moral questions. They disrupt the traffic of marriage[19] by placing mental health into circulation, leaving multigenerational systems of exchange in crisis.

I accompanied Manavi to the old Kolkata suburb of Sovabazar to evaluate the mental health and family situation of Rita, one of her family court clients. Rita's father met us at the bus stop, and we walked to a beautiful, crumbling old house, where numerous families (some related) inhabited a few rooms each. First on Manavi's list was an older man, a landlord and ally for Rita's family. "We never had these things in our culture, this taking responsibility and then throwing (someone) away later. It's in foreign cultures, not ours" (*Eshob amader modhye kokhonoi chchilo na, ei je dayitto niye porey pheley deoa; foreign culture-e achchey, amader noi*), he said almost immediately, recalling other Occidentalist specters of the "bad" family. He talked generally for a while about how "joint families," including his own, got along with "respect." As an example, he cited his grandfather and his two wives, who all "behaved like one family." We were joined by Rita's uncle by marriage (*meshomoshai*), who had been instrumental in setting up the match and was close to her husband, Sanjay. The discussion continued in the same vein: times had changed, now birthdays involved pizza and cake instead of *payesh*,[20] and liquor was ubiquitous. Both men testified enthusiastically about how much they liked Sanjay: he was always pleasant, dropped by with seasonal fruits or sweets, and was friendly with his brothers-in-law (*bhairas*).

According to the men, Sanjay and Rita had seen each other socially four or five times before the wedding and had blood tests "as they do nowadays" (they did not specify what was tested, but there is no such test for mental illness). They disputed his allegation of mental problems by pointing to the prior acquaintance, and cited her B.A. degree as further proof of sanity. Their explanation, then, was that the death of his maternal uncle had changed his behavior, as he became interested in working on the uncle's farm and getting closer to that family. Rita's problems, they contended, were "adjustment" problems that lots of newly married women go through; the landlord claimed that his wife had been similarly afflicted but recovered after seeing a psychiatrist. Manavi had told me, however, that Sanjay alleged a fundamental lack of intimacy: Rita's affect was often strange (*udas*—perhaps better translated as "disengaged"), and she did not let him approach her sexually at all. He had taken her to a psychiatrist, bringing her father along, but her father later persuaded her to stop taking the medicines, telling her they would turn her completely mad (*pagol*). "What about my life? What's going to happen to my life?" Manavi reported Sanjay asking repeatedly (*amar jibontar-i ba ki hobey?*). "Life" is tied to sexuality here, more broadly an expectation of marital intimacy, echoing the legal standard that being capable of sex and procreation is not sufficient if a spouse is "unfit as a life partner due to his/her abnormal and erratic behavior."[21]

We observed Rita coming and going, bringing us tea and snacks without saying much. Rita's mother (whose mental health was also the hushed subject of rumor) peered out from the next room. Manavi skillfully fended off energetic persuasion from the men to prioritize reconciliation; she was just looking into maintenance questions, she demurred, and this was a "complex" matter. Her final strategy was to assert that she didn't want to put Rita in further danger ("Okey aro bipoder mukhey pheltey chaina"), deploying a familiar mode of "protecting" women even though no violence or danger had been raised here. In parting, she told Rita gently not to worry, to be self-reliant ("Sho-nirbhor, nijer paye daratey shikhtey hobey"), that her life would not be over even if this marriage didn't take ("E biye na holey ki hoyechchey, tomar jibon ki hoye gelo?"). She had found out through another source that the family applied for and received a "self-reliance" (*sho-nirbhor*) government loan in Rita's name for her to run a small business. Her father used the funds instead for an underwear shop he ran on College Street, hence her financial dependence had not been alleviated in the process. Manavi's use of the word *sho-nirbhor* in her parting advice was thus both literal and a subtle reminder to the family of the scope of her vigilance, putting them on notice to do right by Rita.

Another case, mentioned in chapter 3 for its connotations of speech and silence, circled around similar questions of financial and social liability in behind-the-scenes negotiations. The epigraph to this section, from this case, highlights the judge's exasperation in dealing with Shobha, a litigant whose lawyer was a no-show. As with Madhu, questions of mental ability were not explicit, and hence the judge's frustration might have been related to the question of her legal standing. The most significant backstage negotiation, however, was going on that day between Shobha's father and the counselors. Manavi and Champa, the counselors assigned to the case, called me into the counselors' room to listen.

Champa explained in Shobha's father's presence that she had been talking with him about whether he wanted to send his daughter back "where she would not get respect as a wife" (*jekhaney o stri hishebey marjada ba shomman pabey na*). Champa's suggestion that he figure out a lump sum to constitute a maintenance settlement was taken by Shobha's father as an implied recommendation for a divorce. He retorted angrily that Champa was taking the husband's side and not advocating reconciliation, and they continued arguing in circles. When he accused Manavi of calling his daughter "insane" (*pagol*), she denied using that word, claiming she had merely noted that Shobha had been unable to say anything in court. Shobha's father said that she was not insane (*pagol*), and her husband knew this because he had seen her several times before the wedding. Champa muttered to me that these are fleeting social occasions, during which the bride doesn't usually say anything. These were all really "adjustment" problems after marriage, he insisted. Manavi had shared with us earlier, in his absence, that Shobha's in-laws alleged she did not know how to put on a sari until her mother-in-law taught her, and that sexual overtures upset her completely.

Shobha's father contended mainly that he could not have his married daughter back home. He had two grown sons at home with college degrees but no jobs, and repeatedly insisted, "One can't keep a daughter at home after her marriage" (*Meyekey biyer por baritey rakha jaye na*). Despite the counselors' arguments that his daughter had as much legal right to stay in the natal home as his sons, he kept repeating that position, then added with finality, "I can't keep the girl at home, I will have to get her married." It seemed this last overture indicated that he needed money to get her remarried, meaning he was opening the door slightly to negotiate for a better settlement, though he would not name the figure yet.

The counselors contended that they could only begin negotiations with the husband once they had an amount to work with, and there was really no way to stop the divorce on certain grounds (Champa didn't say which). "He's not the type to volunteer to pay if he doesn't have to" (*O sherokom chchele noi je nijer thekey debey*), Manavi slyly added, as if to discredit the husband, and urged the father to act firmly so that Shobha was not simply left with nothing. He looked battered by the conversation, and was further perturbed when Manavi offered that he was welcome to send his daughter instead. They had been speaking to him as a courtesy, she strategically reminded him, but Shobha was their real client (especially because, according to him, she had no problems with mental capacity). Alarmed, he asked them not to say anything to the daughter, because she was most "depressed" by the situation, and they left with his reluctant promise to come up with an amount.

The counselors expressed frustration after he left, accusing him of wanting to repeat the cycle of getting her married even though he understood her mental condition. Champa argued excitedly that she believed such weddings should be treated as "fraud marriages" and annulled. She vividly recalled another case, where a woman's husband and father sat in the room negotiating between Rs. 10,000 and Rs. 300,000, bargaining in increments of Rs. 5,000 rupees, the woman between them giggling crazily and repeating, "Am I potatoes and onions? Am I potatoes and onions?" (*Ami ki alu potol? Ami ki alu potol?*[22] referring to bargaining for vegetables at a market).

Questions of kinship and transaction, intimacy and familiarity permeate these two cases. Women's families used the language of long-term bonds, a kinship established through marriage rather than the narrow relationship of the couple, referring to usufructuary notions that the care of the feeble or disabled fell to the family in which one "belonged." This perspective contrasted the ideal Indian family, seen to include a complex swath of familial bonds and cycles of ritual exchange, with the specter of Western norms, symbolized by pizza, cake, and liquor, and equated with a structure where individuals could be cast aside. Women's natal families thus fixed the wedding as the moment for transfer of economic responsibilities. Individuals' needs were sublimated in the joint family, where everyone had a place, even cowives. Daughters-in-law's "adjustment" problems were routine, temporary, and fixable. Whereas modernity was marked by prewedding meetings and medical tests, these were brief, modest, and formal, though convenient as evidence to stave off legal accusations of fraud. Other registers of the modern state, such as daughters' legal rights to parental property and economic support, were conspicuously absent.

Men's families spoke in terms of optimal conjugality, of a "fulfilling married life," both sexual and emotional, evoking the couple at the core of postcolonial marriage law. Sexual aversion was posed as an essential impediment, based on the signal importance assigned to heterosexual "consummation" as the fundamental "corporeal yoke linking law and marriage" (Brook 2000, 140). Prescribed deviations from optimal female behavior were used to supplement these allegations, justifying husbands' abdication of financial responsibilities.

Notable here is the contrast with discourses of extended family obligations and conjugal expectations explored in the previous sections. In those cases, husbands commonly pled that they were financially liable for a broad range of kin, and wives that they were entitled to conjugal intimacy and separation from patrilineal affinal households. The inverse emerges in these cases of putative mental disorder, with husbands pleading for "married life" and wives' families sanctifying the extensive economic shelter of the joint family. However, these are not in fact *opposite* ideologies: they are linked by the overarching logic of patriarchal relations in which (family) property and resources are male entitlements. If women's connection to property is primarily developed by staying married and being part of an exchange of sex and labor and affect, the chain of exchange is broken in marriages where soundness of mind is in question: a woman incapable of delivering the required labor or reproduction is placed outside the resource/property base of both families.

The women litigants central to these scenarios were almost entirely silent (whether as legal strategy or not) and often deemed to be pathologically so.[23] Their constructions of the marital home or intimacy, or their opinions about economic entitlement, never appeared in negotiations. Rather, their sexual lives and domestic experiences were folded into the discourse of "bad adjustment" said to be common in early years of marriage.[24] Unlike wives discussed earlier, whose affective claims to conjugality marked them as contractual subjects in court, Rita and Shobha's agency was beyond representation. Given the perceived impossibility of assigning them to any category of the familial or conjugal contract, the only productive advice coming their way involved opting out—in counsel about self-reliance, possibilities of economic independence, and the irrelevance of marriage, a dramatic contrast to normative repertoires for other women. Recalling Cohen's (1998) analysis of the joint family as an unassailable affective trope but also a prime locus of resource transmission, I suggest the putatively unsound mind of the wife as a significant point of fracture to that trope: it destabilizes the familial and foregrounds the transactional nature of marriage. It is tempting to see here the crazy giggle of the woman who felt she was equivalent to a bargain over vegetables as poignantly marking one of these sites of excess, showing up the economic exchange at the center of marriage and the unreliability of customary regimes of care.

THE ABLE BODY: MAINTENANCE, CLASS, AND PROPERTY

Eta ki alu-begun-potoler dokan je dam komaben? [Do you think this is a shop selling potatoes and brinjals and *potols* that you can bargain here?]
—Irate judge to a man asking for the maintenance amount to be lowered after decree

Two young and dusty-looking men, handcuffed together at the wrist, came running up the stairs of the Kolkata Family Court one day, singing a hit song from a recent Hindi film with deliberate raucousness. A portly policeman in his uniform of starched white shorts and shirt followed behind, trying to keep pace, occasionally prodding them with his long baton in an attempt to control their display. These handcuffed men were "criminals" of the family court (where few people are brought in as "criminals"): husbands who had repeatedly failed to comply with court orders to pay maintenance to wives or children and had finally been jailed for their recidivism. In this court, where failure to pay maintenance regularly (across a range of social classes) was more routine than not, they had not prevailed in their arguments, most likely because of their financial situations, thus becoming disciplinary objects of the system's seemingly serious intent.

The effusiveness of these men marks another site of excess—a legal, economic, and social paradox around maintenance as the solution to marital troubles. Imprisonment is the only threat that can be held over husbands to enforce the legal responsibilities of maintenance, but it is of symbolically punitive rather than tangible economic benefit to wives, who can expect no financial help when a husband is in prison, though in theory his debt remains.[25] The threat might be more effective in engaging middle-class men's fear of loss of face than in motivating men with scant earning opportunities, whose attempts to cope with economic marginality might routinely bring them close to imprisonment. Moreover, gender and class privileges are validated rather than undone: while the economically marginal man is publicly punished as an example of irresponsibility, middle- and upper-class men's role as family saviors is highlighted. The state's benevolent power exercised on behalf of women is notoriously visible but limited in effect. Most problematically, maintenance and its minutiae of accounting come to stand for women's property; their economic partnership in marriage is invisible.

In the media, maintenance is often represented as benevolent protection, a token of modernity, with an undertone conveying excessive benevolence, suggesting that the law favors women too much. The headline "Post-Divorce Upkeep Scales New Heights" introduces a story about an unusually high maintenance payment of Rs. 25,000 a month imposed on an Indian Airlines pilot, in the face of charges of habitual adultery and "torture."[26] A doctor living abroad is reported to have paid 40 lakhs to his ex-wife when her innovative lawyer, well known for her work on women's rights, asked that the woman who negotiated the match be arrested until he paid up.[27] In a recent judicial flashpoint, maintenance rights granted to wives were extended to other sexual and economic relationships deemed to be "in the nature of marriage" as additional "contractual" rights.[28]

Indian case law on maintenance seems to justify such media reports in its apparent sensitivity to gender and material conditions. Men and women are entitled to claim maintenance under some personal laws,[29] proudly depicted as a "radical" feature of Indian law that goes beyond the British legal notion of maintenance as married women's economic dependence and near "tutelage" to husbands.[30] However, men must prove long-term disability when asking for maintenance from employed women and are exempt only if "old and infirm."[31] Unemployment or lack of income does not cancel men's maintenance obligation, nor does women's income (typically low) or their parents' status: "It is duty of the able-bodied person to earn enough to discharge his legal obligation to maintain his wife and to provide for the subsistence so that the wife is not driven to destitution even when the husband is not earning sufficient money."[32] In a case where both parties claimed maintenance from each other, the Supreme Court acknowledged that they were both "able-bodied" and possessed earning capacity but argued that the female situation was harder: "In this patriarchal society like ours that weaker sex is to face various troubles to find out a suitable job for maintaining herself"; the husband was deemed responsible for costs and interim maintenance because he had launched the case and failed to prove his unemployment.[33] In a new twist of gender-neutrality, a woman's equal able-bodiedness was held as grounds to cancel her maintenance order.[34] These decisions appear sensitive to both nominal and substantive equality: there are rights to maintenance across genders but also a recognition that gender neutrality can be blind to inequities of the market. The man's "able body," as a gendered vehicle of labor and hence of fulfilling kinship entitlements, dominates the discourse (in contrast to the female unsound mind, which is capable of neither appropriate labor nor tasks of kinship or conjugality).

But maintenance quintessentially illustrates the ambivalence of protection in the marital contract. Successful maintenance claims, portrayed as compensation for broken conjugal promises, hinge on women's performance of conjugal responsibilities. Moreover, maintenance is often granted at a subsistence level, at best an amount befitting a certain standard of living rather than shared income. The "economic dependency" generated by marriage and the costs of litigation are invisible (Agnes 2011, 120). Awards typically ignore marital property built up through women's labor or other resource contributions (the only exception being a return of dowry goods upon divorce) and disregard marriage as a site for shared property based on homemakers' production and (biological or social) reproduction in the household. Maintenance therefore comes to stand for moral and behavioral leverage, and a distribution that assumes women's primary economic resource lies elsewhere (in the labor market or the natal family).

In contrast to media reports and appellate cases, advocates of women's legal and economic rights have pointed to the dismal practicalities of maintenance. In a survey of separated, deserted, or divorced Indian women conducted by the Economic Research Foundation, only 47.4 percent of women applied for maintenance, 42 percent of divorced women had no income at all, 80 percent of women with children to support lived below the poverty line, and children lived with the mother in 86 percent of cases (with the father in 7 percent). While limited by sample size,[35] the study usefully identifies some structural obstacles. Wives are required to produce income certificates to validate their claims; however, most women have little idea of their husbands' incomes, getting income certificates is bureaucratically laborious, and determining income for the nonsalaried, including business or self-employed income, is almost impossible.[36] Lack of jointly held marital property exacerbates this situation, further complicated by the fuzziness between men's share of joint family property and individual property. The realistic possibility of getting substantial livable payments is therefore low.

In the cases I observed, several women who were satisfied with their jobs and felt their natal kin to be supportive did not put forth maintenance claims, though some did so as a reminder, a mark of the wound or of childrearing responsibilities. Sandhya, who felt her children were thriving in her brothers' care, still looked to maintenance "so that he has some trouble at least, so that he can't forget." More often, women framed their claims in terms of the economic constraints of their natal families or their own income potential. Ruby desperately needed maintenance or a lump-sum settlement, according to the counselors, because she lived with her father as his sole caregiver. The house was owned by her brothers, who were unlikely to let her stay on once their father had passed, though presently her labor was convenient. The dual threat posed by women's habitual lack of natal and marital property is evident here.

Maintenance claims, dominating the work of the Kolkata Family Court, at 43 percent of the court's caseload (Agnes 2004), exemplified these dynamics. They were explicitly regarded by judges and counselors as the principal socially beneficent aspect of their work, and were the focus of a majority of courtroom hearings, counseling negotiations, and appointments with the registrar's office to set up payment schedules and monitor recidivism. Bargaining over maintenance followed a predictably gendered script. Men claimed to have little to no income at the moment and alleged that their wives had informal income through tailoring, tutoring, or other small tasks. Women claimed to have no personal income and little support from their natal family, and alleged that their husbands had profuse informal or illegal income (popularly called "black money") or that they enjoyed the wealth of their extended family.

Postdivorce maintenance for Muslim women has been an incendiary political issue (Pathak and Rajan 1989; Basu 2008), regarded as a zone of exception and abjection, but in practice, Muslim women faced the same principal problems: lack of natal or matrimonial assets and recidivism in payments. Since 2004, lots of Muslim women have come to court seeking (pre- and postdivorce) maintenance under S125CrPC.[37] Their use of the law increased as the minimum amount granted under S125CrPC tripled, and the differential with women of other communities effectively disappeared. One judge of the Kolkata Family Court claimed in 2005 that he had even given awards of Rs. 25,000 as "fair and reasonable provision," and was consistently granting maintenance at one-third to one-fourth of income (the other judge did not follow that norm). The decisions provided welcome relief to women (though many of these amounts were modified in appellate settings), even if they might also have served as hegemonic claims of progressive legal equity (from Hindu judges) in reining in Muslim men's perceived economic advantage (Basu 2003).

However, as with other maintenance awards, the main difficulty lay in executing them: a Muslim man who had accumulated Rs. 31,000 in unpaid maintenance (from a monthly requirement of Rs. 1,500) was one of the worst defaulters in the court. *Mehr*, or dower in Muslim marriages,[38] visualized as the optimal alternative to maintenance, did not prove powerful in practice (Agnes 1999; Vatuk 2008), with *mehr* amounts often set too low to make any difference or brides "persuaded" to "forgive" the *mehr* permanently as an act of generosity. While *mehr* recovery was often the only recourse for a woman who was already divorced, the logistical difficulties of determining the terms of forgiveness and payback tended to stump litigants and counselors.

Judges and counselors often bemoaned the ways the gigantic parallel economy and incommensurable lines within family wealth complicated their task, as they cannily struggled to assign value across a gamut of jobs. When a man claimed that the small *sharbat* (sugared drinks) shop he ran was his mother's and he received none of the income, the counselors were asked to check the name on the ownership certificate and trade license; they acknowledged that he might well have been managing the property and retaining the profit even if it was formally in her name. Another, whose plaint said that he was a transport broker in a business shared with his two brothers, the business making about Rs. 75,000 a month (his share thus being Rs. 25,000), argued that this business now belonged to his two brothers and that he had started his own, which made Rs. 5,000 a month at best.

As the epigraph to this section indicates, husbands' routine attempts to bargain inevitably irked judges by challenging their authority. In that case, the man was warned that he was in imminent danger of being found in contempt of court and was asked to appeal to a higher court if he was so dissatisfied, both warnings indicating in the strongest possible way that he had lost the judge's sympathy. Similarly, recidivism and partial payment were sternly reprimanded: to a man who had brought Rs. 700 of the Rs. 3,050 he owed, having failed to pay for over four months, Judge B said with angry sarcasm, "Do you think you are just giving out any amount you want out of charity? [*Apni ki doya kore ja khushi dichchen?*]. What is the point of having a court order if you bring any sum you please, as if there is no order?" He was asked to pay that afternoon or be sent to jail and finally negotiated a two-week reprieve, a tactic his wife contended he had tried before.

Judges themselves routinely bargained about income, with no profession seemingly beyond their knowledge. Judge K argued with a vendor who sold peanuts on trains and was contesting the very small interim maintenance order of Rs. 250. He claimed to be making 5 or 10, at best 20, rupees a day, which is only about 600 rupees a month, while his wife claimed he made Rs. 7,000–8,000. The judge contended, "Look, I used to be the rent court judge. I know how much things cost at Howrah station. Anybody who gets a window seat on those trains is going to buy some peanuts from you. I know the state has now restricted hawker travel from train to train but you still must sell a lot." To the wife's protests and allegations of violence, she responded in turn, "Now what can I do? Look, I didn't ask you to marry this person." After much altercation, the husband's father intervened to get him to agree to the amount.

At the other end of the income scale, a man who owned a factory claimed to have fallen on hard times because he had had throat cancer for about ten years. Judge B interrogated him about everything from the questionable validity of the documents he presented as income statements to his fragile health to his claim that his wife's determination of income was based on the businesses of his nephews and tenants, in which he was merely an investor. When he asserted that he avoided the factory because of dust and expected to live only five to ten years longer, the judge refused to enter the statement into the record, saying, "Cancer researchers at SSKM and Bombay and other places are now saying that treatment for cancer now prolongs life for eight years plus, so there's no point to that statement."

Judges often echoed case law about the able-bodied man's accountability for maintenance whatever his employment status. Judge K retorted to a man who claimed to be earning only about Rs. 500 a month doing casual labor and electrical work and who pled that he didn't have any money because he didn't get far in school, "Look, you may not have studied, but when you had the two children, you became responsible for feeding them and for sending them to school, so don't tell me about that." When Subhashish contended that he was unemployed and lived with his brothers, working their land without income, Judge B pointedly asked, "Why was it all right to marry in that case?" then granted Rs. 500 monthly maintenance. He summarily rejected Subhashish's testimonial of unemployment written by the head of the village *panchayat* (a local governance body) as invalid proof, the very offer of such proof indicating the creative routes of establishing income tried out by litigants. Subhashish's wife, Manu, minimally literate and who had not even realized she had been divorced ex parte until it was too late, tried to work as a medical helper but had trouble because of her reading skills; she lived with her mother, who barely supported herself with a small stipend from her son. The irony lay in Manu's desperately poor family's interest in the match on the basis of Subhashish's prosperous joint household and his ostensible ownership of a small *paan* (betel leaf) stall; as Manu told me, "We were too poor to be choosy about what he looked like or was like. The family's situation [*obostha*] looked good, and we couldn't turn it down." That is, *joint* family property works to married women's usufructuary advantage, whatever the husband's income, when she shares in the wealth of the joint household. In determining maintenance upon divorce, however, the standard switches to husbands' *individual* income and property, and women are cut loose from the prime resource base of the joint household.

Maintenance is the primary solution for divorced women's economic support, even though it is contingent on women's conduct and the practical difficulties of recovering money. Feminist legal experts in India have emphasized these deficiencies, advocating division of marital property on divorce as a far better solution that avoids the monthly runaround and the norm of conduct, while acknowledging women's labor contributions to marriage: "While maintenance can be viewed as a sustenance 'dole' for basic survival, which the prevailing social conditions necessitate, matrimonial home and property can be construed as 'rights' which would economically empower a woman and redeem her from the situation of perpetual dependency" (Agnes 2011, 207). Recent judicial and legislative moves to institute "irretrievable breakdown of marriage" as a no-fault ground of divorce have added urgency to these theories, as they enable walking away from a marriage without any economic division.[39] Indian women's rights lawyers argue that fault-based divorce, despite its negative energy, has provided one of the only wedges for leveraging beneficial economic arrangements; they insist that resource division must be considered in the new law before it can be finalized.

Global studies of no-fault divorce bear out these worries, despite its reputation as the gold standard for eliminating needless conflict and blame, decluttering courts, and realistically linking financial needs and awards (Wardle 1991, 79; Nakonezny, Shull, et al. 1995, 478). Significant problems include accentuation of the "inequities in the economic consequences of divorce," indeed an exacerbation of difficulties caused by delinking divorce from the distribution of assets (Wardle 1991, 79). No-fault divorce disproportionately affects custodial mothers and women without significant incomes, when "the reality that homemaking is both gender-specific and career-costly clashes with the rhetoric of equality underpinning no-fault divorce laws" (Starnes 1993, 70–73). The fear that no-fault divorce might essentially eliminate economic entitlements in marital dissolution thus precipitates urgent deliberation on matrimonial property in India, given women's reliance on marital assets. The Irretrievable Breakdown of Marriage Bill presently awaiting legislative debate addresses these concerns by giving judges power to consider matrimonial property (including ancestral property) "compensation" in cases of "irretrievable breakdown" divorce. It is a subject of controversy even among feminists, with some deeming it too narrow yet allowing too much latitude to judges, and others saying that it is too broad and fails to specify criteria for determining property rights.[40]

When wives preferred property settlements to monthly maintenance, the benefits of receiving more substantive assets were obvious, despite skepticism from court officials. Arun challenged the Rs. 500 per month that Seema and her two children received as maintenance, claiming his total earnings in casual labor to be about that much; his wife contended he had about triple that income. He was in major arrears for over a year at Rs. 6,900. Seema offered a quick alternative, keen to move on with her new partner. She proposed to count the arrears canceled if Arun transferred the deed of a piece of land to her name, to which she estimated she had contributed half of the Rs. 10,000 over time by tailoring "sari falls." Judge K asked her in cross-examination, "How will you manage this piece of property? Won't this new man beat you up and take it away?" Seema wanted to get the land in her name with a deed transfer, but according to the legal rules for these claims, arrangements were made to sell and then divide the proceeds between them. While the judge and counselors viewed her aspiration for property ownership with suspicion, depicting her as too confident about her economic future, they facilitated the outcome nonetheless. Equally splitting assets was far preferable to the constantly rotating wheel of maintenance arrears, but the problem is that few people have such convenient assets available to split. The ambiguities of separating individual income and assets from the joint family pool or determining business or self-employed income also pose formidable obstacles to proposals to institute matrimonial property division upon divorce. Maintenance therefore continues as the norm, marking women as economic dependents rather than asset generators in marriage.

CONCLUSION: MARRIAGE AND MONEY

Though "modern" marriage and the "traditional" family are set in opposition, the point is that such conjugality is not radically modern nor is the extended family that outdated; both are dialectically, actively contested and formed through these discourses. The patrilocal extended family faces challenges as a viable unit but continues to carry affective power as a site of economic pooling and social strength; alternatively, it embodies oppressive violence and tension. Conjugal compatibility, while prominent in marriage law, must nonetheless be optimally reconciled with women's harmonious, skillful melding into the conflicted space of the extended family. Litigants strive to inhabit both realms, while exposing the dissonance between the two through their claims.

Fundamental questions of women as sharers of their natal and affinal family's resources and as contributors to the fund of conjugal assets go unanswered in this opposition between kinship and conjugality. Trouble to marriage is posed as an unprecedented problem of adjustment and a threat to intergenerational resource transmission, as the cases relating to the unsound mind and the able body (maintenance) demonstrate. Men, as sons and husbands, become accountable for fulfilling the expectations of *both* extended *and* nuclear families, but their gendered burdens of income and care are balanced against their entitlement to property and (usually) superior positions in the labor market. However, women's claim to intergenerational and conjugal resources, based on their kinship position *or* their labor, is not met either in the extended family or in the companionate nuclear family. The default economic arrangement for them is to bargain hard to receive subsistence or slightly better, if they can demonstrate appropriate gendered behavior.

CHAPTER 6

Sexual Property

Rape and Marriage Conjoined

At present it is not possible to confirm whether she was raped or not since the victim is a married woman.

—West Bengal police officer, regarding a 2012 Katwa gang rape where a
   woman was dragged off a train for protesting against hooligans

Rape, feminist movements have iterated for at least four decades, is a profound violation of bodily integrity and hence self, an archetype of "sexual violence," and a mark of patriarchal dominance. Focusing attention on rape as violence has been one of the most significant global successes of women's movements, achieved through protest in the streets and reform of state institutions. These movements have helped expand the definition to include college dates, conjugal beds, and weapons of war, as well as dark alleys; they have codified it as a crime of assault and not property. They have influenced national legislatures and international bodies to produce documents such as the UN Declaration on the Elimination of Violence against Women (1993). The disappointments of botched prosecutions or shaming ideologies and the intransigence of law notwithstanding, feminist analyses have substantially shaped the discourse of rape.

This is not to say that rape has gone away, nor would it be difficult to launch a chapter on rape with an account of continuing and emergent rape cultures. I focus here, however, on how feminist principles used to reform rape law may become dangerously aligned with discourses of marriage, property, and protection, thereby buttressing systems of privilege. In particular, this chapter focuses on the ways rape laws are used to discipline the conjugal by drawing upon notions of compensation and consent, thus complicating feminist critiques of power and agency. The goal is to consider the embedding of rape within systems of exchange—in property and marriage.

I explore these concerns through rape prosecutions in which marriage appears as the Other of rape, as a solution to rape. To this end, the epigraph locates discourses of rape as always already located within marriage (rather than the related but narrower question of marital rape as violence). In this case, where neither sex nor violence were in dispute, the police officer's mystifying comment refers to the (now proscribed) popularity of testing the hymen for signs of a woman's "habituation to sex" to determine rape (Baxi 2014).[1] Such techniques of knowledge production, including medical evidence and judicial precedent, make clear the obsession of rape prosecutors with virginity and harm to systems of alliance (Das 1996) rather than with survivors' testimonies of violation or force. At the heart of this chapter are rape allegations in which sex is considered a form of women's property, allowing them access to the material privileges of heteronormative conjugality.

A highly publicized media event in a Kolkata theater in 2004 provides an ideal scenario for thinking through these questions, in its confusion around meanings of rape, consent, coercion, and compensation. I read this case against other ethnographic examples, appellate cases, and media accounts, to trace the ways codified rape law allows people to negotiate the economic and cultural expectations of marriage. In particular, I look to rape prosecutions that proffer marriage as an optimal benefit (for women), to analyze their problematic constructions of gendered subjectivity and kinship. To plot where a feminist jurisprudence of sexual violence might lead, I argue for greater attention to the circuits of property exchange in compulsory heterosexual marriage, within which rape is often encoded.

The ambivalence of state protection figures at the core of such problems. In compensating for the violence of rape with the capital of marriage, the state exemplifies what Wendy Brown calls "prerogative power," or "self-affirmation through displays of power and prestige," in which "women are cast as requiring protection from the world of male violence while the superior status of men is secured by their supposed ability to offer such protection" (Brown 1992, 25)—that is, acting in the name of women's interests sediments the patriarchal power of the state. As Pratiksha Baxi's analysis of Indian legislative debates around rape suggests, the object of rape law may be "not to deter rape against all women . . . [but] to control normal levels of violence against some women and increase disciplinary power over all women" (2000, 1196). Because the state provides the only feasible protection, no matter the embedded assumptions, it has to be engaged in the hope of mitigating harm: "The prerogative of the state, whether expressed as the intervention of the police or as incessantly changing criteria for welfare benefits, is often all that stands between women and rape, women and starvation, women and dependence upon brutal mates, in short, women and unattenuated male prerogative" (Brown 1992, 26). Feminist jurisprudence therefore has the difficult task of enabling better state recognition and enforcement, while challenging the equation of rape with passive feminine victimization and advocating for gender (and sexual) equity as the condition of full citizenship.

STAGING RAPE, STAGING MARRIAGE

In a dramatic postshow performance in January 2004, Kolkata police gathered in the wings of the Academy of Fine Arts as the play *Phataru* drew to an end. They were waiting to arrest actor Rudranil Ghosh on charges of rape brought by fellow actor Oindrila Chakraborty. The actor gave them the slip that night, but for the next few days the papers were full of the alleged rape, and highly excitable conversations erupted all over about the mysterious circumstances and the actor's reputation.[2] The case galvanized public discussion about "appropriate" modes of arrest; actors and artists wrote about destroying the "sanctity" of the theater, and the chief minister spoke out against the "unbecoming conduct" of the police.[3] Questions of violence, morality, and sexuality were center stage.

Newspaper accounts of the foiled arrest relied on evoking a stereotypical rape rampage involving an actor with loose morals, such as this sarcastic condemnation of police excitedly charging into women's changing rooms ("greenrooms"): "They may have thought that an actor charged with rape rushes to the women's greenroom at every free moment to continue his favorite activity, or, in all the excitement they had forgotten the gender of the alleged rapist, or, they thought that he had hidden in the women's rooms. That is what they would have done under similar circumstances, probably."[4] But the charges, it turned out, were sensational in their ordinariness. Rudranil and Oindrila had been romantically involved and cohabiting for a while. Though she was going through a divorce when they first started a relationship, she had since become free to marry; in the meantime, Rudranil had changed his mind about marriage, though he willingly continued the cohabitation. Oindrila, in bringing a rape case against him, relied on a body of case law where men who had sex with women through "false promise of marriage" were deemed guilty of rape based on fraudulent "consent." Rudranil did not challenge the fact that he had promised marriage but contended that he had rethought the decision over time.

The matter also leaked into my fieldwork spaces: Rudranil would have been brought to the Women's Grievance Cell of the Kolkata police, where I was at work observing domestic violence claims, and hence the area was abuzz with excitement. It appeared that the police felt some sympathy for Rudranil's fugitive status but did not want to be seen as minimizing a high-profile rape case, given the visibility of the unit, and were being careful in framing the case. The parties' actor and journalist friends dropped in periodically over the next few days to make inquiries; Rudranil himself called on a friend's cell phone. I heard a police officer advise one of these friends on the phone, "Once the case has become so public there is not much we can do. Try to talk to your common friends and get her to withdraw the case, or else make arrangements for bail. It's a hot time for 376 [rape][5] cases these days [Ajkal 376 case-er gorom abhaoa cholchchey]; there's nothing the police can do." Another friend came by to let the police know that they were trying to get friends together to convince the couple, or else "the lawyers' bellies would get bloated over it for ten or twelve years" (naholey dosh-baro bochchor dhorey ukiler pet phanpabey). Oindrila's one condition was that he marry her, so the friends were trying to see if they could arrange anything.

The police put the arrest on hold, and Rudranil applied for anticipatory bail. The High Court judge declared in the subsequent plea hearing that they "should be able to settle their dispute through peaceful discussion" in five days: "Both of you are in the same profession and know each other. You should be able to sort out your differences through discussions. The court should not interfere in the matter."[6] Following this, they met in the prosecutor's office to work out an agreement. The case then dropped out of media circulation, presumably in private negotiation, with no tidy "ending" available for our consumption. I became fascinated by the ways the putative solution of marriage in this rape case intersected with the quotidian mediation of domestic violence allegations with an eye to reconciliation that I had observed at the Women's Grievance Cell (chapter 7) and the Family Courts (chapter 4).

The actors' case presented a frustrating representational problem. Though people often discussed the opaqueness of the legal process and our scant knowledge of Oindrila's subjectivity and motivations or Rudranil's alleged claims that he had lost trust over time, they tended to treat the rape charge with distinct skepticism. In women's organizations and feminist groups, there were many troubled conversations about the case's adverse effect on other rape prosecutions, about class and uneven justice, and about how to read agency. One set of arguments went something like "one shady claim does not mean that other charges of rape are also fabricated," not too subtly dismissing this rape charge as a misuse of law, in fear that it would cast doubt on other, seemingly more justifiable, charges. Oindrila's claim, in other words, called up the specter of the vengeful false accuser who cries rape—or, even worse, who is really out for money—and admits to sex instead of being mortified into silence.

The case also fit with the prevalent analysis from women's organizations (which I often heard applied to family court prosecutions) that middle-class and elite women are sometimes able to manipulate law to their advantage, while poor women have scant access to legal remedies. Oindrila's identity as educated, middle-class, urban, a professional actor (and therefore subtly seen as having a looser moral scale), and a divorcée who had subsequently taken up cohabitation, perfectly cast her as a figure whose alien ("Western"?) values of promiscuity, immodesty, and public forwardness wrought chaos upon Indian society. Her allegations skated close to making a mockery both of the feminist work of vigilance against rape and of cases (described in a later section) where women were persuaded to have sex in the belief that they were or imminently would be married. To feminists, other actions seemed off key, such as the seeming prudishness of invoking cohabitation as a form of rape, the erasure of her own sexual agency in seeing her long-term relationship as consensual only if marriage rendered it legitimate, and her insistence on marriage despite her professional success. As Nivedita Menon opines of a similar case, it is possible to sympathize with women being "cheated and exploited" in some cases of false information, but "if as feminists we were to see it as rape, we would be participating in a discourse that sets up sex as legitimate only within the framework of marriage" (2004, 124). This widespread unease is useful for our purposes, repeatedly demonstrating the links among rape, marriage, resource acquisition, shame, and consent, and the dilemmas these present for feminist organizing.

RAPE CULTURES

Across the political spectrum, the Oindrila-Rudranil case reveals the fear of a postfeminist world, where feminist legal reform can be surreally applied to entrap and hassle, "real" cases of rape having been satisfactorily curbed. It validates the alarm of those who imagine that feminist influence has gone rogue, as well as those who fear that feminist critiques are being cut off from serious consideration without having secured a foothold. Let it be abundantly clear, however, that this case did not take place in a postrape world; it is, rather, embedded in a history of stark violence at local, national, and global levels that continues despite (even through) feminist interventions against rape.

Rape in India drew global attention in December 2012, following mass protests in numerous cities over state accountability and complicity, after Jyoti Singh Pandey died from injuries sustained during a gang rape on a bus she had boarded after a late night movie with a male friend (Roychowdhury 2013). But there has been no dearth of cases over the decades that demonstrate the prevalence of rape, often deployed for gender, caste, class, and religious domination, for marking public space or enforcing political pressure. Indian feminist mobilization around questions of rape harks back to the 1979 Mathura case, in which the Supreme Court deemed a fourteen-year old girl's rape by two constables to be consensual based on her lack of injury or audible protest and her alleged sexual experience.[7] Several legal reforms, including strong sanctions against "custodial rape" (by police or other authorities) followed, but there has been no dearth of spectacular horrors nonetheless: the rape of a mentally challenged twelve-year-old in a suburban Mumbai train while seven passengers looked on,[8] the rape of sathin (social worker) Bhanwari Devi in front of her husband as "punishment" for her work in preventing child marriage,[9] rapes of Dalit women by landed upper-caste men citing their failure to vote for a particular candidate in the panchayat (village-level) elections,[10] vicious rape-murders of Muslim women during the 2002 Gujarat riots to mark Hindu religious-nationalist domination abetted by state power (Sarkar 2002), and the punishment of Soni Sori, a teacher from a Chhattisgarh scheduled tribe community, through penile rape and penetration by stones, for protesting human rights violations.[11] In protest marches following the Delhi rape, persistent chanting of these women's names marked litanies of failure.[12] In West Bengal, Oindrila and Rudranil's state, several recent rapes grotesquely rival Pandey's in horror,[13] including a schoolgirl burned alive after being gang-raped twice (the burning and second rape allegedly in retaliation for her police complaint)[14] and a rural laborer gang-raped by village officials on a public viewing platform to avenge her failure to monetarily compensate them for an adulterous affair.[15] In these scenarios, where the penis and its proxies are used to humiliate, brand, and terrorize, it is hardly difficult to affirm MacKinnon's assertion that "sexuality is central to women's definition and forced sex is central to sexuality," so "rape is indigenous, not exceptional, to women's social condition" (1989, 172).

The responses to such violence further underline the ambivalence of state protection; calls for stringent punishment affirm the state's prerogative power, while other violence becomes invisible. Notably, married and virgin (not yet "married") women are extended full-blown state support while women free of marriage are ripe for suspicion. In recent West Bengal cases, the rape of a "housewife" from an outlying suburb of Kolkata who was trying to get home late at night from visiting her sick husband in the hospital merited police alacrity.[16] But shortly before, in the Park Street case, a similar incident of multiple men raping a woman in a car was met with overt police suspicion: the victim's presence at an expensive nightclub around alcohol, her labor history of working at a call center (at night), and even her ethnicity of "Anglo-Indian" (meaning part-white) were deployed to signal sexual permissiveness.[17] The new (female) chief minister cast this case as politically motivated and an attempt at extortion,[18] similarly maligning[19] another victim (described in the epigraph) who had been dragged off a train.[20] This survivor was cast as guilty both by inappropriate assertiveness in public space and by association with widowhood—that is, for being outside marriage and hence unrecuperable for systems of alliance (Das 1996). Jyoti Singh Pandey's case from Delhi gained international notoriety through representations of her as a "modern, rights-bearing subject" of a "global consumer economy," in contrast to the rapists, who were depicted in terms of traditional rural hierarchies inconsistent with urban modernization, despite little difference in their ethnicity and class (Roychowdhury 2013, 283). The Barasat case in West Bengal, while involving the rape and death of a student of similar age, did not cause a national outcry, likely because of its periurban location, but was disturbingly highlighted by Hindu fundamentalist groups making political capital of the Muslim rapists, and was yet again dubbed a political conspiracy by the chief minister.[21]

As Pandey lay in the hospital, outraged crowds and conservative politicians called for capital punishment or castration for rapists, while many communities responded with more stringent curbs on women's mobility and clothing. Feminist analyses emphasized, however, the ways such prerogative power to punish pumped up the state as vigilant arbiter while doing little to alter the perceptions through which rape testimony was typically heard or rape victims offered up as spectacle.[22] Even landmark trials leading to judicial reform draw their power of sanction from the "sexualized spectacle" of the trial (Baxi 2014, 1–2). Representations of rape as dishonor and social death inscribe women primarily in terms of sexual honor and shame, fixing their value within circuits of patriarchal kinship.

Rape law, through the centuries, centers around trespass and property compensation for women's bodies to their male kin, women's subjectivities absent from the discourse. In the colonial jurisprudence of rape in India, Kolsky argues, reliance on victim testimony was rapidly outpaced by the turn to external evidence, the outcome of a perfect storm where "English common law presumptions about the frequency of false charges and a suspicion of women's claims" combined with specific prejudice toward Indian victims, "based on ideas of native mendacity and manipulation of law" (2010b, 1095). Colonial legal paradigms for proving rape read like a checklist of feminist objections: legal strategy was guided by women's sexual history, evidence of force, and prompt complaint, and juries were read the Hale warning, that rape "is an accusation easily to be made and hard to be proved, and harder to be defended by the party accused" (Kolsky 2010b, 1097).[23] Medical jurisprudence and "ethnographic knowledge" about class, caste, and body size rose in prominence "to locate truth in and on the body" (Kolsky 2010a, 112) rather than in women's enunciations of bodily integrity (Das 1996), accruing "truth value" through adjudication (Arondekar 2009, 85).

Feminist critiques have attacked the logic of such evidence, establishing alternative paradigms. In global feminist discourse since the 1970s, rape is characterized as "sexual violence," a form of assault parallel to other bodily injuries and a result of discrimination and inequality affecting women as a group,[24] "an obstacle to the achievement of equality, development and peace" according to the United Nations' Forward Looking Strategies (1985). In postcolonial India, some of the most prominent interventions of the women's movement foregrounded rape as a fundamental aspect of patriarchal violence (Kumar 1993). Recent legislative debates over the new Criminal Law (Amendment) Bill (2012) considered gender-neutral definitions of rape, more complex notions of consent, and the exclusion of victims' prior sexual history—almost full circle from the Hale norms.[25]

That these laws serve a strategic and prerogative function rather than a deterrent one is demonstrated by Indian statistical data showing a large rise in the rate of reported rape at a time when other violent crimes, such as murder and robbery, seem to have declined. Statistics from the Indian National Crime Records Bureau record 2,487 reported rapes in 1971 (first year of data gathering), 10,410 in 1991, and 24,206 in 2011; moreover, estimates are that three-quarters of rapes are not reported.[26] However, few of these rapes are prosecuted, dropping out before the chargesheeting process (when formal charges are filed after the initial complaint). Even fewer result in convictions, about only one in five cases at the national level (falling steadily from 23.8 percent of chargesheeted cases in 2004 to 20.3 percent in 2010), and far less in West Bengal (varying between 4.4 percent to 10.8 percent). The gap between chargesheeting and conviction rates points to the obstacles to obtaining rape convictions, including families' unwillingness to have victims testify after the passage of time and remarriage (Baxi 2014), and families' use of rape law to manipulate marriage choice, as explored in later sections. The backlog of cases (only 14.5 percent pending rape cases were disposed of in 2012)[27] and logistical problems with enacting new procedural reforms further indicate the symbolic power and practical failures of rape prosecution.

Agents of the state, moreover, are regular perpetrators despite the extra punishments attached to custodial rape, such as a police constable in Bombay who raped a teenager out with her friends,[28] or the Soni Sori case in Chhattisgarh, where terrorism was used as an alibi for detention and sexual violence. Police attitudes, disturbingly, echo rape as justified male domination of public space, whether in Delhi police commissioner R. S. Gupta's infamous statement that "crime against women will drop by 50 percent if they are careful in the way they dress, if they know their limits and if they do not exercise unsafe behavior"[29] or in *Tehelka* magazine's investigative report on the Delhi police, where the problems officers cited included "everything from fashionable or revealing clothes to having boyfriends to visiting pubs to consuming alcohol to working alongside men." The officers contended "that genuine rape victims never approach the police and those who do are basically extortionists or have loose moral values," thus framing the rape charge as in itself a lack of appropriate modesty. The officer who conflated women in pubs with sexual availability complained that "the day somebody uses force, it becomes rape,"[30] depicting sex and rape as indistinguishable, with women's public presence in the sphere of male lust as the central problem and "force" merely a logical excess.

Other nations have faced similar obstacles to bringing rape under legal control despite elaborate institutional mechanisms and activist vigilance. Some of the primary stumbling blocks across nation-states are prevailing cultures of honor and shame, globalized ideas of sexuality, impunity against prosecution, and rape myths among judges and officers (Westmarland and Gangoli 2011). The Indian police officers' attitudes above indicate why persistent calls for better sensitization and enforcement in these countries go nowhere. Emergent legal notions of "gray rape" (as "sex that falls somewhere between consent and denial")[31] or "post-penetration rape" (or sex that continues after intercourse has started and one person desists) (Ehrlich 2011) make understandings of violence yet more complicated. In response, feminist advocates have begun to formulate standards that further clarify questions of power and violence. Questions of choice and coercion are so often manipulated that perhaps the central paradigm of "consent" might need to be set aside (Cowan 2007). Alternative visions include the consideration of whether assent was obtained by "coercion," the notion of wartime rape as part of a continuum of violence rather than an exceptional circumstance, a "consent-plus" standard requiring an explicit token of acquiescence, or a more nuanced norm of "sexual integrity and sexual self-determination" (Burman 2010; Kelly 2010, 117; Munro 2010). These ongoing global struggles to curb rape through law indicate, most importantly for this chapter, the double-edged nature of protection from the state, which tends to emphasize rape in terms of honor and modesty rather than bodily integrity and affirmative consent.

VIOLENCE, EMBODIMENT, RESISTANCE

The aggression, pervasiveness, and persistence of rape, as laid out in the previous section, explain why radical feminist theories have seemed persuasive. In this tradition, exemplified in the work of Mary Daly, Catharine MacKinnon, Susan Estrich, and Susan Brownmiller, rape is a marker of ultimate patriarchal power both globally and historically "paradigmatic of women's larger oppression." It is "the most blatant example of systematic misogyny and masculine dominance" (Cahill 2001, 15). Global policy documents often echo this perspective despite their generally liberal call to define gendered violence as impediments to ending discrimination and furthering equality. Feminist groups in India have similarly argued that rape is "a critical instrument in the subjugation of women and their confinement to private spaces" (Kannabiran and Kannabiran 2002, 157). Ann Cahill usefully identifies two strands of this approach. The first is typified by Susan Brownmiller, who argued that rape was violence and not sex, that "it did not arise out of a sexual need" but "was an act of power that sought to dominate and degrade the victim." The second is represented by Catharine MacKinnon, who famously asserted that rape was sex, but because all heterosex was violence and dominance, "rape was in fact continuous with most heterosexual sex and could not be distinguished from it by mere reference to coercion or violence" (Cahill 2001, 2–3).

While the rhetorical impact of these views, which posit rape in terms of a ravaged body and thus a destroyed self, is undeniable, these perspectives are also implacable and deterministic, typically homogenizing political and cultural specificities. In counterpoint, analyses that see rape not as universal and uniform but as variant constructions of embodiment and violence are useful for tracking particular codings of rape. They depict women not as a priori hunted objects of intimidation through sex, but as embedded in worlds of belief, negotiation, and resistance.

Is it self-evident that a penis is an instrument of torture and violence, or is it enabled as such in cultures that assign particular valences to the gendered body? Like other anthropologists who have challenged the universality of rape culture (Watson-Franke 2002; and most famously, Sanday 2003), Helliwell (2000) thinks outside the familiar box of overdetermined patriarchal violence. She starts with an astonished question from a Gerai woman who challenges her concern that the woman may have been subjected to a rape attempt the night before by saying, "It's only a penis. . . . How can a penis hurt anyone?" Helliwell argues that the terms of rape are not *biologically* determined, but rather that *cultural* constructions of gender difference, in particular ideas of "sexual polarity" in which societal "disparities of power and status" are attributed to bodily difference, construct the power to violate through rape: "Rape itself produces such experiences ['of men's genitalia and sexuality as inherently brutalizing and penetrative and women's genitalia as inherently vulnerable and subject to brutalization'] and so inscribes sexual differences onto our bodies" (796–98, 812). Rape cases accordingly constitute scripts that dictate *through their actions* gender-power dimorphism and sexuality as central to subjectivity. Discourses of sexual difference further rape's power to create terror and subjugation in public space, or to sediment caste and religious hierarchies.

Given the persistent difficulty of legal remedies, the focus for more recent feminist theorists has been on solutions beyond legal deterrence. Sharon Marcus famously advocates foregrounding the discursivity of rape, "understanding rape to be a language," and thence undoing the power of the "gendered grammar of violence" (1992, 387). While Marcus has been criticized

(Mardorossian 2002) for overemphasizing the healing power of language, as well as for the victim-blaming implicit in making overcoming rape a matter of mental resistance, I read her as arguing for changing signifiers of violence and embodiment in ways that seem congruent with Helliwell's argument: "Social structures *inscribe* on men's and women's embodied selves and psyches the misogynist inequalities which enable rape to occur" (391). Other feminist analyses similarly argue for noting the ways in which the body is inscribed, while leaving room for agency beyond dominant scripts. Cahill recommends seeing "the feminine body both as a site for the inscription of patriarchal and misogynist truths and as a fluid, indeterminate set of possibilities" (2001, 13); Mardorossian proposes to "supplement feminist accounts of women's experience with a contextual analysis of the ways in which experience is given meaning at a particular time and place" (2002, 748). Accounts of rape are forceful reminders that harm and intimidation are all too often corporeal rather than linguistic, and that legal protection is embedded in hegemonic codes of gender. These alternatives, however, fundamentally contest the power of rape to wound, by purposefully emphasizing inscriptions of body and language and highlighting the (material and discursive) resistance of survivors.

Consider the role of embodiment in the following examples of organized resistance in India, which highlight *discursive* challenges to rape. The rape of *sathin* (social worker) Bhanwari Devi became a prominent rallying point for antirape activism; in the subsequent protests, other *sathins* named their own experiences of sexual assault, and slogans mocked the rapists' loss of honor (Menon 2004, 133; Kannabiran and Menon 2007, 145). Another landmark event, the 2004 rape and murder of Manorama Devi in Manipur (in northeast India), thinly constructed by the army as the capture of an insurgent, was followed by a memorable protest in which "15 middle-aged women demon-strated naked" in front of the armed forces' headquarters (Kannabiran and Menon 2007, 170): "'Indian army, rape us!,' they shouted, challenging the authorities by drawing graphic attention to the shameful violation of women's bodies by them. By saying, 'We are Manorama's mothers,' they as good as declared that her rape was tantamount to raping them, and by extension, all Manipuri women and all mothers" (180–81). This protest set off a prolonged agitation against the armed forces' impunity in northeast India, justified by their depiction of the region as mired in ethnic unrest, terrorism, and sexual license. The strength of moral claims based on maternity aligned these women with other South Asian groups, such as the Naga Mothers Association (also in the northeast, working on armed forces' persecution and sexual violence), the Association of the Parents of Disappeared Persons in Kashmir, and the Mothers' Front in Sri Lanka, which chose public cursing as their mode of protest (108, 180), as well as internationally renowned groups, such as the Madres de Plaza de Mayo in Argentina. The Naga women transformed a custom in which women bring about an end to feuds by whipping off their sarongs to evoke shame (109), thus recoding meanings of assault through their bodies. In a very different context, the 2009 Pink *Chaddi* campaign by the urban Consortium of Pubgoing, Loose, Forward Women, which protested assaults on women by the fundamentalist Hindu group Ram Sene on Valentine's Day, asked women to mail pink underwear to the offices of the group,[32] deploying the shame of the female body against itself.

Visceral alterity was most dramatically demonstrated in the embodied resistance of the women of Kasturba Nagar at the courtroom remand of Akku Yadav, who had terrorized the town with his gang by raping numerous girls and women, maiming and murdering, extorting money, and walking on bail after each arrest. Some of these women, "ordinary slum-dwellers and daily wage-earners," stormed the courtroom with stones, sticks, and chili powder, and attacked, castrated, and killed him (newspaper accounts commonly use the word *lynching*). They declared their act a "freedom struggle," an act of "social justice" rather than "murder," retorting to those who were horrified by the vigilantism that "there is no justice for the poor. What if this had happened to a minister's wife or daughter? So, we decided to do it ourselves."[33] In a remarkable strategy of plural culpability, scores of women claimed to have been the perpetrators, so the police were unable to arrest any specific women for the crime (and even alleged that perhaps some men did it and the women were protecting them).[34] The Kasturba Nagar women's actions suggest a retaliatory use of bodily violence not just to harm or kill but to transform the signifiers of victimhood, class, and legal protection. While the specter of scores of enraged women wielding sticks, stones, and chili powder replicates the stock image of the (Indian) female avenger pushed to the limit and taking back the problematic value of "honor,"[35] these women challenged the power of rape through a collective, coordinated, visceral response that elides legal punishment, in blatant mockery and rebuke of the law.

The Kasturba Nagar revenge reminds us, however, that moments of resistance are necessarily embedded in the same linguistic and corporeal signifying systems as the assaults they resist, making discursive analyses problematic as the frontline of attack. Nonetheless, most of these strategies did succeed in transforming public understandings of gender and violence by challenging connotations of masculinity, femininity, modesty, shame, and power, even if they did not stop military impunity or transform judicial assumptions or administrative retaliation. Images of naked middle-aged women daring soldiers to rape them or a group of women with sticks and chili powder taking over a courtroom affect the ways gendered scripts of rape can be thought about, displacing the centrality of law.

In contrast, Oindrila's inscription of harm and violence is a more uncomfortable fit for feminist challenges to rape discourse. Not only is there is no obvious pain, or coercion, or humiliation, nor triumph, no turning law on its head, but moreover, it is a gesture designed to evoke the punitive gendering of law, relying on the protectionist state to deliver the prize of marriage to helpless women. It complicates resistance by disempowering women's sexual agency and affirmative consent. However, in common with these other cases, it does lead us to look through and beyond the body in rape. Oindrila's actions, and the following cases on rape and marriage, signal the complex cultural matrices within which understandings of rape (and hence body and consent) draw meaning, in particular the legalities through which marriage is instituted. Feminist struggles to theorize sexual agency and sexual victimization, equality and difference, are deeply, contradictorily embedded in such legalities.

MARRIAGE AND RAPE

The Rudranil-Oindrila case is most significant in this chapter not for debating whether "real rape" happened, or whether or not law is being "misused," but as a node that exhibits the deployment of sexual violence charges for negotiating material and cultural needs. Like other cases in these chapters, it demonstrates the arsenal of strategies litigants routinely use to deal with marital trouble, including playing off civil and criminal claims against each other in multiple venues. Parallel to domestic violence cases, which can provide leverage for better alimony (chapter 7), or criminal law provisions for return of dowry, which can be a proxy for recovering matrimonial property (however little), such rape charges also point to the advantages of criminal over civil law (or the benefits of using both simultaneously).

Criminal sanctions by the state, which rely on essentialized notions of female victimization and sexual passivity, are advantageous in offering broad protection. In contrast, civil remedies deliver few punitive solutions to failure to provide maintenance or housing. Criminal provisions offer protection by highlighting gendered *difference* (although women's chances of accessing these criminal remedies vary widely depending on their class, caste, and religious position, and judges or law enforcement officials do not necessarily follow through on the spirit of these laws). Civil marriage law, on the contrary, is more gender neutral, even though in effect it reinforces patriarchal economic and social power, with divorce exposing the economic vulnerabilities of marriage (Fineman 1991), as chapter 5 explores. The limited "civility" of equal marriage can thus be rattled by criminal law, one of the few forms of leverage, albeit through protectionist logic. Criminal law displays the state's prerogative power while civil law veils the material base of the state's patriarchal relations.

One such case, which illustrates the ways rape and marriage work in each other's shadow, came from a day at the Women's Grievance Cell. One morning I saw a large man, wearing a fancy safari suit and prominent gold jewelry, waving a huge file of legal papers at the police officers and agitatedly reporting a call that morning about "Supriya's" attempts to set up a meeting and have him bring her money. Some officers explained after his departure that he claimed to be in media and to have been set up by a group of gangsters, drugged and entrapped with what they termed a "professional" woman (likely meaning a professional con artist rather than a professional sex worker). Unaccountably, he continued to be involved with the group and the woman, Supriya. He had set her up in a flat, had a child with her, and lived there quite a lot of the time, all the while claiming that he had been coerced into a registered marriage.[36] His fifty-four-year-old wife had recently threatened divorce on grounds of adultery if he did not quit this relationship. Supriya had threatened to file an S376 (rape) case on the grounds that he entered into a formal bigamous marriage with full knowledge that it was invalid and hence fraudulent, thereby continuing a sexual relationship with her under circumstances she would not have knowingly consented to. The police officer told me that in their meetings she had stressed to him that she needed to be fair to both women's claims. The women bitterly opposed each other but had separately framed their claims with tidy strategies. His best recourse, the officer believed, was to use persuasion or his ample financial resources to extricate himself, though joint family property and alleged gang involvement would pose some obstacles.

Like Oindrila, Supriya evokes rape in the context of a long-term cohabitation, claiming a sudden violation of chastity. She too is not solely dependent on marriage for economic sustenance but sees it as a form of social legitimacy (with obvious economic benefits). The case similarly causes uneasiness in its erasure of female sexual agency and its evocation of social status conferred by marriage. But it also illustrates the ways criminal complaints help express "civil" issues of marriage entitlements. Several organizations dealing with violence against women in India report cases, often from similarly educated, employed women, who see rape laws as a way to bring charges after relationships (often with married men) have ended. Some feminists express their discomfort with such charges, which assume marriage as an outcome even when women voluntarily entered nonconjugal relationships.

Such cases draw their force from well-worn legal trajectories in which rape prosecutions turn to marriage as a compensatory solution. They not only represent rape as sex rather than violence but view it as a violation of property to be made whole by restoring the woman to marriedness—that is, to the benefits of marriage that premarital sex cut off. The two main "patterns," a recent article suggests, are that "either an autocratic system, like a panchayat, intercedes to force the union or the accused, in a bid to avoid punishment, offers marriage in exchange," often accompanied by payment from the groom's family. These are similar to cases filed by women when men bring long cohabitation to an end or promise marriage in order to have sex; as in Rudranil's case, police officers mediate these unions. That these marriages often end in further violence or desertion seems unsurprising.[37]

Such cases synecdochally inscribe marriage as the form of property at stake in rape: women rely on being married for security (whether or not they accrue individual wealth), and violence is erased by compensatory marriage proposals from rapists. The Goa High Court set aside Rafik Taksir's imprisonment for rape and kidnapping in 2002 after he declared that he had married the rape survivor following conviction, deeming that "it is true that the scars of trauma suffered by the victim cannot be erased from her memory but the evidence on record does indicate to a certain extent that the appellant and the victim were in love."[38] A Delhi court acquitted a man of rape and kidnapping (originally charges of gang rape were filed against him and three of his friends) when letters from the woman and pictures of their wedding ceremony were presented. The judge commented that "if one goes through these letters, there remains no doubt that the prosecutrix was deeply involved with the accused"; her pictures in wedding attire served as evidence to prove that she did not marry under coercion.[39] Kanhu Panda "expressed his desire to marry the victim despite belonging to a different caste" and was granted bail to marry at the Bhadrak temple where "their well-wishers had also hosted a grand feast to mark the occasion," then went back to jail as a prisoner under trial "hop[ing] his wife will withdraw the case against him and look[ing] forward to a married life outside jail."[40] Remarkably, these judgments emphasize visual rather than oral evidence of consent (old love notes, wedding pictures, community presence) and validate past or future relationships rather than the time and context of the sexual act at issue. In effect, they erase violence from rape, ground agency in marriage rather than sex, and dismantle the very notion of consent. With women's consent to sex viewed as tantamount to consent to marriage, women's articulation of their own sexuality is altogether irrelevant.[41]

A blatant equivalence in currency between marriage and rape marks the 2005 case of Bhura, who worked as a ward boy at a hospital. He raped a nurse, gouged out her right eye and severely injured the left, locked her up, and left her for dead. After conviction and prior to sentencing, he sent in an application saying, "To save the life of the victim as well as the lives of both of the families, the convict, from the core of his heart, without prejudice to the merits of the case, is ready to perform marriage with the victim." The nurse vociferously responded that he should be accorded the maximum punishment instead, or even hanged. Feminist organizations berated the judge for admitting this application. "The court should not be a marriage bureau for criminals," political activist Brinda Karat scolded.[42] But the application, while a desperate last-ditch bid for clemency, also represents a reward that a man with the worst of prospects has the power to grant. How could we not believe in genuine repentance and integrity if marriage was on offer?

A few recent global examples show that such seemingly archaic practices are neither isolated nor rare, marking dangerous emergent collusions between law and custom. After the 2012 suicide of sixteen-year-old Amina Filali (who had been severely beaten after a forced marriage following a rape),[43] Moroccan women's rights activists protested a penal code provision that allowed a rapist to marry his victim to "preserve *her* family's honour" (emphasis mine) by permitting a judge to grant consent for marriage on behalf of minors.[44] A 2011 case in Afghanistan, while overdetermined by media hunger for representing the state in terms of primal "tribal" justice, nonetheless demonstrates the limits of new policies on sexual violence in the face of customary law. Gulnaz, raped by a cousin's husband, was jailed during her subsequent pregnancy on charges of adultery. Though later given a presidential pardon from criminal charges, she was still likely subject to the customary Pashtun resolution to rape, a trade of women in which the rapist would find a wife for one of her brothers and pay a hefty fine to them.[45] Gulnaz's resigned entrapment emerges in her statement, "If he can't find a wife for my brothers, I'm not crazy about marrying him. . . . If I have a good life with him, that will be fine." In contemporary Taiwan, rapists' proposals to marry had widespread social and legal endorsement. Though women reported worries about fear of disclosure, loss of virginity, guilt, and blame following rape, they occasionally entertained the offers as strategies to save their businesses and reputations, or in one case to get foreign residence (Luo 2000, 589–90). These offers, Luo argues, reinforce the virginity fetish and the sexualization of rape, and worsen trauma among survivors. As with the Indian cases, these strategies do not strengthen survivors' sexual agency and heighten rather than ameliorate the status of rape within patriarchal relations.

On the other hand, judgments that directly addressed questions of female sexual desire demonstrated the pitfalls of highlighting women's agency. The 2006 case *Vishnu vs. State of Maharashtra*[46] was hailed as a landmark judgment because the rapist was convicted on the sole testimony of the "prosecutrix." But the decision was saturated with deeply gendered understandings of shame and chastity: "The statement of the prosecutrix, in our view, is quite natural. . . . In the traditional non-permissive bounds of society in India, no girl or woman of self-respect or dignity would depose falsely, implicating somebody of ravishing her chastity by sacrificing and jeopardizing her future prospect of getting married with a suitable match. In doing so she not only would be sacrificing her future but also would invite the wrath of being ostracized and cast out from the society she belongs to and also from her family circle." While this "prosecutrix" happened to get the benefit of the doubt, partly because she was viewed as innocent and virginal, others who fit the mold less well in terms of perfect chastity or class would not, by implication, warrant the same protection, as earlier examples demonstrated. But when a more complex notion of women's sexual agency was deployed in the 2003 case *Uday vs. State of Karnataka*, it served to dismiss naïve belief in "promises of marriage": the court determined that the woman had willingly consented to sex "not because he promised to marry her but because she also desired it," having been "overcome with emotions and passion" and "succumbed to the temptation."[47] The ascription of sexual agency to the woman was, unsurprisingly, a legal disadvantage for her, illustrating Baxi's contention that the desiring woman complicates the drive of rape prosecution to establish harm to society (2014, 344). Is this case to be commended as an equitable recognition of women's sexual passion or a pathway for dismissing rape charges by putting women's desire on trial?

The counterpoint to courts' support for marriage offers is the punitive zeal directed at men who managed to get sex by promising marriage down the road (the precedent that Oindrila's claim relies upon). "Back Out of Marriage at Own Risk," the *Economic Times* headline gleefully screamed,[48] on the occasion of Kalipada Garu being charged with "exploit[ing] the poverty and physical disability" of a woman who "had been lured by false promises of a happy married life and agreed to sleep with him," then learned later that he had married someone else, after they spent many weekends at tourist hotels. A Nagpur woman filed a case of rape against a Delhi man she met after placing an Internet matrimonial ad, citing his lies about his life and the abortion he forced on her.[49] A Hooghly (West Bengal) judge sentenced a man to seven years in prison, contending a false promise of marriage was "tantamount to rape" and hoping the punishment would "ensure 'that no one in future dares to cheat innocent girls.'"[50] Subhra was awarded a compensation payment for rape on the basis of a false promise of marriage, after Gautam staged a fake ceremony in front of "his God" (Buddha, evoking the horror of religious exogamy).[51] In several similar cases in Bangladesh, women brought attempted rape and deception charges by alleging that they were made to undertake invalid marriages (involving fake authorities or rituals), after they had rebuffed repeated sexual advances by saying they would only have sex if married; these cases illustrate that sex outside marriage "can only be intelligible through the grid of coercion and rape," Siddiqi (2010) argues.

In further legal refinements of what constitutes "false promise," the 2005 case *Deelip Singh vs. State of Bihar*[52] set the standard that women would be deemed to have not given consent "only if it established that from the very inception the man never really intended to marry her and the promise was a mere hoax." The Supreme Court held in 2013 that men's "'clandestine' motives" and "malafide intentions" would have to be proved to establish criminal liability, and that "not fulfilling a false promise" was not tantamount to "breach of promise."[53] Defendants like Rudranil might use such a norm to argue, for example, that there was no plot or conspiracy at the beginning, merely a change of heart over time. However, this norm reflects the defendant's state of mind, with rape prosecuted according to standards of fraud rather than consent.

In several recent decisions, appellate courts have strongly condemned "false" rape cases for harm caused to the accused,[54] conflating outright perjury with a range of other common ways of using laws. But what constitutes the "false"? A common set of cases under this designation involves women being coerced by their families into legal strategies when they return after being missing or were found by police after having run away. Two sixteen-year-olds (legally deemed incapable of sexual consent) petitioned the Delhi High Court in 2005 that after they ran away by choice, their husbands were being falsely accused of kidnapping and rape. The judge granted their petition to deem their marriages valid, to the dissatisfaction of women's groups.[55] A twenty-two-year-old man was acquitted of kidnapping and raping a fifteen-year-old girl in 2013, based on her statement that she ran away voluntarily to get married, even as the court lectured on the perils of early marriage and the need for education.[56] It was established in another case that a betrothed woman's brother had provided a false statement that she was underage and had been kidnapped.[57] These examples point to a growing use of kidnapping and rape law by women's families against men who have eloped with their daughters, particularly where they disapprove of the match on the grounds of caste or religious exogamy.[58] The 52 percent growth registered by the National Crime Records Bureau in the number of registered kidnapping and abduction cases relating to women between 2004 and 2010 strongly indicates the use of kidnapping charges as a popular strategy of controlling marriage choice. Most cases are dropped and few end in conviction; the number of chargesheeted cases is only about half the registered cases, and the conviction rate of chargesheeted cases hovers around 18–20 percent.

Public acknowledgment of sexual violence appears to be less stigmatizing in such cases than the possibility of a permanently transgressive marriage, tidily illustrating Veena Das's argument that rape law in India tracks "offences against the system of alliance" (1996, 2416). Women's choices are deemed moot, with rape law deployed to solidify caste and religious hegemonies, "the identity of the family . . . traced through its capacity to bring punitive measures against errant daughters" (Baxi 2014, 257). Unlike "love matches" compatible with systems of alliance and kinship, where "love" is often rendered by the families into the form of an "arranged marriage" (Mody 2008), marriage in these cases cannot secure appropriate kin and property relations, and therefore rape must serve as residue. Women are charged with theft and violence by their families to coerce their cooperation or punish them, surreally serving "as a victim, witness and accused in the crime of and for planning to kidnap, abduct and rape her own body" (Baxi 2014, 275).

In the alarming emergence of so-called honor killings, women's transgressions across categories of alliance are met with social (and literal) death.[59] While scholars have argued that the rationale of honor is used to mask local class, land, and property disputes (Hossain and Welchman 2005; Chowdhry 2007; Basu and Bhatt 2010; Puri and Dogra 2010), the point is that the murders are considered acceptable violence in the face of threats to alliance. Ironically, feminist groups may inadvertently support the logic of such families when they campaign for making marriages below sixteen, the age of consent, void. Agnes argues[60] that such campaigns become complicit with state protectionism of hegemonic formations of "caste, community, region, religion," challenging the affirmative consent of "women who exercise active agency to defy convention [and] pose a threat to the established social order."

Postrape marriage, promises to marry that constitute a firm contract to the property represented by the woman's sexuality, and accusations against women as being party to their own rape and abduction have not been at the heart of feminist conceptualizations of rape, but neither are they bizarre aberrations or primitive trade-offs. They demonstrate, rather, "the particular discursive form . . . that gives rape its particular meaning and power in these contexts" (Helliwell 2000, 796–98). Within the particularities of their "sex-gender systems" (Rubin 1975), these scenarios reveal the ways rape works within kinship structures, labor patterns, and religious and caste endogamy: they reflect and reinforce women's reliance on compulsory heterosexual marriage and, within this system of transaction, on sexuality as a commodity that secures its acquisition. Where rape is depicted as patriarchal control over sexuality, sex can be nothing other than rape given women's lack of meaningful choices (MacKinnon 1988). In these cases, too, there is no distinction between sexual activity and rape other than through the shadow of marriage, which is the proxy for consent and future security. If (appropriate) marriage is the only possible beneficent future, rape is the trauma of closing off access to those benefits.

THE VIOLENCE OF MARRIAGE

Swallowing the idea of marriage as a solution, no matter how strategic a solution, is virtually impossible within feminist theory. Materialist feminist theories, famously going back to Engels, contend that marriage serves as a linchpin consolidating patriarchal relations through the control of labor, reproduction, and property (see chapter 1). Marriage laws inscribe gendered heterosexual subordination under the sign of economic and moral protection. Inequality is constructed through marital ideologies that imprint pleasure and consent "deep into the bodies, thoughts and identities of individuals" (Chambers 2005, 330).

Carole Pateman (1988, 2) provocatively attributes gendered socioeconomic difference to the inherently inequitable contract of heterosexual, patriarchal marriage, which is at odds with the social contract of democratic participation: "Men's domination over women, and the right of men to enjoy equal sexual access to women, is at issue in the making of the original pact. The social contract is a story of freedom; the sexual contract is a story of subjugation." In her reading, women are excluded from the social contract, which is marked as both neutral and masculine, and participate only in the subordinate sexual contract: "Only the marriage contract can turn use of sexual property . . . into the use of a person. But it is the husband who has use of a person, not the wife" (172). The sexual contract undergirding marriage, property, and sexual expression is invisible and hence impossible to negotiate, meaning marriage is fundamentally intractable to contract although apparently located in democratic space.

While Pateman has been critiqued for her broad, essentialized depiction of paralyzing oppression, I find her argument useful for thinking about how rape and marriage are linked as forms of sexual property. In these cases, sex as property has transaction and exchange value: men's relationship to marriage is one of either shirking full value or paying up on such property. Women embody these forms of property: typically excluded from inheriting within circuits of natal and matrimonial property resources, their only access to those resources comes via the commodity of sexuality (and related productive and reproductive labor). They lose their control over this embodied property through rape and need to recapture it to be part of the marriage economy, where their economic survival lies. Where their status as the currency of transaction supersedes their identities as subjects of law, consent is moot. Marital rape is a categorical impossibility given the irrelevance of women's consent.

Pateman's model most clearly fits early rape law, where "criminal law supported marriage law" in "protecting the authority of the custodian (the father or other male relatives) to arrange a maiden's marriage by making the seduction of an unmarried girl a crime" (Kiesiläinen 2004, 170).[61] Contemporary rape laws may seem very different to the extent that they evaluate violence based on consent rather than property, but they nonetheless posit the violation of rape in terms of precluding futures in which marriage opens up the primary means of survival, according with Pateman's perspective. Consent is specious if it is evaluated in terms of legal sex rather than perceptions of bodily integrity, validating Pateman's contention that women are not quite able to be full participants in a social contract of full and free exchange, given their primary affiliation in terms of the sexual contract of limited agency. This is not to say that individual women do not negotiate their own lives by using the logic of transaction against the grain, but usually this is best achieved by ideological assent to gendered dependence, as Oindrila's case illustrates.

The state looms large here in bestowing marriage with entitlements and punishing rape for interrupting that scheme. Rape interrupts the patterns through which circuits of kinship are rendered sacred; norms of kinship are restored through state-sanctioned legal categories, including marriage. Some scholars contend that (patriarchal) kinship is the primary sphere of transaction and violence monitored by the state, establishing "an insignia of the extent to which politics between men [in kinship] are always already also the politics of exchanging, violating, protecting and dominating women; the one constitutes the imperatives of the other"(Brown 1992, 25). The gendered subordination of kinship systems is continually reproduced in state governance of marriage, even though sex is rarely specified in any pronouncements (Stevens 1997, 66).[62] The above cases of kidnapping, rape pardoned by marriage, and lack of marriage equated with rape, exemplify the state's strong support for kinship hierarchies. Even the feminist turn to the state to enforce age of marriage, which seemingly challenges kinship authority governing customs of child marriage, ironically aligns with families who seek to proscribe less-than-ideal alliances.

But marriage as a solution offers scant equity after all. Laws regarding sexual violence rely on marriage. In state sanctions of marriage to rapists, the use of rape law as a tool to punish defaulters to marriage, or Oindrila's and Supriya's attempts to make sex criminal unless converted to marriage, we see the privileged status conferred by marriage, despite its failure to provide distributive equity. Proffers of marriage to compensate the harms of rape cannot transform the ideologies of sexual passivity or socioeconomic dependence that are part of rape's discursive force; rather, they enhance the effects.

CONCLUSION: BEYOND LEGAL PROTECTION

It was clear from the massive crowds rallying in the wake of Jyoti Singh Pandey's assault in December 2012 that rape was eliciting vociferous public outrage in India. Marches and testimonies have continued since that time, fueled by newer cases, with demands for greater state sensitivity and vigilance, and calls for swift and severe punishment for rapists. Some legal decisions and policies reflect these demands: a Jodhpur fast-track court created legal history with its speedy convictions of two men accused of raping a German tourist in 2005,[63] while in 2006 a Bihar court handed down a rape conviction in five hours.[64] The Indian National Commission for Women is putting together a Criminal Injuries Compensation Board at the directive of the Supreme Court, with substantial financial remuneration if the rape is proved, plus legal aid and protection during trial, as well as medical and psychological help.[65] In a dramatic decision (an about-face from the colonial norm), "the Supreme Court has advised all trial courts to take a victim's testimony as gospel truth, unless it is tinged with a motive to falsely implicate the accused," citing women's hesitancy to bring rape to public notice,[66] following an earlier recommendation to lower courts to use their power for reducing sentences sparingly.[67] These decisions cast the state as prompt, active in addressing women's sexual exploitation, and attentive to women's voices. They also (realistically) highlight women's status as victims and their economic neediness, underlining the protective welfare function of the modern nation-state.

However, rape-related policies that are "beneficial to women" can only be superficially sensitive, because the structures of sexuality, reproduction, and property through which they are constituted are not challenged. Oindrila's claim, for example, was a solid legal strategy (or at least an effective bargaining strategy), relying on precedents invoking female vulnerability and innocence in the face of male predatoriness. Calls for drastic corporeal punishment further validate the prerogative power of the state to avenge rape through ideologies of shame and honor and eye-for-an-eye justice. Similarly, demands for swift resolution ignore the complex deployments of rape law by families and the state, where fast outcomes may mean hasty investigations.

The irony is that after having struggled for decades to have sexual violence recognized within law, some feminist legal theorists and activists find themselves urging caution and context while the public bays for revenge over rapes. At issue are the very notions of gendered harm once used to argue that sexual assault is a crime—specifically, the representation of femininity as vulnerable and requiring special protection. The dilemma is the terrifying one of abandoning legal "protection" based on such "difference" for a norm of "sameness" where the effects of gender systems might be invisible. If rape can only be inscribed as harm to a special group, as "a sexual offence the psychological and social consequences of which are so unique, severe and rooted in age-old power relationships between the sexes that a gender-neutral law would fail in important ways to deal with the world as it really is" (Williams 1997, 77), then how can that group also make a claim for empowered equitable citizenship in other social areas? "Do we want equality of the sexes—or do we want justice for two kinds of human beings who are fundamentally different?" (84), Wendy Williams asks, echoing Helliwell's worry that insistence on gendered legal difference *creates* untenable scripts of gender and codes female subjectivity as passivity and dependence. Williams favors the "equality standard" because it lines up with full citizenship (and hence full access to the social contract, in Pateman's terms), arguing that feminists should support gender-neutral rape legislation "because it resists our segregationist urges, and affirms our common humanity" (77).[68] Nivedita Menon, striking at the heart of the difference claim, suggests "demystify"ing rape, in order "to begin to see it not as a unique and life-destroying form of violation from which one can never recover, but as (merely) another kind of violence against persons, many of whom could be men" (2012, 140).

But picking any one side of this binary is trouble, because short- and long-term remedies are thereby in conflict. Herein lies a fundamental feminist dilemma, "the familiar paradox of demanding that the law both privilege women's difference *and* overlook it in different contexts, according to the ends of real and substantial justice" (Rajan 2003, 33). To critique the notion of protection may mean that state protection is substantially retracted as a result, with even less accountability for violence. Thus it may not be practicable to move beyond the emphasis on women primarily in terms of their sexuality, especially where crimes deploy those very associations. As Smart fears, "Feminism may not be able to articulate alternative accounts because of the real fear that law will snatch back the minimal protection it offers. . . . [A] feminist discourse which might attempt to construct rape differently, which might attempt to deconstruct the biological/sexed woman, is silenced by the apparition of law's sexed woman to whose survival it is unwillingly tied" (1995, 86–87). Can we afford to criticize the essentialist constructions of the gendered body in rape legislation, after rape has come to be legally recognized as an act of violence that relies on social categories of sex, thanks to feminist movements? Yet the related question is, can we live with marriage as a form of compensation for rape claims, or indeed with marriage as any kind of compensation at all?

The recent frontier of legal reform around sexual assault in India, the Criminal Law (Amendment) Act of 2013, exemplifies these dilemmas. Though it tried to reconceptualize violence, it faltered at the difficulty of this task given that violence is experienced through culturally inscribed harms and forms of embodiment. It included long-overdue updates, including a broader list of categories of sexual assault, an expansion of rape beyond the penis-penetrating-vagina paradigm, and more nuanced notions of consent. But it failed to include same-sex violence or marital rape, in part because these categories complicated conceptualizations of gender difference and consent. Although it was essential for feminist groups to be actively engaged with the shape of this potentially far-reaching reform, they were strongly aware of these contradictions.

The mirroring of rape and marriage traced in this chapter reminds us that feminist interventions are necessarily lodged in these difficult encounters: while they attempt to influence forms of state vigilance, they cannot control the meanings that emerge in judicial governance, nor people's use of laws for their own ends. The best hope is to destabilize rape within or outside law, ultimately to not be undone by the harm that rape seeks to wreak. In responding to whether there has been any "progress" in controlling rape since the 2012 agitations, Flavia Agnes pointed to a recent survivor's expressed wish to move on with her life: "The biggest change is that nobody is calling her a *zinda laash* [living corpse] or saying that her life is now over and what will she do and where will she go? That in itself is a sign of our making some form of prog ress."[69] Uncoupling rape from marriage, kinship, and honor is critical to this process of combating sexual violence by challenging its signifiers rather than embracing its logic through law.

CHAPTER 7

Strategizing Spaces

Negotiating the Violence out of Domestic Violence Claims

I arrive at my in-laws' home, *ledikeni* [sweets] in hand
My wife says there's no chance [she's coming back]
My enraged wife asked me for a divorce
Her figure swelled up like she's from the Border Security Force
It's true I did plead [with her], do consider our case
And that's when the scandal of "torture" got tagged to my name.
—Bhoomi, "Photik Ekhon"

Poor Photik. He is humiliated, assaulted, and pronounced dead, all on account of his disastrous marriage, able to escape being cremated alive only by sitting up on the funeral bier and telling his story. In the song, the well-meaning Photik shows up at his in-laws' with sweets, to encounter his enraged wife (her eyes like molten lava, a huge puffed-up body like that of a military officer) and her family (gigantic in size and temperamentally unsuited to any love/ *prem*). She demands a divorce, and when asked to consider her decision, files charges of "domestic torture" and breaks his jaw with her fist. Her rage, he posits, is in response to the crime that he is a simple man ("content with plain tea"), with no extra income from bribes. He decides to fake unconsciousness, then death, to escape this "tigress's paw." Once rescued, he vows never to be a son-in-law again.

Photik is a recurrent character in the songs of Bhoomi, a renowned Bangla music group. He appears as an amiable simpleton not quite ready for life's responsibilities. In an earlier song, he uses up the family grocery money on sweets and is roundly beaten by his father, then wins the lottery and is abandoned by his wife, who takes with her the new saris and jewelry he bought.

176

His relationship to money, in other words, is inappropriately careless, making his exposure to family violence always imminent. While this chapter follows the everyday life of domestic violence rather than such popular representations, it will become evident that people negotiate their claims in the shadow of these tropes: the beleaguered, burdened husband in the clutches of law, the shrill, greedy wife who turns to the law for revenge, and particularly the ubiquitous presence of "torture" or domestic violence charges in sites of marital trouble.

The "torture" suit filed by Photik's wife is likely a reference to S498A, a notorious legal provision at the heart of the discursive conflict around domestic violence—to some, a powerful measure to help women negotiate physical violence and economic well-being; to others, a way to torture husbands by manipulating law. The number 498A, referring to the Indian Penal Code section under which domestic violence, both physical and mental, is prosecuted, has acquired a totemic quality (reminiscent of Indian usages of 420 to connote a shady person, a cheat, or a thief, corresponding to fraud offences under the Indian Penal Code); it has become a colloquial way of referring to persecuted men, avenging women, and the power of governance feminism. I began to notice the distinctive affective culture of S498A during divorce proceedings and marital mediations. Male litigants in the social camaraderie of the family court corridor would check in with each other, "How did your 498 go?" assuming a shared legal torment. Police officers frequently remarked, "You can't save the marriage once there's a 498." "How can she blame me for the marriage failing when she has filed a 498?" a family court counselor asked rhetorically. Male litigants used the number to mark unease with their affinal kin and their own entitlement to property, while female litigants believed it useful for accessing resources and marking troubled relations in extended households. Judges, counselors, and police most often took S498A cases to be not about punishing violence, but rather about negotiating the social and economic entitlements of marriage.

In this chapter, I focus on the cultural life of S498A, especially the ways in which it is used to express issues of marriage and property, with criminality functioning as a lever of civil negotiations. It is, of course, impossible to determine the veracity of any of these domestic violence claims, or to deny that criminal charges add a level of threat to civil remedies. However, as the cases show, the crux of S498A's potential is that it seems primarily successful when deployed against the grain to obtain civil remedies, rather than to end or reduce violence. The question of violence, as a result, is continually deflected. Criminal allegations of domestic violence ironically become a conduit cementing the material and symbolic power of marriage. As with rape charges, criminal law's potential to redress violence is contrarily deployed to secure dominant notions of domestic order.

S498A takes its place within a decades-long powerful transnational critique of gendered violence, which claims freedom from violence as a human right. However, the global discourse is often unevenly translated into local idioms, as communities may have different criteria for social justice, and international norms may be tone-deaf to local understandings (Merry 2006a, 1). "The deeper social transformation of gender orders and gender relations" (Kelly 2005, 491) that needs to happen alongside law has also proved intransigent, with some difficulties related to the very success of feminist institutionalization: the state and civil society organizations appear to be sensitized to domestic violence but nonetheless work through prevailing discourses of gender roles, family cohesion, and authority (Merry 2009). Forms of structural violence (tied to race, ethnicity, or class) compound the gendered effects.

In "the battering state," to use Adelman's provocative phrase, the effects of domestic violence are felt at the intersection of "1) the organization of the polity; 2) the arrangement of the economy; and 3) the dominant familial ideology expressed normatively through state practices" (2004, 46). Ethnographies of domestic violence in a variety of nation-states perfectly substantiate her formulation. Vietnam's signature on international treaties and constitutional provisions for gender equality signals its modernity as a state, but it is also immersed in neoliberal policies and a contradictory promotion of familialism. Vietnamese women seeking help from state venues were most often sent to reconciliation committees that emphasized women's central role in the family, and hence national harmony (Kwiatkowski 2011, 25). Sonja Plesset's (2006) study of domestic violence in Parma, Italy, similarly suggests the contradictions between public campaigns to stigmatize domestic violence and the problems women faced with their families, police, judges, and shelters, who asserted the validity of normative conjugal roles and viewed violence as domestic discipline. Shelters in various countries replicate gendered labor and patriarchal authority, and become subject to bureaucratic practices (Plesset 2006, 167–202; Bumiller 2008, 4). Laws, targeted police stations, and shelters were in place in Lima, Peru, but poor migrant women found them inhospitable and were compelled to either continue violent relationships or face the dangers of shantytown living (Alcalde 2010). Women in Trinidad were frustrated by legal process but also dropped cases because they preferred a "successful" (often economic) outcome beyond legal remedy (Lazarus-Black 2007, 163). As Adelman suggests, class and gender vulnerabilities enhance the difficulties with state governance of violence.

S498A: PROTECTION AND PERSECUTION

Domestic violence (often connected to dowry) and rape were central to the Indian women's movement in the 1980s (Katzenstein 1989; see also Phadke 2003), which radically emphasized violence within the family (Gangoli 2007, 99). S498A was enacted at this time as part of a package of measures to curb violence in the home: Minister of Home Affairs Venkatasubbaiah introduced it with the Criminal Law Second Amendment Bill to "cover cases of cruelty on account of dowry or otherwise,"[1] in recognition of the ineffectiveness of the Dowry Prohibition Act (1961).[2] Several legislators faulted the bill during debates for its incipient inadequacies in addressing dowry excesses and women's economic problems, seeing it as not punitive enough. Those who opposed it represented women in terms of victimhood and noble motherhood (reminiscent of the marriage debates), and objected to the feminist critique of the home (Gangoli 2007, 105–8). These worries about women pursuing cases as *agents* (not victims) and challenging domestic hierarchies are mirrored in later responses to S498A.

S498A expansively defines "cruelty" as "the intentional infliction of severe pain or suffering whether physical or mental," and is explicitly gendered in scope given the above historical context, addressing "cruelty by a *husband* or *his* family towards a married *woman*." Its other provisions similarly carry the whiff of common modes of domestic violence in the 1980s: its four categories of offenses include driving a woman to suicide and harassment for money or property; husbands and affines are named as potential perpetrators; and people other than the victim may file charges (since victims may be unwilling, injured, or dead). Women's organizations saw S498A as "groundbreaking" because it identified family (and not just spousal) violence as criminal behavior, provided for the accused to be arrested without a warrant and held without bail,[3] and instituted non-compoundability or the inability for a case to be settled between parties (Mitra 1999, 21). It constituted a "major breakthrough" in conceptualizing violence, transforming "cruelty" from a gender-neutral ground of divorce in civil law to a criminal "gendered act, directed specifically against women within the space of the Indian matrimonial home" (Lawyers Collective 2009, 2).

The necessity of such intervention is amply demonstrated by the prevalence of family violence in India, as depicted in government statistics (typically believed to undercount violence). The National Crime Records Bureau, which counts criminal charges, records S498A cases as 41.5 percent of all charges in the "crimes against women" category, with 81,344 cases recorded in 2008.[4] The 7.1 percent rise in rates over the previous year points to robust use of the provision, despite the practice of avoiding such charges if possible (as the following sections will show). In the National Family Health Survey, based on survey data from large national samples, 37.2 percent of respondents reported having experienced "physical and/or sexual violence," and 39.7 percent reported "physical and/or sexual and/or emotional violence." Husbands were overwhelmingly cited as the most common perpetrator of violence toward married women (85.3 percent), although in-laws were named in a third or more cases (Gangoli and Rew 2011, 421).[5] Reported family violence typically hovered between 30 and 40 percent across age groups, urban–rural divisions, educational levels, employment statuses, household structures, and marital states (International Institute for Population Sciences and Macro International 2007, 509–10),[6] consonant with studies from international and national research organizations (Mitra 1999; Visaria 1999, 10; Pande 2002, 344; Centre for Social Research 2005, 2).

These statistics, as well as the provisions of S498A lauded by women's groups, are the focus of attack from a well-organized contingent of men's groups, who counter that S498A is disastrous social engineering designed to trip up husbands. Many of these organizations, who valorize the extended family and downplay violence within it, issue repeated warnings that laws are killing marriage by making men fearful, disgusted, and marriage-averse.[7] Their names reflect these perspectives, from Pirito Purush Pati Parishad (Harrassed men and husbands' forum, Kolkata) to the Patni Atyachar Virodhi Manch (Forum against torture by wives, Delhi), and most famously, the India-wide Save the Indian Family.

While much can be said about the misogyny that informs some of their material, most relevant for our purposes here is that the core of their ire is directed at the fluid possibilities of using criminal law. Most MRAs (men's rights activists) join the movement when faced with a cocktail of civil and criminal cases, their outrage fueled by the admixture of charges combined with high demands for alimony or property, under threat of embarrassment, imprisonment, and unemployment. S498A is their prime target, given the scant evidence it requires to file an arrest warrant and its potential for sending a husband and affines to jail with no provision for bail, believed to make it ideal for revenge and extortion by women and their natal families. Its low conviction rate is cited as further proof of its use in bad faith (rather than a reflection of the difficulty of getting a conviction). Media reports on these men's groups are often overtly sympathetic: the headline "Harassed Husbands" prefaces a story on "a desperate band of men who claim to be victims of dowry laws, hang out together, fighting legal battles and helping each other in this 'pro-women legal world'";[8] the piece "Mujhe biwi se bachao" (Save me from my wife) argues that "many 'poor men' . . . are tortured by their wives through anti-dowry laws."[9] This is the archive that Photik's narrative draws upon.

These movements might be allied with global antifeminist backlash, but the capricious potential of S498A and its related failure to curb violence also worry many feminist activists. Maitreyi Chatterji of Nari Nirjaton Pratirodh Mancha (Forum against torture of women) contends that in her experience, elite women have been able to use their influence to have police act on S498A, creating dramatically humiliating scenarios for husbands and in-laws, whereas women without socioeconomic resources continue to have a hard time getting police to file complaints. She recalled a case where a woman's in-laws bribed the police, who refused to press charges.[10] Police, lawyers, and judges claim there is misuse by "educated and independent minded women" (Centre for Social Research 2005, 10), saying that S498A signals the rise of "Frankenstein's monster" (Lodhia 2009, 115). Recent appellate decisions have begun to define guidelines for prearrest investigation to monitor thin or corrupt applications of the law.[11] Judicial decisions have, however, echoed the class-differentiated effects, with certain women (often elite) believed to be entitled to a broader slate of rights, while for nonelite women, "domestic violence has often been legitimized as natural to the institution of marriage" with recommendations that women should be more forgiving and "have a greater biological capacity to tolerate adversity" (Mehra 1998, 68, 71). Other "practical constraints" to filing a case under S498A, despite its expansive provisions, are that "the complainant cannot realistically hope to gain access to her matrimonial home once she files a case. Thus, women without alternate shelter and financial support cannot exercise this option. The husband's family also often proposes withdrawing the case as a precondition for an easy divorce" (Mitra 1999, 22). That is, even those who are sympathetic to the law recognize logistical and structural obstacles.

The number of convictions under the law is extremely small in any case. Solanki (2001, 84) found 100 percent acquittals among the cases that were filed in a particular women's cell in Mumbai. In another district of Maharashtra, only 2.2 percent of cases in a six-year period resulted in convictions (Mitra 1999, 22). At the Delhi crime cell, 53.98 percent of complaints recorded under S498A and S304B (related to dowry) failed to progress to formal cases; 74 percent of cases combining S498A and S304B were challenged in court; and 87 percent of cases decided by courts resulted in acquittals (Pande 2002, 346). The Women's Grievance Cell I visited pursued only four cases out of 470 petitions as formal charges in 2004 (about 230 became "counseling" or mediation cases, and the rest were dismissed). A Centre for Social Research report found that convictions were rare when charges were filed solely under S498A (they improved when S302 for murder or S304B for dowry death were also included),[12] the biggest legal obstacle being the difficulty of providing evidentiary proof of cruelty, especially mental cruelty.

Still, Nishi Mitra (1999) perceives S498A to have critical deterrent value, ranking it among best practices for addressing domestic violence. A 2005 Supreme Court decision also argued that potential for abuse did not erase the need for the law, because "the court, while upholding the provision of law, may still set aside the action, order or decision and grant relief to the aggrieved person" (Shukla 2005). Even if the best argument is that "middle-class and lower-middle-class women have been predominant beneficiaries," the amelioration of violence in their lives is not insignificant (Katzenstein 1989, 67). Nor is the advantage that S498A "offers a small section of women some leverage to negotiate for their rights" inconsiderable, given that this leverage is of critical importance in the absence of "matrimonial property rights for women in Indian law"(Solanki 2001, 84). Despite the instrumental misuse ascribed to the law, its scope and advantage even to its proponents are limited, narrow, symbolic, and strategic.

"EK KE SAATH CHAR MUFT" (FOUR FREE WHEN YOU GET ONE): PLURALITIES AND CONTRADICTIONS

Criminal law, our focus in this chapter, ranks low on the list of strategies people turn to when trouble breaks out in a marriage, given its public nature and fearsome reputation. Litigants' search for the optimal venue is commonly referred to by scholars of legal pluralism as "forum shopping," a pleasantly consumerist phrase implying a set of equally available "purchasing" options. However, we see in later sections that people navigate between invariably difficult choices. The options often involve overlapping and sometimes contradictory directives, a delicate choreography with potentially disastrous long-term consequences. Men's rights activist (MRA) Zahid's sarcastic comment "Get one, get four free" refers to the frustration many men's rights groups articulate, of having multiple cases piled up for obvious leverage. The language of consumer choice is experienced as coercion here, as well as in the frequent MRA mockery of multiple cases as "a gift hamper" of assorted goodies.[13]

"You've played it excellently, like Zidane, so far; don't ruin everything at the end like him," family court counselor Manavi advised her enraged client, Shibaji. Shibaji was being scolded for having slapped his wife in the court corridor, in the presence of witnesses, after the last hearing, potentially turning the legal case against him. It was the summer of 2006, with the (football) World Cup on everyone's mind in Kolkata: Shibaji's rash and foolhardy behavior was here being compared to Zinédine Zidane's aggressive head butt (allegedly in response to an Italian player's racial slur) in the World Cup final, where France's loss was attributed to a penalty brought on by the superstar's behavior. Shibaji, anxious to be reunited with his wife and children, was equally melodramatic about his legal performance. In a perfect film hero romantic speech, he portrayed his own grand generosity and the harsh punishments in return: "Three punishments for three mistakes I made: 498 because I trusted her, 125 because I loved her" (*Tintey bhuler tintey shaja, bishshash koreychchilam boley 498, bhalobeshechilam boley 125*).[14] That is, in the course of a divorce case, she had filed two criminal complaints, an S498A charge and a 125CrPC case for maintenance. The exchange demonstrates the routines of resolving marital trouble explored in this chapter, requiring just-so cultural performances and carefully timed movement among civil, criminal, and mediation venues, and suggests the bafflement and anger attendant on working through these multiple processes.

Court typically appears late in the game. A common first step in marital trouble is to involve extended kin to draw attention to trouble, warning or shaming parties into early modification.[15] Other early informal solutions include approaching organizations that function as fictive kin, including neighborhood associations, local branches of political organizations, nongovernmental organizations (which may effectively be political networks), or autonomous women's organizations. Civil courts are usually approached at a later stage, often to negotiate alimony before, during, or after divorce. Domestic violence complaints may be taken up in civil courts (such as family court) as grounds of cruelty in divorce (committing the violence or falsely alleging violence may both be construed as cruelty); cruelty may be cited as a justifiable basis for claiming alimony while staying away from the household. Criminal law options include making a GD, or "general diary," at the local police station (thus creating a track record of the complaint but requiring no investigation or corroboration), or pursuing a case under S498A, either at a local police station or a Women's Grievance Cell, sometimes in combination with dowry recovery charges under S304B. Once a case is deemed a potential criminal offense, a formal FIR or First Information Report is registered by the police. However, criminal venues may also use mediation rather than filing charges. More recently, Protection Officers who administer the Protection of Women from Domestic Violence Act (PWDVA, 2005) work out civil remedies, including property, residence, custody, and maintenance orders, with additional powers to enlist criminal law to issue notices, enforce orders, or pursue remedies against violence (Lawyers Collective 2009).[16]

Having multiple legal and quasi-legal options for dealing with gendered violence in marriage can be difficult, facilitative, or ambiguously beneficial. The advantage of customary options or informal community groups lies in their familiarity and innovation, in working like the law and beyond the law (Holden 2008; Vatuk 2008; Grover 2010; Solanki 2011): "It is imperative for the local forums to resemble the law and yet devise different strategies of gaining familiarity to the case and enforcing accountability from the parties. The accountability is local and depends on the coercive force that issues from the public hearing of the dispute coupled with the respect and status of the leaders" (Nagaraj 2010, 443). Solanki is also optimistic that the hybridity and porosity of "polycentered legal settings" in India facilitate "formal and substantive gender equality" at individual and collective levels (2011, 78, 89), and help transform the public sphere through women's claims (83).

However, customary dispute resolution forums are notoriously difficult for women (Hirsch 1998; Moore 1999), posing "structural and practical constraints such as the lack of information about law and legal options, the lack of resources to pursue legal forums, coercion from communities and the family, the lack of family and affinal networks, domestic violence, violence and threats from strongmen, and religious fundamentalism" (Solanki 2011, 78). Law is often inadequate for addressing the solutions women prefer, such as transforming a marriage without breaking it or reforming the nature of marriage itself (Suneetha and Nagaraj 2006, 4359). Of particular concern for this chapter is that questions of violence are either deliberately elided to preserve marriage for social and economic security or, contrarily, brought up (only) to enforce economic settlements. That is, domestic violence becomes a legal strategy rather than a harm. The following portrait of the everyday life of domestic violence complaints shows that plural options relying on the shadow of law are more flexible than legal bureaucracies in using local political and kin connections and calculating specific solutions. But the limits of plurality are revealed when short-term material goals are met at the cost of ignoring family violence.

Rayna's situation exemplifies the problem of going directly to police and law. An educated, middle-class woman in her twenties, she was highly unusual in having gone to the police station herself, asking to begin a GD to record the violence by her affinal family. The officers told her they would not pursue the matter as an S498A domestic violence case, though they did not explain why; it was unclear whether the husband's family's political influence was in play here or whether a solitary woman at the police station (unaccompanied by an organizational representative) got scant attention. Dissatisfied with this outcome, Rayna took another unusual step and found a lawyer herself, who drafted a petition under Section 156.3 of the Criminal Procedure Code to the magistrate in lower-level civil court, resulting in a court order directing the police to investigate. This order caused a puzzling legal situation that she brought to the mediation organization, seeking further advice.

The organization Rayna sought out was known for its ability to use political connections with the then-ruling left party to facilitate cases, but this problem had the mediator-counselors stumped: they worried that Rayna would not be able to file an S498A case because the petition her lawyer had drafted referred only to dowry recovery and not to violence. Rayna recounted to the mediators that she had married against her parents' wishes, with no wedding costs or dowry, but that over the years as relations mended, her husband asked her parents (through her) for money to fund various projects, adding up to Rs. 4 or 5 lakhs. She reported much physical violence both within the nuclear unit and in the extended household. But her petition referred only to the extended dowry harassment of coerced and repeated payments, with no mention of physical violence. The lawyer had likely chosen that approach on the assumption that dowry laws were a more promising way of pursuing a criminal case than domestic violence laws, given the latter's notoriety. But, as one counselor explained passionately, given the usual police reluctance to prosecute domestic violence, the police were unlikely to later add the charge of violence when not explicitly directed to do so in the petition. The group strategized about possible ways to add an S498A amendment to the 156 petition, while supporting and reassuring Rayna: "Remember this case is only one thing; it is not your life. Whatever happens with the case, you need to take care of yourself." Rayna's case thus demonstrates the problems of seeking criminal sanctions when lawyers routinely treat domestic violence claims as paths to other solutions, such as alimony, return of marriage gifts, or reconciliation. Her class privilege was diluted by her solitary pursuit of options. The political clout of the group from which she sought help was limited by the confusion between dowry and domestic violence claims among police and lawyers,[17] the rigidity of petitions, and the cultural atmosphere of suspicion against S498A cases.

Madhumita's situation, by contrast, illustrates the potential of exploring plural options in the shadow of the law. Madhumita had approached a long-standing autonomous women's organization that explicitly took on feminist antiviolence work. One evening in 2006, she narrated to the counselors that she had left her marital home in Kolkata without her one-year-old child, frightened by the behavior of her husband, who allegedly suffered from "bipolar mood disorder." Asked what outcomes she would prefer, she said she wanted to be back with her child, to have money to live on, and to be in the affinal family home despite their collective verbal, financial, and emotional violence and the erratic behavior and impotence of her husband, if only they could be warned to behave a little better. She had chosen this autonomous organization because her parents had been loath to involve extended kin given the greater wealth and connections of her in-laws, and hesitated to approach women's wings of local political organizations because her mother-in-law was believed to be powerful in those circles.

In response, the counselors proposed various arms of the state she could engage: she could create a GD record at the local police station, approach a Women's Grievance Cell to file an S498A case, or file a divorce or maintenance case at the family court. The mediators promised to accompany and assist her, but cautioned her that each of these should be launched with a precise recognition of the consequences. The subtext was that asking an avowed feminist organization to intercede or threatening criminal or civil proceedings might well be perceived by already dissatisfied in-laws as a point of no return. Desperate to be back in the affinal home before her child's birthday in a few days, Madhumita ended up taking the quickest and most pragmatic step: she simply called her mother-in-law, who asked her to move back. However, she let the organization know that she would file a GD at the local police station when she was at her parents' home, in case they needed a paper trail for a later S498A or divorce case. We do not know whether she did so, but the message seemed to indicate that she knew long-term problems had not been resolved.

Informal and formal, community and civil and criminal venues functioned here as alternative and parallel options, each with potential advantages and risks. If the desired outcome was money to live on, access to a child, or social respectability, violence could only be brought up as part of a delicate calibration: it had social leverage when raised by women's kin if a reconciliation could stave off public scandal, but the scales tipped when women's organizations, police, or courts were involved. Respectability and shame are the tokens of this currency. In Madhumita's and Rayna's cases, several seemingly woman-friendly options (neighborhood associations, Mahila Samitys) were closed off because of the in-laws' influence, a reminder that some perpetrators (here mothers-in-law) could also use community networks to their advantage. Madhumita's chosen strategy hedged these options: she took the least intrusive path (if the least transformative and most dangerous one), while leaving open the possibility of initiating a criminal record in anticipation of future legal leverage and continuing the relationship with the organization. Rayna, having forgone these networks initially, was more vulnerable to legal jeopardy. She was also more socially vulnerable in publicly resisting violence and financial extortion, in contrast to Madhumita, who seemed to have temporarily found shelter in marriage.

The following sections illustrate other permutations, along with their contradictions and trade-offs: engaging civil and criminal options simultaneously, playing off criminal sanctions for civil leverage, or losing civil benefits as a result of making criminal complaints. This chapter moves from legal venues with the greatest punitive sanctions—civil courts and police—to a quasi-governmental entity, to nongovernmental and autonomous organizations with no formal enforceability. Remarkably, mediation is omnipresent across this spectrum. Violence comes up as an available (if disapproved) strategy for settling economic issues in marriage rather than as a gendered crime; remediation or cessation of violence is discussed as an impossible hypothetical solution.

THE "AXE" OF DOUBLE-DIPPING: FAMILY COURT

We return to the family courts here because they are the main *legal* node for working out alimony and residential and custody arrangements—that is, the later venues in this chapter try to approximate this court's capabilities. Violence was insistently cited in these courts as part of divorce, separation, and maintenance cases. Judges and counselors emphasized that they were the official space of alternate dispute resolution when they heard clients' S498A cases. They regarded litigants' use of plural venues as an affront to the scope of the court's work, depicting criminal complaints as "garbage cases" (Merry 2009, 65) that disrupt the considered settlement of civil courts. Counselors proudly narrated "reunions," often featuring family torture (chapter 4), where they secured the best economic and social solutions for women *within* marriage, with hopes of behavior modification by husbands. Notably, parallel criminal claims had *not* been filed in these cases, such that reconciliations were still possible.

While judges were scrupulously attentive to issues of maintenance, these concerns seemed secondary when they knew that women had filed parallel charges under S498A. They depicted such cases as a willful destruction of marriage, an unforgivable embarrassment to the husband and affinal family, and an arbitrary demonstration of power. One of the celebrities seen in court, Arushi, a singer and teacher, exemplified such power in the case she brought against her husband, a prominent senior government official, with the ensuing publicity believed to have brought them to the brink of extreme vendetta and bitterness. In a perfect example of the difference that social class makes, neither judges nor counselors sought to interrogate her on her claim or talk her out of exploiting every legal avenue to the fullest, despite their wariness about her motivation.

Rima's allegation (chapter 3) that she had been slapped when she refused to go out provides a telling contrast (her husband, Prasun, had claimed she was insane and had also hit him). Judge K asked Rima jocularly, "Are you sure you didn't smack him [*chor mara*] about something? We women do this to our husbands all the time." Rima had asked to return to her affinal home despite the alleged violence and claimed maintenance if she was not allowed back. Her S498A case resonated as doublespeak to the family court because her maintenance petition expressed an intention to continue the marriage. The civil suit for financial support was treated as misguided and incompatible *because* she had already made the violence explicit. Her counselor's rhetorical question to me, "How can she blame me for the divorce if she filed a 498?" signaled the S498A case as a failed strategy, while the judge dismissed it as miscommunication. In Rima's mother's rendition, her daughter saw domestic violence as a condition of marriage, and marriage as the only possible living situation. She whispered to me that Rima had said, "So what, if I die I die. Women belong in their affinal homes and ought not to live at their parents' after marriage. A Hindu woman gets married only once" (*Ki ar hobe, morey geley morey jabo, meyeder to shoshurbaritei jayga, biyer por baperbarite thakte nei, ar Hindu meyer ek bar-i biye hoi*). Elided in this picture-perfect rendition of Hindu women's ideological assent was, of course, her mother's inability to support Rima financially or to convince her son (Rima's brother) to support Rima in the long term.

Shibani and Hemanto's case trenchantly demonstrates the prejudice against S498A as one of successive strategies. Unlike Rima, Shibani said in her petition that she could not go back to the affinal home because of violence; she sought maintenance to live on her own. Her previous S498A case, which resulted in Hemanto's immediate suspension from a government job (and could have ended in firing), was dismissed because none of the neighbors testified. Judge K began the day's hearing by asking Hemanto about possibilities for separate space in his extended family home in a town a few hours from Kolkata, after a long detour on her knowledge of old houses. Hemanto, perhaps sensing a sympathetic hearing, tried to strike a note of compliance, saying he was willing to increase the interim maintenance slightly, "whatever you decide." He showed his Railway Department salary certificate for Rs. 3,000 per month as proof of earnings, with additional earnings in months when he got a travel allowance. The judge kept describing his wife as having "axed" him (*kop diyechche*), referring to the fact that the S498A case had almost gotten him fired.

In cross-examination, Judge K began by asking Shibani whether she had any questions of Hemanto, to which she was silent in the manner of many litigants. The judge continued to repeat the query with growing irritation, yelling, "These things women do!" (*Ei meyeder karbar!*). Shibani finally said in a very low voice that she had left the house because she was "nirjatito" (tortured, a word brought into this discourse primarily through feminist activism). Judge K responded, "But you're the one who was able to give him the axe [kurul diyechchilen]—you filed the 498. Because of you, he was about to lose his job, and this is a railways job. If I send a qualified person to you, can you get them a railways job? Is it so easy to get?" She paused dramatically, smiled broadly, and said with an ironic twinge, "But you want your maintenance claim, don't you? [Khorposh ta to chan?] You're not willing to live with him under any circumstances, but you still want maintenance. You tried to have it both ways by filing a 498 while the other case is going on. If he was convicted, you would have lost all the money, so this strategy of playing both things would not work. You're not some simple dumb woman [sadashidhey bokashoka non]—you were able to put him through this process, so I know you know what's going on and you must respond in court."

Shibani had asked for Rs. 500 as interim maintenance instead of the present Rs. 225, an amount far below subsistence. (Judge K had asked Hemanto earlier if he could perhaps raise it to Rs. 300, a negligible difference). Asked about the alternative of "permanent alimony" ("from now till the end of your life," in the judge's words), she was silent again for a long time, to the judge's visible anger, then suddenly burst out in a rush that she wanted Rs. 2,500 per month. "What do you eat?" Judge K inquired rhetorically, and then inquired about a lump-sum payment Shibani could settle for instead. She thought for a minute, and said, "Ten lakhs."[18] There was an audible gasp in the courtroom, and the judge's clerk surreptitiously flashed his palms in surprise to me ("Ten?! Ten?!!"). Judge K said sarcastically to Hemanto, "So, do you have ten lakhs in your Provident Fund?[19] It would have to be a very different sort of government job than mine!" Hemanto merely smiled in agreement. (Meanwhile Shibani's brother muttered from his bench, "We don't want anything at all, we're just happy she got out of the torture," but only we could hear him.) Judge K gave out two hearing dates in the following month to finish the case and was unsympathetic to Shibani's request for a delay given her brother's illness, saying, "Your brother's health is no concern of the court. You must be there. You can't rely on your brother for the rest of your life—you need to know what's going on."

The paradoxes of multiple legal forums are illustrated here: were S498A complaints presumed to be genuine (rather than assuming a priori that they are false or manipulative), the filing of the dual claim would be entirely valid.

The recommended corollaries of job suspension and possible job loss are meant to signal the seriousness of the offense rather than serving as modes of revenge. However, given women's economic dependence on marriage for survival, the conundrum is that claims for maintenance are made to the person against whom one is filing criminal charges. Conviction would negate the earning power that is relied upon in the maintenance claim. The two provisions are located in separate legal niches for different remedies, but the onus of resolving the contradiction falls upon the female litigant. Each remedy works only if the other fails: either violence complaints must be forgone to maintain the cash flow, or economic support must be forgone if symbolic redress of violence is deemed more important.

Legally "enterprising" behavior such as Shibani's is viewed with suspicion, eliciting demands for a new package of legal subjectivity and female agency. Judge K treated Hemanto with apparent sympathy, validating his sense of entrapment with the metaphor of *axing*, thereby ironically casting Shibani's verbal accusation of physical violence as the *more* violent, harmful act. The lack of testimony from the neighbors was read as lack of evidence of violence, even though such avoidance might well signify disinclination to be involved in a legal process. The judge devoted quite some time to residential arrangements, in an attempt to work out a way for Hemanto to offer his wife conjugal space away from extended family. Shibani's refusal to move back could then be read as failure in her domestic duties, and her maintenance claim as a further burden upon his resources. Hemanto would be able to claim desertion as a ground of divorce, paying little in maintenance because desertion would put her at fault.

The maintenance and lump-sum amount Shibani named seemed to turn courtroom opinion against her, as if that made the torture claim spurious, the assumption being that a genuine victim would not be thinking about money. It is relevant to point out here that the payments she was receiving would cover no more than a few day's food. Hemanto's seemingly generous gesture to double it (to a sixth of his stated income) made him appear amenable to the judge, but this was still grossly inadequate to live on. Most people in the room would be aware that a railway salary was, more often than not, plentifully supplemented by an under-the-table income, making the salary certificate useless for determining income. Shibani's brother publicly protested the violence and wanted her "home" without any maintenance, possibly to avert criticism of his own role in financially supporting her. But her financial dependence was also related to his own entitlement, sons being preferred heirs of natal property, despite laws to the contrary. The judge was irritated with Shibani's silence (as when she exclaimed, "You're not some simple dumb woman") because it seemingly contradicted her active invocation of criminal law. Her refusal to change the hearing schedule and her admonition to Shibani that she should be independent and not rely on her brother jibed at this alleged aggression. However, the maintenance amounts she deemed appropriate were so low that they would, ironically, make Shibani reliant on her brother or require new skills for the labor market.

Judges and counselors regarded the family court's evaluations of physical violence en route to granting divorce or alimony as superior, contextually nuanced, socially sensitive solutions. Women's best interests were believed to be secured through the court's benevolent patronage; thus women litigants' assertiveness in ways that were at odds with their roles as economically vulnerable entities in need of the court's protection were deemed manipulative and insulting. Domestic violence was effaced as a crime and depicted as a nuisance getting in the way of the court's real work.

"BE CLEVER, DON'T BE STUPID": POLICE COUNSELING

Women's police stations—that is, special police cells staffed by women trained to deal with crimes against women, in particular crimes of gendered violence— have been popular as feminist solutions since the UN Decade for Women. They have been institutionalized by various countries in Latin America, Africa, and Asia, most famously and extensively Brazil. Based on "the essentialist assumption" that female police officers would prove more sensitive to female victims, they are imagined as safe spaces free of custodial revictimization, often praised for increasing reporting on violence and connecting victims with a variety of support services beyond the law (Santos 2004, 50). Ethnographies of their quotidian work, however, reveal systemic obstacles, such as their marginalization within police systems, erratic state support, and the ironic realization that policewomen in these units are unsympathetic to feminist approaches to gender violence and enact hegemonic gender and class ideologies (Santos 2004; Hautzinger 2007; Alcalde 2010).

Women's police stations in India are part of this transnational history, with the first one established in Chennai (Tamil Nadu) in 1991 to "make it easy and comfortable for women to approach the police station with their problems at home and talk to a woman police officer."[20] There were 442 police stations by 2011,[21] with regular rebukes from the central government toward the thirteen Indian states and union territories that lagged behind. Created in the wake of antidowry agitation, their initial thrust was to be "dowry cells" attending to family violence and return of marital gifts, but they are meant to cover a broad range of "crimes against women" (including kidnapping and rape, as in chapter 6), with a renewed call for active vigilance following the 2012–13 rape agitation.

While these police stations signal state sensitivity to gendered violence, their tendency to prefer reconciliation and mediation dilutes their mandate of pursuing criminal sanctions. The Women's Grievance Cell of the Kolkata Police enthusiastically embraced "negotiation" as an effective and efficient mode of operation. The officer in charge (OC) explained that they added mediation to their array of tactics soon after they opened in 1995, in response to the deputy commissioner's vision that counseling could help some violence cases: "He said to us, 'Listen to them, hear their problems'; and I soon understood too when I applied my own smarts to it that a third-party intervention often resolves things [mitey jai]."

At the time I visited them, the staff of four undertook both investigation and counseling, but (like the family court counselors) they highlighted the reconciliations they had effected, pleased with their unpolicelike tasks and proud that they had registered only 4 of the 470 petitions that came to them in 2004 as S498A cases. "We prefer counseling because you can't have a home if there is a 498" (498 case holey ar ghar-ta hoi na, tai counseling prefer kori), OC Samaddar claimed, a statement often iterated by her staff as common-sense knowledge. Samaddar framed S498A cases in terms of performance and manipulation—"Let me tell you how the game works" (Khelata apnakey boli)—insisting that S498A cases are used by litigants "to apply pressure" (pressure debar jonyo korey). The staff acknowledged that in a small number of exceptional cases, they helped couples draw up agreements for mutual consent divorces and, much more rarely, filed formal S498A charges. As the following case reveals, both litigants and investigators acted within a familiar orchestration: they foregrounded the primacy of economic needs in the dissolution of marriage, emphasizing delicate timing and treating claims of violence as a strategy toward those goals.

I met Rekha one morning sitting with the OC, describing her five-year-long marriage to a pilot for a foreign airline. With his high income, a father-in-law who was a bank manager, and a brother-in-law who was a dentist in the United States, her husband and his family were considerably better off than hers, her father being a retired college professor in a small town. His family had been very opposed to the marriage, she contended, and her father-in-law had become increasingly verbally abusive. He accused her of being from a bad (*kharap*) family, cursed her as ill-behaved and unruly (*oshobhbho beyadob*), preferred her to be confined to her room, and arranged an abortion of her second pregnancy. Her husband, too, had withdrawn his affection in the last few years, and several months earlier they had demanded she leave the matrimonial home, since which time Rekha had been living at her parents' house with her three-year-old child.

The OC checked and found that a divorce case had been filed in which her father-in-law accused her of "behaving badly" (*kharap byabohar*). The husband's family had thus far failed to come in to talk to the police despite three summons. The tempo abruptly changed after this formality, with a visceral alteration in the OC's interrogative mode: in a too-casual tone, cleaning her ring, she asked Rekha, "What do you want out of this?" (*Ki chaichchen?*). Rekha replied with the English word *settlement*. The word seemed to imply divorce by mutual consent with an alimony agreement, because in response Samaddar reminded her that it took a year for the divorce and that "settlement" was difficult in cases such as this, where she had an "irritative" [in English] nature and there had been disputes (*jhograjhanti*).

Notably, Rekha's allegations of physical violence only emerged at this point. She said she had been thrown down in the bathroom, but had not told her parents she cracked her skull. The OC went on with her earlier thought: "Your case is legally weak, so now all we can try is counseling." It emerged that the only documentary record of violence was a GD filed shortly before the divorce was initiated, whose timing was thus inherently suspect. Rekha's father recounted, "The local police station wanted to use counseling to make him less rigid; that's why they recommended filing a case." The response at this point illuminated the cell's pride of place in the hierarchy of criminal justice, as well as the power assigned to criminal over civil measures. Samaddar retorted, "The *thana* [local police station] doesn't know these things, they don't need to know, but *we* know that filing a case creates more rigidity." Another staff member chimed in: "When you make a report at the *thana*, that means the husband promptly puts in a 'mat suit' [matrimonial suit or divorce case] to counter the police claim." These police officers asserted, in other words, that Rekha's mistake lay in leaving a formal record with the local police station in the form of a GD. This lower-level station, which they depicted as less sophisticated in these matters, had by its insistence on a paper trail irretrievably damaged any possibility of reconciliation and thereby made divorce inevitable.

Samaddar interrogated Rekha about whether she had been rough with her father-in-law and postulated that this might have also turned her husband against her—"If you reacted [badly], the son will not go against the father—I would not either." Samaddar contended that the divorce case might have gone beyond the possibility of an amicable outcome, the in-laws' ire having been provoked as much by Rekha's putative aggression at home as by her summoning the law/police. These suspicions pitted the criterion of physical violence, typically asserted as violence to a woman's body, against the standard of emotional abuse. The final advice to Rekha and her father invoked the strategic power of legal forums and depicted women as having new agency only if they put it to use in the right way, such as under the cell's guidance: "You can't just start a criminal case in a naïve way [bokar moto]—you have to win it. She should have been more 'intelligent' and patient [shohonshil]—now she has poisoned her husband's mind against her."

Whether OC Samaddar's questions about Rekha's "nature" were a pro forma interrogation of facts, a "bad cop" performance, or merely a narrative strategy, during the interview Rekha was accused of being (at least partly) responsible for the demise of the marriage. There was remarkably little discussion of physical violence in the conversation: the police officers discussed it as relative strategy, and Rekha mentioned it only at a particular moment of negotiation, implying that it would worry her parents and that she was loath to upset her aging father. This faint and awkward articulation of physical violence was ostensibly the primary reason for being at the police cell, but it functioned at best as a double-edged route to better terms in divorce.

The OC's grudging offer of help was that they would try to "set up the home again, since there is a child—but everything has been delayed because of the case." Rekha and her father asked the police to talk with the other parties before the court hearing in two weeks, since they could not talk directly while the matrimonial suit was under way. She promised they would try and that an S498A case could be filed later if the counseling failed, but likely the chat would not go well if the divorce judgment went against them in court. The final question from Rekha's father, seemingly in response, was "How much could maintenance be?" Again the answer was deeply circuitous: "Time will be needed. If the police try to achieve something good, then it takes time. We have to show the police are involved in 'social welfare.'"

This case exemplifies the delicate call-and-response between divorce and criminal cases, requiring an impossible management of temporalities. The police cell entrusted with monitoring S498A declared that launching a case under S498A delayed matters, precipitated divorce proceedings, and wreaked irreparable damage. The only good S498A case was one that did not quite become an S498A case; the only smart reason to file such a case was if all other avenues of mediation and reconciliation had been exhausted. Rekha's father's question about maintenance at the end was thus not, as it seems, a non sequitur to Samaddar's suggestion about a 498 case down the line but the driving force of the meeting with the police officer. It was an opportunity to make an urgent case for Rekha and her child being in need of a home and financial sustenance, with violence evoked as an opportunity for leverage.

"WE COULD JAIL YOU FOR THIS": LEVERAGING VIOLENCE IN COMMUNITY MEDIATION

There were high hopes for community mediation, *shalishi* in Bangla, during my 2004–5 fieldwork. Encouraged by the proliferation of alternative dispute resolution methods in courts and among nongovernmental organizations, and hailing a history of village-level arbitration forums, the state government and ruling party envisaged a network of local *shalishi* forums to supplement *and* complement formal legal settings. Given that people often took their complaints first to influential locals, or to neighborhood party offices or women's organizations, long before they sought formal legal sanction, structured venues of semiformal mediation could be helpful.[22] Some women's NGOs also got involved in "women initiated community dispute resolution mechanisms" (Talwar and Shramajibee Mahila Samity 2002, 2).

The Paribarik Paramarsho O Shahayata Kendra (Family advice and assistance center) in a medium-sized town about an hour from Kolkata held arbitration sessions lasting three or four hours every Friday. Located inside one of the police posts in the town (which also advertised the Mahila Pulish Tadanta Kendra, or Police investigative center for women), it focused exclusively on *shalish* or arbitration, sending people with criminal cases off to a different police station across town (which functioned as a Women's Grievance

FIGURE 9. The semigovernmental mediation center in a city near Kolkata, housed in a police station. The sign reads, "Paribarik Paramarsho O Shohayota Kendra" (Family advice and assistance center).

Cell of the kind described above). On one of my first visits, when I was being shown around by one of the constables, a motorcycle pulled up with two women and a man. Approaching the constable, one of the women introduced herself as being with a nongovernmental organization and said of her companion, "She is having some trouble at home and wants to report it." The constable responded, "Ekhaney, jara shongshar korben tader jonyo" (my translation, "this place is only for those who want to pursue the marriage," does little to capture the sense of *shongshar/sansar* as embodying notions of family, domesticity, and worldliness), recommending that she go to the other police station to register a complaint or seek maintenance. To approach this unit was thus to have reconciliation in mind. This means that while almost every case I observed here dealt with domestic violence, they were invisible to any criminal record keeping maintained by the police cell.

The "counseling board" consisted of a local female magistrate of the lower courts, a male doctor, a female lawyer, the male supervisor of the center, and the female officer-in-charge (OC) of the cell. The board had the authority to summon witnesses and draw up arbitration agreements but no civil or criminal enforcement authority beyond that. However, the OC and a magistrate who served on it seamlessly invoked their professional roles during proceedings. The spatial configurations were conspicuously different from the previous settings: the board members sat in a row of chairs behind a wooden screen, across the table from the couple, while every other available seat was occupied by family members and even neighbors, and a continuous row of heads peered over the top of the screen. Projecting itself as an unofficial venue within a formidably official setting, this center signaled its alternative nature by incorporating family and community participation, indeed encouraging families and community members to attend.[23] This liminality allowed it to simultaneously deploy and circumvent formal legal provisions, while extending its quasi-legal reach through community surveillance.

In marked difference from the previous two settings, allegations of domestic violence were often front and center in women's complaints here, uncontested by the accused or their families. The board's formal position was to condemn the criminality of violence in the strongest terms, while using the condemnation as leverage to design solutions to economic and other social problems, holding criminal sanctions in suspended abeyance.[24] Mirza appeared at the hearing in a brashly defiant mood, readily admitting to drunkenness, drug use, battery, and bigamy (the last being legally valid for Muslim men). His wife Fariza listed her complaints about eighteen years of marriage as follows: "Getting high, cursing, beating [me] up, selling off [family] land each year" (*Nesha bhang, khisti, maar, bochor bochor jomi bikri*). In her iteration, the physical violence was seen as part of a linked chain of behavior, at least on a par with economic abuse. She foregrounded two main triggers of the violence: her objection to her husband's family marrying off their daughter too young to a groom she deemed unsuitable, and her daily complaints that there was no food at home. Bigamy did not feature in her list of complaints. Mirza, on the other hand, foregrounded equitable treatment of his two wives and his responsibility to provide for them both, possibly in some space in the same house if the children agreed: "One lives in a two-story hut and one in a two-leaf hut," he kept muttering in rhyming Bangla.

The adjudicatory board responded to a variety of issues, likely in line with their stated purpose of working toward holistic community solutions. Various members expressed regret about the daughter's marriage: "She could have got a good job as a Muslim girl, have you seen the [good] jobs other girls are getting?" They began with the proposition that they would try for a *mimangsha* or solution, with the declaration (or threat) that a legal case would follow if they failed to resolve matters; Mirza said he wanted to avoid a legal skirmish at all costs. The doctor reminded him that in that case it would be advisable to follow their recommendations, suggesting (almost threatening) that compliance would be in his best interest because he had admitted to domestic violence, which could mean an imminent jail sentence. Occasional bouts of strong-arm negotiation followed, with a defiant Mirza saying, "Fine, jail's what I want" or "Now they'll see how much I can drink," and the police OC, the magistrate, and the doctor making moves as if to put him away immediately, irritably proclaiming that a night in jail would do him a lot of good. The criminality of domestic violence hovered over these negotiations as an imminent threat.[25]

The solution provided economic sustenance for Fariza by laying claim to landed property that Mirza had been selling off, such that only six bighas (about two acres) were left. Mirza was notionally willing to let his children from Fariza, though not Fariza herself, have access to half his land, claiming the other half would be for the other wife and his business. The board closely examined the land documents, deciding that much of this family land had not even been his to sell and rejecting his notion of making an informal transfer through his father. Instead, they came up with a strongly patrilineal solution (far below considerations of gender parity in Muslim personal law): Mirza was to formally pay to register two-thirds of the land in his son's name, with his daughter having access to it until marriage and his wife in her lifetime. He was to return to the board with legal documents showing he had completed the registration in his son's name. Other conditions specified that the second wife was not to be brought back to this marital residence, Mirza was to be responsible for providing food for the household; and Fariza was to be able to choose or consent to her daughter's marriage partners. Both the husband and in-laws protested vehemently at this last condition, among other reasons saying, "What if she picks a dark person?" but the board prevailed, at least in writing.

The board gave Fariza much overt support to use their resources and to come back whenever there were problems, also urging relatives on both sides to report any domestic violence to them. But they simultaneously negotiated a set of conditions that reinforced patriarchal authority over her mobility and decision making. Fariza's access to the land and monthly maintenance was conditional on her returning to her marital residence immediately, living there peacefully (*shantimoto*), and obtaining permission from her husband or in-laws to visit her natal home. Mirza's discursive strategy was to speak to the rights of his absent second wife: his counteroffer was to allow Fariza to visit her parents only if the other wife could come to the marital residence. He protested that Muslim wives were not to leave home by themselves, but promptly followed that up by refusing to shop for food for her, saying she could go to the market herself. The board roundly berated him for the latter, reminding him he was required to provide food, but the former injunction was never directly challenged. As the magistrate said to Mirza, "Remember you've signed things here—if you beat her up again, you'll find out what the results are for you [*petaley bujhbey ki phol*]." She followed this up by advising Fariza to "get along with others [*maniye nao*]" and "be less agitated/rambunctious" (*lomphojhompo kom diyo*, which might literally be translated as "don't jump up so much over everything").

Despite these complicated contractual exchanges, uneasiness prevailed as the group left. Fariza expressed fear that he would now beat her a lot because she had brought these issues to the board. "Why did you do it then?" a married female neighbor chimed in, even as the board urged Fariza to calm down and seek help when necessary. The magistrate commented wistfully on their departure, "Let's see them 'united' first, let them stay together first—there are a lot of problems from 'broken families.'" I asked in the interlude between cases whether they thought their intervention would stop Mirza's domestic violence. "It may decrease a bit," the doctor responded.

The possibilities and circumscriptions of community mediation through official boards become evident here. The board had the skill and resources to leverage criminal legal sanctions and the civil authority to design a contract about maintenance and property that mirrored remedies constructed in the family court. They articulated righteous if jaded anger at domestic violence, consistently condemning it and perhaps hoping some injunctions would stick as a result. The optimal conjugal family and the companionate marriage where partners have an equal say in family decisions, as imagined at the heart of postcolonial family law, were reflected in their negotiations to allow women a say in their children's marriages, to imagine that sharing a home with a cowife is humiliating, and to refuse to sever women's relationships with their natal families. But correspondingly, they were governed by related ideologies of conjugality: that a "united" family is optimal for mental health and social harmony, that women need to defer to authority structures in their affinal homes, and that women fare best when they act without undue agitation or strident claims.

LIVING BEYOND VIOLENCE: WOMEN'S MOVEMENT ORGANIZATIONS

The arc of this chapter might indicate a teleological hope in this final category of interventions by women's movement organizations. Alas, no such simple magic is on offer. Women's movement organizations are highly heterogeneous; though they typically lack official sanction, they work through informal political and social channels and creatively devise extralegal contextual solutions (Grover 2010, 202). They are, however, keenly aware of the limitations of intervention and the necessity of compromise; sometimes the best they can do is to provide "practical advice" and "emotional support" (Gangoli 2007, 104). Despite their antiviolence ideology, they find domestic violence difficult to redress and can at best proffer less patriarchally coded solutions.

The two organizations profiled in this section arose from different legacies of the women's movement, which affect their access to resources and networks, as well as their institutional personalities and forms of comportment. The first is a group affiliated with the then-ruling left coalition (and hence state government), which foregrounds class rather than gender as its political mission; the second is a feminist collective often in opposition to the state. The ideological differences in conceptualizing marriage are salient here: the group that emphasizes gender as the primary axis of subordination identifies the economic impoverishment of marriage and violence as tools of control; for the one that marks economic inequality as the fundamental problem, women's economic self-reliance, whatever the state of their marriages, is critical. However, solutions may not line up with ideological missions in practice.

Suraha (literally "solution," known also as the Socio-Cultural Research Institute), officially a nongovernmental organization with deep ties to the state and to left politics, exemplifies contradictions in gendered power within left organizations. It is autonomous but closely tied to the women's wing of the ruling party, having been founded by a powerful former president of the wing. The benefits of its nongovernmental status lie in getting access to special categories of party funds, while it is also able to draw upon its regular political networks and government connections (Ray 1999, 92–94). However, as a party organization, it may be constrained from radical actions by "loyalty" and "deference," and is often required to "self-censor" (92–94).

Located on a primarily residential street in south Kolkata, Suraha was open for mediation and consultation three evenings a week. "Counselors," mostly but not exclusively women, including several lawyers, family court counselors, and other party allies, sat at clustered tables, almost continually busy with problems such as physical and financial harassment by families, defrauding attempts, and intimidation from neighborhood goons, in addition to marital troubles. Quite often, people came with explicit referrals from local political representatives, and counselors sought the active assistance of Mahila Samitys, in a seamless connection between NGO and party.

Ideologically, the organization foregrounded social justice through class empowerment, with gender as a secondary concern. Prioritizing class over gender produces rich contradictions, as exemplified by Ray's interview with a prominent woman leader: "Feminist or womanist groups believe in gender oppression. We do not. We believe in class oppression. Like us, there are men who are oppressed. But it is true that social oppression is a little higher in the case of women because as a section of society, not as a class, women are backward. It is true that family and society are male dominated. I prefer to call it not oppression but domination" (77). This relegation of gender to a "postrevolution" priority in favor of the primacy of class (Sen 2005) is ironic in the predominantly middle-class milieu of the organization (counselors are middle-class, though not necessarily clients). Its work focuses on intrafamilial discord and violence rather than the remediation of class-based inequities, but it ideologically assigns gender inequity as a lower-order problem ("not oppression but domination").

At Suraha, there were no obvious attempts to repair marriages at all costs or to tolerate violence for the sake of economic stability. The organization was not under any legal directive to favor reconciliation (though some family court counselors were also mediators here). Sessions generally focused on advantageous legal strategies for clients, with outreach to personal, political, and professional networks as needed. Consideration of women's economic resources often loomed large in planning strategy. A senior member mused in an interview that she was most bothered by women clinging to marriage: "Why are you just waiting for the maintenance award? If you were illiterate and you had no means of supporting yourself that would be one thing; cut off all relations and stand on your own feet." There was a long discussion, one evening, of the livelihood possibilities of a recently widowed client whose in-laws were trying to seize the marital house and bank assets. Suggestions included bringing a paying guest into the home or finding a job with daily wages, in addition to other legal moves.

Twenty-three-year-old Padmini's case better illustrates the organization's multiple forms of support. Padmini, who had begun a diploma in computer administration after her B.A., brought allegations of severe emotional abuse and control of mobility and privacy against the husband and in-laws. She emphasized her Marwari ethnicity, describing Marwaris as a small and conservative community; her affines played to this fear by telling her repeatedly that for the community, divorce meant "a big ugly mark on the forehead" and that she would not be able to remarry. In answer to the counselors' question, "Do you still love him and want to stay?" Padmini said vehemently, "No, I feel hatred." Various counselors chimed in with recommendations for action preparatory to filing a dowry recovery and violence case: she needed to ask her mother to draw up a full list of wedding expenses and gather all jewelry receipts (which were her property even if given by the in-laws). Padmini sought restitution of wedding expenses of Rs. 40 to 50 lakhs, to use toward a business or further education. A lawyer clarified that large expenses related to hospitality could not be claimed, though they could try for the rest. She was to report back after these steps for further guidance. One of the counselors said in parting, "There is no such thing as a stamp on the forehead from divorce." "If there is, lots of Marwari boys have that stamp too," another added.

These sessions focused on legal strategy and economic self-sufficiency, with implicit assumptions that marriage was not necessarily the optimal solution, that deference to in-laws or violence from them need not be a norm. It was Padmini's choice that drove these suggestions, but she was never pressed to consider marriage as the inevitably better option. Though it is impossible to know whether this advice was affected by Padmini's class, education, and job prospects, or her ability to pursue legal remedies energetically, the organization's focus on living beyond marriage was conspicuously different from other venues. Moreover, advice offered here echoed Ray's finding that grassroots "frontline" women workers are often sympathetic to the problems posed by domestic violence, even though leaders in left parties prefer to downplay domestic violence, sexual assault, or the gendered division of labor, and deal with such problems internally (1999, 89). Thus Suraha's founder formally endorsed the primacy of class oppression, but the counselors routinely tackled

FIGURE 10. Offices of a feminist organization in a residential neighborhood, ready for Friday counseling.

the materialities of gendered violence and the intersectionalities of gender and class, and promoted women's autonomy. Their quotidian work, while ideologically grounded in very different political rhetoric, thus ended up in practical alliance with explicitly feminist organizations.

Autonomous feminist organizations often adhere to a more radical gender politics than party affiliates, but the trade-off in West Bengal is that they are marginal to the priorities and funds determined by the ruling party, limiting their scope and effectiveness (Ray 1999, 95). The organization profiled here, Nari Nirjaton Pratirodh Mancha (Forum against oppression of women, most often called Mancha, meaning "platform/stage") is a long-standing autonomous women's organization with the reputation of being stridently vocal in seeking state accountability.[26] Antiviolence work is central to its identity, both through public awareness campaigns and support for individual cases. The core members are a mix of age groups and classes, including professors, journalists, office workers, informal sector workers, and career left political activists, who often study and debate together.

Counseling sessions look remarkably similar to the previous venue: sheets are laid out on the floor of a residential apartment on Friday evenings, and members gather to hear clients as a group, with an occasional private session. There is an explicit commitment to having women narrate their own accounts. Emphasizing women's control over their own lives, however, also means ceding to their choices, sometimes with unsatisfying ideological accommodations.

One evening, Molly brought her eight-year-old daughter, her brother, and a married neighbor couple to the session, so that they could "explain things in case she can't say it all properly." Her brother knew one of the senior members of the group and had been invited to bring his sister. The men and the little girl were artfully dispatched to the next room, supposedly to keep the child away from this conversation, though they later told Molly that they considered it best to let a woman tell her own story. She then narrated a happy marriage of ten years ("the normal happy conjugal life" [khub shukher dampatya jibon, jerokom hoi], ironic as that sounds in this context) until her husband's elder sister moved back into town, to which she dated a recent sharp deterioration in marital relations. Much of her husband's present ire seemed to be violent jealousy over a friend of Molly's brother who had helped them to navigate the house mortgage. He also refused her household money, locked her in the house when he went out, and regularly asked her to leave him. She had finally moved to her parents' home. His sexual dissatisfaction had become a constant complaint: "He is not happy with conjugal life, not satisfied with sex" (O bibahito jiboney shukh pachchey na, sex-e satisfied noy), she said with some difficulty. He had lately begun saying he wanted to marry someone else and thus needed a divorce. She recounted that her in-laws had been pleasant at the outset and claimed to want no dowry; even though her parents did provide all "proper" goods nonetheless, the in-laws now harangued her constantly about poor quality and scant goods. Molly complained that her father-in-law and sisters-in-law drank all day, and that once her father-in-law had behaved so badly toward her that she had to leave. She had recently stopped going to her new job at a direct marketing company after her husband started coming to the office and throwing loud fits. Her boss said they liked her work but she should put her marriage first for now, possibly meaning she was creating too much disruption, although she could go back later.

Sujata, an experienced member in her forties, a professor by occupation, succinctly laid out three trajectories of advice for Molly on behalf of Mancha, to consider later and discuss with her family. First, she assured Molly that the question of maintenance was not closed simply because her husband proclaimed she could not get a *paisa* of his money. Because he had a government job, they could help her file a 125CrPc order to attach part of his salary according to the judge's determination. By way of assuring Molly that the stigma or impoverishment of divorce did not have to be her only path, Sujata emphasized that maintenance was not claimed only in the context of divorce, but was also an entitlement while married. Second, she argued, if her husband was not going to pay her expenses, he could not object to her working. "How long is he going to keep you locked up?" she queried. "Just go out when he goes to work. He'll eventually get tired of harassing you at work if you keep going." She contended that Molly might be surprised to find out that many people in that company were likely to be in similar positions, so Mancha advocated that she keep her boss apprised of the potential trouble and hope it would eventually end.

Third, and interestingly last, Sujata asked Molly what outcome she sought. Molly repeated that she wanted to continue the marriage. On behalf of Mancha, Sujata proffered that in that case, they believed her position would be much stronger if she went back to the marital home. There would be violence, but she would need to learn to deal with it and stand up to it. "You smack him a bit too next time" (*Apnio duto merey deben porerbar*), she suggested provocatively, speculating that he would be really startled by that and might hit her harder that time in retaliation but would think twice the following time. The group's usual weighing of legal options then followed; they considered whether it might be time to register an FIR in addition to the two GDs that Molly had previously filed. It was decided that Molly would benefit from keeping the party women's wing in that area apprised, given the organization's reach and surveillance, and a Mancha member warily offered to make contact. Molly was also told that the best thing her family could do would be to drop in on her every evening, as a reminder to her husband of their vigilance. Amid the cacophony of parting suggestions, Sujata returned to her original advice: "You might be wondering what sort of women's organization you have come to, with these suggestions of running out and beating husbands up. But what we want to say to you very clearly is, you need to be strong [*shokto*] here. Unless you confront him strongly yourself, there won't be a good resolution for you."

The feminist politics of this group is clear in their insistence on women telling their stories and managing their futures, in their respect for women's agency and decisions, even those they consider physically or ideologically unwise. Contrary to popular images of feminist groups, they did not lead with recommendations for a drastic break or extol the benefits of divorce. They offered practical advice about legal maneuvers and workplace etiquette, even showing a willingness to approach, for Molly's sake, the party women's unit they were wary of, thus working strategically both through state solutions and with powerful political allies of the state.

There were no comfortable solutions to offer, however, and the message was fundamentally one of tough love, building (economic and social) independence, and living with one's chosen decision as strongly as one could. In effect, they sent Molly back to the violence (at her will), but with full knowledge of its inevitability, indeed with the remarkable idea of retorting in kind so as to rise above fear and intimidation even in the face of injury, to make livable room for herself in her violent world. They recommended not the imagined outcome of domestic bliss, as did the reconciliation narratives, but alternative forms of support, including her natal family and economic resources such as maintenance and wages. The organizational imperatives of ending violence against women and radical feminist critiques of patriarchy seem to conflict with these solutions, but they advanced their vision on other fronts: they foregrounded the client's subjectivity, worked to maximize legal potentialities of maintenance and criminal law (a legacy of women's movement mobilization), and pushed the boundaries of gendered meanings of work, mobility, and violence.

These two organizations highlight different goals: transformation of class relations versus a primary focus on antiviolence work. In practice, however, neither their client bases nor the trajectories of action line up neatly with their ideologies. Rather they work with a canny sense of the possibilities of institutional options, legal and political but also familial and community based, their strength lying in the very "adhocism" that Gangoli (2007, 104) finds troubling. While they condemn domestic violence and emphasize the critical importance of women's access to economic resources, they must acknowledge the practical benefits of sustaining a marriage even as they evoke alternative futures outside it.

THE DISAPPEARANCE OF VIOLENCE: CONCLUSION

Photik fakes death to escape his wife's blows, physical and financial, echoing popular discourses of domestic violence featuring the harangued husband and the empowered wife who manipulates law to her own material ends. West Bengal ranks at the top of S498A filings, men's rights activists tell me repeatedly, implying that it is therefore open season for monetary extortion. Global and national policies and laws around domestic violence appear powerful and effective in these representations; they seem to support women's experiences of violence, in defiant challenge to patriarchal norms of marriage, property, and authority. The state is depicted as being conspiratorially allied with or cowed into submission by the women's movement.

Indeed, as this chapter indicates, there seem to be plenty of options for pursuing grievances: police, courts, arbitration boards serving as quasi-courts, NGOs, and movement organizations. Domestic violence is legally condemned as a crime in all of these sites. The state is on record as having exercised more than due institutional diligence and having welcomed informal modes of resolution. If anything, the problem is one of plenitude—of the coexistence of mutually contradictory options. As a recent report on the Protection of Women under Domestic Violence Act said with ironic understatement, "Lack of coordination amongst various stakeholders remains an issue of concern" (Lawyers Collective 2009, 57). Regardless of their mandate, many venues pursue marital reconciliation as the default option, and even those who resist this ideology may be forced to align with it. There are no clear answers as to how best to take advantage of the options or how to optimally navigate spheres of influence: lawyers or police or community activists assist in many cases and fall short in others. While mediators and lawyers feel that this confusing landscape allows for leveraging possibilities, for using state sanctions to their advantage, these solutions are most often economic ones.

These structural dilemmas highlight a fundamental problem of gendered violence: with violence located within marriage and marriage the primary pillar of women's economic well-being, redressing violence and providing economic solutions stand in mutual contradiction. Violence is evoked to signal marital trouble, but it has to be erased if marriage is to be resutured as the optimal solution. Cases like Madhumita's, in which violence is strategically ignored, uneasily leave open other avenues. S498A cases are nuisances to judges, counselors, and police because they interrupt the work of reconciling marriages by launching the specter of criminal humiliation within the protected space of conjugality. They are convenient for opening up conversations about alimony but typically in self-destructive ways for the accuser, and they may easily prove to be a bad tactic. As Mirza and Fariza's situation illustrates, discourses of hegemonic masculinity and patrilineal authority dominate even when overt violence is condemned: violence is characterized as episodic, as individual moral failure, unconnected to the ways other contiguous patriarchal discourses validate power and authority.

An effective domestic policy in line with the UN Rapporteur's vision, Dempsey argues, goes beyond the due diligence of state prosecution; the goal should be to empower victims by pursuing either law or settlements that keep them safer but, more importantly, "to lessen patriarchy in society more generally" and address its "structural inequality," thereby improving the state's "moral character" (2007, 919–20, 926). The prosecutions explored in this chapter produce the opposite of these ideals: while they provide women with seeming tools of empowerment and help individual women with economic arrangements and freedom from violence, the overall effects are to strengthen patriarchal control and ideology. S498A is huge in the popular imagination as a useful institutionalized tool to feminists and a symbol of terror, persecution, and impoverishment to those who oppose them—but it ultimately demonstrates the difficulties of negotiating plural options in the face of gendered material inequalities and proves to be weak in remedying violence.

CHAPTER 8

The Trouble Is Marriage

Conclusions and Worries

The December 2013 cover of *Outlook* magazine sports an Indian version of Rosie the Riveter: a woman wearing a red sari, blue blouse, and red bindi, with flowing hennaed locks and flexing her biceps in the signature "We can do it" gesture, proclaims, "Don't mess with us." The cover story announces the efflorescence of "Feminism 2.0" in India "as men tremble," with the horrible pun, "Hear That She-Bang?"[1] It claims a widespread change in consciousness and action among Indian women, urban and rural, young and old, around issues from land rights to public harassment to marriage choice. The outrage is manifest not just in the protests following Jyoti Pandey's rape and murder in Delhi in 2012, but in other memorable strategic actions such as the War against Railway Rowdies, the flash mobs on the Delhi metro, or the Moochi (Moustache) Walk in Bengaluru, where women marched in fake mustaches to challenge feminine stereotypes. Laws created through feminist agitation are perceived as crucial to this empowerment, their power to challenge impunity most dramatically demonstrated in the final months of 2013, with sexual assault investigations and prosecutions leveled against a prominent religious figure, a former Supreme Court justice heading a human rights tribunal, and the editor of one of the best-known progressive investigative magazines. India is newsworthy here because of its inevitable association with abject patriarchal subjugation, but the mood of the article mirrors other recent journalistic analyses, such as Hanna Rosin's *The End of Men* (2012), which predicts a fundamental global shift in material and sexual empowerment for women and a corresponding decline for men. It might seem that the processes set in motion by the UN Decade for Women (1976–85) have finally gained momentum.

Is it time to celebrate this mainstreaming of feminism, with the affirmation of feminist jurisprudence as its crown jewel? Did law primarily help us get where we are? One can, of course, respond with predictable cautions: that dramatic arrests do not necessarily end in just outcomes; that there is a huge gap between arrest and conviction rates for crimes related to gendered violence; that certain categories of victims receive far more receptive responses from law; and that the visibility of feminist movements is met by backlash before any substantive gains can be recognized. But the imprint of feminist legal interventions around the globe is undeniable: people's everyday experiences of work and home, love and sex are shaped through the reputation of and negotiation with such laws. "Governance feminism" (Halley, Kotiswaran, et al. 2006) is a palpable force, used by the state (and ruling parties) to exhibit democratic outreach and protection of vulnerable groups. The state's smug "prerogative power" (Brown 1992) was typified for me a few months ago when an otherwise unflappable and organized member of the domestic staff at our home in Kolkata walked in deeply distressed; unwell and rushed, he had mistakenly entered the special women's compartment on the train and promptly had his phone confiscated until he returned to pay a hefty fine. Such intransigence in certain visible areas (particularly toward those perceived to be economically weak), matched by indifference to other vital concerns, typifies the state's patronage of women's causes.

I wish I could conclude a book on the legacies of feminism-inspired institutions by dusting off our collective palms in congratulation for a job well done. Yet the effects are more complicated. While the changes have enabled some new ways of engaging the state, they have also precipitated situations that require fundamental introspection on gender, justice, and marriage, both within and outside feminist politics. These include state recognition entrenched in ideas of feminine vulnerability and state protection, an inability to imagine women as economic and sexual actors. By way of conclusion, I lay out some of these conundrums. Before we take energetic social movements and new laws to be tantamount to a new "Feminism 2.0," we ought to be mindful of how the law is lived, the injustices it might spawn, and the characteristics of the woman the law ideally seeks to help.

A primary goal of this book has been to explore how multiple laws work, compounding each other's benefits or conflicting with each other. How do they shape novel ways of being, even as they are shaped through older ways of knowing? The anxieties expressed when laws are encoded often continue to erupt in adjudication (chapter 2). Other unforeseen contradictions begin to emerge through judicial interpretation, filtering down to everyday usage. Particular legal provisions become popular as strategies, even (or especially) when used against the grain: domestic violence law used to gain alimony, rape law to induce marriage, kidnapping law to control marriage choice, family court to reconcile feuding couples. Outrage that certain laws are "misused," which I trace across several chapters of this book (chapters 6 and 7 most explicitly), is a reaction to such innovation, drawing on the notion that every law has a "correct" intent and application and can narrowly fix a specific social problem, seemingly unmoored from the corpus of other laws and practices. Anthropologists would contend that legal rules serve as tools of transaction or that laws help people strike bargains, but creative attempts are popularly marked as abuse of legal process and, in particular, as women's cynical manipulation of rules biased in their favor.

Marriage is one of the most obvious sites where law has transformed cultural practices in India. Understandings of law loom large in shaping norms of agreement and harm, gifting and coercion, residence and labor within marriage, whether or not people intend to comply with such norms, ignore them, or circumvent them, and whether or not marital trouble is in the offing (chapter 5). Laws around marriage are perhaps no more contradictory than laws in other areas, but they occupy an overdetermined space in the popular imagination (and hence in adjudication) as "law gone too far."

Marriage is popularly believed to have been weaponized through law. S498A, the criminal provision for domestic violence, is regarded as synonymous with thin and fraudulent prosecutions. The Domestic Violence Act (2005), which was meant to offer an alternative through civil provisions, is viewed as a parallel tool of extortion, scarcely more acceptable. Rape law is seen as a means of pressuring men into marriage or punishing them for having sex outside marriage, on the one hand, and as ending consensual runaway marriages and enforcing caste and religious endogamous marriage through rape and kidnapping law, on the other.

A counterview to the assertion of the weaponization of marriage is that these strategies exemplify the fluid hybrid solutions possible through legal pluralism (de Sousa Santos 2006; Solanki 2011). The cases in this book demonstrate that mediation is critical for navigating potentially contradictory civil and criminal laws, whether in state institutions like family courts or police, state-governed community boards, or diverse organizations (chapters 4 and 7). The balance between civil and criminal penalties creates the leverage to move negotiations forward. The advantages to women claimants seem to lie in obtaining better alimony or settlements in divorce cases by raising the specter of criminal sanctions of domestic violence or rape law. Law can be used effectively as a currency to avoid law, exemplifying the benefits promoted in mediation materials, from saving time and cost to customized solutions.

However, these practical solutions often come at the cost of broader gender justice: the cases I followed affirm critics' foreboding that mediation works best in the language of economic compensation and is inadequate whenever violation, pain, or anger is in the mix, which is all too often in marital disputes (chapters 3, 4, and 7). Alimony settlements for women are frequently made under conditions of marital compliance and community surveillance. Violence, hypervisible in the problems of marriage, is downplayed in mediation to maintain marriage (and related social relations) as the optimal economic base for women.

Moreover, disparate laws are popularly treated as mutually constitutive trouble, as the confusion between (civil) divorce and (criminal) dowry and domestic violence law in the following cases indicates. A Kolkata professor recounted at a recent conference that a domestic worker, after being injured during a household errand, was referred by the hospital to the police for further inquiry. "Are you married?" they began by asking. When she replied in the negative, they sent her home, proclaiming there were no concerns about violence. Here, the priority accorded to marital violence cases erases all other forms of violence in the domestic and extradomestic realms. Soon after, my cousin, who was recounting the physical and verbal harassment his friend had faced from her mother-in-law, replied to my question about whether she had filed for divorce: "No, but she has gone to the police station to lodge a report (GD)." He referred as common-sense knowledge to the conflation between the domains of criminal and civil law and informal negotiation: the first step in a divorce is perceived to be a criminal case regarding violence or dowry recovery—an oblique, tortured way to access the economic entitlements of marriage.

My most graphic reminder of the rationale for these laws came a few months ago, at the offices of an organization renowned for its legal assistance to women. A client entered seeking divorce assistance: the staff lawyer noticed that she was severely bruised and elicited that above all she wanted an end to violence at home. The lawyers told her that what she needed in the short term was a protection order under the Domestic Violence Act, to have a deterrent while she continued to live in her home; the staff made contact with the protection officer and sent her off. Divorce, they advised, was a long-term process with specific strategies which they could help with later. This injured woman is the fundamental motivation for instituting such laws, to keep domestic violence victims as safe as possible; but even here, as the client's approach indicates, the understanding of trouble is always mediated by the near inseparability of divorce and violence.

Ultimately, such routine conflation is counterproductive for reducing violence. First, the widespread atmosphere of suspicion around S498A and the related low conviction rate make the police unreceptive to victims trying to lodge complaints, especially if they are socioeconomically marginalized. A law with a 2 percent conviction rate (for officially filed cases) effectively offers little to no protection. Second, because marital reconciliation dominates as a mode of resolving such cases, women are often sent back to violent situations in the hope of protecting their economic interests. Third, the ubiquity of evoking violence as a platform for negotiating the economic issues of divorce reduces complaints to strategic maneuvers, and the goals of curbing domestic violence as a violation of bodily integrity or will are not advanced. Crime is mostly salient as a tool of mediation. It becomes impossible to determine the extent of violence, to legally punish it, or to contemplate modes of redressing violence.

Widespread social consternation about the cynical misuse of multiple laws comes not just in the shrill outrage of men's rights activists, but increasingly in appellate judicial pronouncements on rape and domestic violence, which strongly condemn the routine use of these laws as negotiating tactics. While backlash against feminism is no reason to abandon reform, notable here is that many feminists also express discomfort with the thinness and instrumentalist use of these cases for other ends. It is immensely worrying that violence cannot be identified or redressed through the laws written to curb it, with such laws primarily used as a convenient tool of police harassment, and secondarily as a mode of leveraging alimony. Approaches to curbing violence need to be directly addressed, not simply as a proxy for marriage and economic compensation. The hybrid possibilities of legal pluralism seem insufficient cause for optimism when they come at the cost of turning a blind eye to violence.

Many feminist scholars are troubled not just by legal process, corruption, and harassment, but more fundamentally, by the representation of gender undergirding the laws. We can rest assured, as the cases in this book show, that women are exercising legal agency, at least as measured by their use of the law to solve marital problems. Yet the gendered subjectivity they ideally embody is profoundly problematic. Laws interpolate a female subject who has no salary or property, whose economic benefits lie in being part of a marital household, who is sexually naïve and wont to give consent only within the bounds of marriage, who is a recipient and not a perpetrator of violence. These characterizations do realistically describe a wide swath of Indian women, and as the chapters trace, these ascriptions may be strategically advantageous for those fitting such norms. However, by extension, they also constrict women by representing them as economically incapable and sexually passive, characterizations that prove dangerous because the protection of law is withdrawn if women's actions deviate from these ascriptions. It becomes difficult to represent the complexities of female lives and personalities in law, to acknowledge that many women are economically devastated through marital dissolution and depend on marital property for survival and others require protection from violence at home, while recognizing that some women may also deploy legal provisions for harassment, pressure to marry, or payoffs.

To see women as irredeemable systemic victims lacking agency is to be unable to contextualize them within the full scope of human possibilities, as capable of bravery and pathos and wit, as well as prevarication or anger or revenge. The feminist analysis of women as fundamentally "different from men" (strongly associated with 1970s and 1980s radical feminism and its avatars in India), needing help and protection, echoes the former vision, counterposed against the criterion of "sameness" or gender equity, which posits women's agency and citizenship on equal terms. While there are short-term advantages to protectionism, ultimately the norm of difference rather than equity sets women in a specially governed and sheltered category of citizenship (Smart 1995; Williams 1997), inscribing them in terms of the primacy of the sexual contract rather than the social contract (Pateman 1988). Agency and complexity are erased: rape and heterosex seem interchangeable; statutory rape denies women's consent; domestic violence law views women as perpetrators only when they are sisters- and mothers-in-law but never daughters-in-law; maintenance or alimony can imagine only a dependent female recipient. Gender is flattened across class, ethnic, sexual, and religious variations, or local advantage, ignoring privileges that certain women might have. The focus on marriage as central to gendered oppression also erases nonheterosexual and nonmonogamous sexual relationships and their economic entitlements. In contrast, a model based in gender equity need not assume that women are de facto equals of men in economic and cultural capital; it ought to be concretely grounded in analyses of structural inequity, mapping subjectivity intersectionally. The fear among some feminists that an equity paradigm might lead some men to cynically harass some women by filing reverse maintenance or rape charges against them is not sufficient reason to treat women as undifferentiated victims.

Marriage is more than one site of structural vulnerability captured in law; it is at the core of gender trouble. The intertwined laws followed in this book reflect the cultural understanding that marriage protects women (and, less obviously, men), economically, sexually, and socially. By this logic, when women legitimately deploy their sexuality in the commodity market of heterosexual marriage, they ought to be set for life: their parents need not consider them entitled to any portion of family resources; they need not engage the labor market, since they are to rely on the income of the husband and affines; they need not worry about having matrimonial property, because if they are good wives they can simply share in the benefits of the household. Such preassigned gender roles in marriage (Borneman 1996) create systematic vulnerability. Either one can access the benefits of being within a marriage through "good behavior," however troubled that marriage might be, or one can claim "good behavior" in courts or mediation to access alimony (substantial or not) in lieu of long-term support through marriage. These narrow formulas leave no room for the desires of men and women, sexual or otherwise, that disturb this scheme; in law, sex is entirely a commodity related to marriage. Similarly, women's labor contributions to their natal and marital households are rendered invisible: they are depicted as undeservedly demanding shares of others' (parents' or husbands') property, rather than retrieving their legitimate share. The state of staying married, in other words, is regarded as their primary form of property.

Divorce, or marital trouble more generally, therefore puts several systems in crisis. Attempts to make divorce easier—establishing family courts to process cases faster and give people greater voice, introducing mutual consent or irretrievable breakdown of marriage as grounds to avoid the negative associations of fault-based divorce, or systematizing alimony and marital property—elide the depth of this disruption. A good divorce seems impossible, whether because of the affective intensity attached to marriage as a form of social being, the awkward exposure of contractual labor and sex, or the strain of public performances in courts and related venues. No-fault divorce, touted as a solution that removes overt conflict, is problematic when it enhances the dependency of those in a weaker bargaining position (typically women) by taking economic distributions within marriage out of consideration (chapter 5). The upcoming bill in India that focuses on matrimonial property in divorce bucks this trend, emphasizing better distribution of assets. The project of making the dissolution of marriage less trouble, however, is not just about such strategic policy changes. Can we, as Menon hopes, "create conditions for marriage to be seen as an option to be chosen freely, with the inbuilt possibility of a fair divorce, for which an equitable partition of household resources is essential" (2012, 39)? It will require broad transformations, such as rethinking the gendered dependency of marriage, the labor market, and generational and conjugal transmission of property and other resources. Indeed, it relies on challenging ascriptions of masculinity and femininity, emotion and comportment, sex and money. Law is only a small, if influential, piece of such rearrangement.

NOTES

1. Camus and de Beauvoir soundly critiqued the association of romantic love with marriage, arguing for meaningful relationships as the ideal alternative (Keefe 2007).

2. An inquiry to the Camus Society confirmed that the quote is a common misattribution.

3. The contradictions between the poems are apparent in literary exegesis rather than to visitors in court, but the point is that the presence of these mismatched ideologies signals a space of competing expectations.

4. The British radical feminist magazine *Trouble and Strife* offers the eponymous explanation that "Trouble and Strife is cockney rhyming slang for wife. We chose this name because it acknowledges the reality of conflict in relations between women and men. As radical feminists, our politics come directly from this tension between men's power and women's resistance." "About Trouble & Strife," *Trouble & Strife*, www.troubleandstrife.org/test/.

5. What to count as law and whether all cultures had "law" have been some of the most contentious debates in legal anthropology (Moore 1969; Roberts 1994; Nader 2002). Malinowski's conception of law as a system of reciprocal obligations implies that all societies have law. Others deduce the existence of law based on judicial reasoning or vocabulary (Gluckman 1955); Bohannan (1957, 57) contends that "the Tiv have laws, but do not have 'law.'"

6. Sally Merry posits that "plural normative orders are found in virtually all societies (1988, 873). On plural orders, see also Auerbach 1983; Griffiths 1986; Merry 1986; Greenhouse, Yngvesson, et al. 1994; Moore 1999; Just 2000; Demian 2003; Sharafi 2008.

7. In divorce, litigants' social and economic capital determines the deal they can make, with "the outcome that the law will reach if no agreement is reached" determining each person's bargaining position (Mnookin and Kornhauser 1979, 986).

8. Such forums are present "in revolutionary socialist states, in fascist states, in capitalist welfare states, and postcolonial socialist states" (Merry 1993, 31).

9. Vatuk's work on Dar-ul-Qza courts in India (2008) makes a similar point.

10. The critical questions posed by mediation for law and politics are lucidly summarized in Goldberg et al. (1999, 11–13).

11. I received it in the same week in July 2006 from a male friend in India and a Nigerian female friend living in the United States.

12. Provocative legal reimaginations include Stark's suggestion to replace marriage certificates with renewable time-bound contracts relating to labor, sex, and property (2001, 1488), or Starnes's partnership law model in which early dissociation from partnership would trigger an equal division of marital property, accounting for the length of marriage and high earners (1993, 71–72). Such solutions highlight the implicit material terms of marriage through comparison with individual contracts but ignore questions of kinship and affect.

13. Yi and Deqing attribute the rising rate of Chinese divorce to women's increased ability "to control economic resources and become economically independent" (2000, 215). Riessman, on U.S. divorces, reports higher depression (from husbands if they don't have enough contact with their children and from wives related to economic "strain" and recidivism in child support, though less if they have supportive kin networks). But on the plus side, women appreciate greater freedom and learning to survive, changing social relationships, and a fuller sense of a whole identity, while men value greater "freedom from obligation" and from "scrutiny of wives," being "less confined," having "pleasure at using money in new ways," and greater connectedness with people (1990, 124, 163, 184, 205, 207).

14. Betzig's (1989) analysis of 186 "societies" found infidelity, infertility, economic issues, and personality issues to be the most prominent causes of dissolution.

15. Goode contends that Western European divorce rates "rise with prosperity— that is, divorce is a consumer good, and people who 'want' it will purchase it when they can afford it" (1993, 26). In combination with labor market changes for women and less remarriage, this means there is less reliance on marriage overall. In contrast, he critiques the socialist legacies of Eastern Europe (particularly the gendered hierarchies of the labor market) for generating economic distress for women in divorce. Malaysia's "stable high-divorce family system" is linked to customary provisions for women's welfare within and outside marriage, as well as a high remarriage rate, while falling divorce rates in Taiwan and Indonesia are associated with the failure of family support structures (218–19, 249).

16. Goode (1993) cites the Scandinavian countries as the exception to the pattern.

17. "The family," rather than being a "little world immune from the vulgar cash-nexus of modern society" is viewed in such accounts as "a vigorous agency of class placement and an efficient mechanism for the creation and transmission of gender equality" (Barrett and McIntosh 1982, 27, 29). Whitehead argues that "inequalities of power between husband and wife become manifest in the various arrangements by which the goods, services and/or income of husband and wife are allocated and distributed" (1982, 114).

18. The Rapporteur's call followed the Inter-American Commission on Human Rights' ruling that the U.S. *government* was responsible for human rights violations against Jessica Lenahan Gonzales and her three children, for failing to protect her against domestic violence.

19. Rai argues that legal reform has been particularly important for the postcolonial state, citing the example of India as having placed "considerable emphasis on the power (or lack of power) of the state to formulate, legislate and enforce laws regarding equality between men and women" (1996, 11).

20. Kannabiran and Menon argue of the IWM that "even the most optimistic of liberals in the movement do not believe that laws alone can change social discrimination and customs, or that the state is an impartial dispenser of justice," but see legal reform claims as part of "broad strategy" and "political practice" (2007, 10–11).

21. Hearings are deemed to be public venues; for in-camera hearings, judges sought clients' permission for my presence, as did counselors for mediation sessions. Access was not granted to files for ongoing cases, but the Kolkata Family Court staff provided aggregate statistics.

22. Baxi (2014) vividly describes the "aporia" involved in listening in on hearings in public courtrooms.

23. Krishna Dutta (2003) describes Calcutta's inevitable association with degradation in several such accounts, including Claude Lévi-Strauss's *Tristes Tropiques* (1955), filmmaker Louis Malle's *Calcutta* (1969), and Günther Grass's *Show Your Tongue* (1988). More recent associations include Zana Briski's 2004 film *Born into Brothels* and Roland Joffe's 1992 film *City of Joy* (based on Dominique Lapierre's novel).

24. Some notable accounts of historical and literary legacies of the city can be found in Moorhouse (1974), Chaudhuri (1990), and Dutta (2003). Some excellent recent ethnographies include Ray and Qayum (2009) and Roy (2003).

25. The shrinkage in population density is better contextualized by remembering that only a small portion of the city proper is in the census count, excluding the largest expansion of the urban population into surrounding districts (Banerjee and Mukherjee 2005, 22).

26. Ministry of Home Affairs, *Census of India*, www.censusindia.gov.in/2011-prov-results/prov_data_products_wb.html.

27. For accounts of the postcolonial Indian state, economy, and politics, see Brass (1994), Bose and Jalal (1998), Deshpande (2004), and Panagariya (2008).

28. The calculation of divorce rates is a thorny discussion for demographers. The problem lies in what to place as the denominator to compare with the number of registered divorces in a year. See "Calculating Divorce Rates," http://serc.carleton.edu/nnn/quantitarive_writing/examples/23804.html; and Bloom and Bennett (1990). In "How to Calculate the U.S. Divorce Rate, Correctly," sociologist Neil Bennett suggests that a best-case scenario is to follow a particular cohort over twenty years to see whether that group's marriages survive, using the marriages and divorces of the same people (*New York Times*, 27 May 1990, www.nytimes.com/1990/05/27/weekinreview/l-how-to-calculate-the-us-divorce-rate-correctly-707290.html). The Indian data is based either on statistics from

family courts (where only a small number of divorces take place) or the total married population as denominator, neither of which really show what percentage of marriages end in divorce.

29. Ministry of Home Affairs, Government of India, "Marital Status by Age and Sex," *Census of India 2001*, www.censusindia.gov.in/Tables_Published/C-Series /c_series_tables_2001.aspx.

30. Anand Giridharadas, "With India's New Affluence Comes the Divorce Generation," *New York Times: Asia-Pacific*, 19 February 2008, www.nytimes. com/2008/02/19/world/asia/19iht-divorce.1.10178712.html?_r=0; Mark Dummett, "Not So Happily Ever After as Indian Divorce Rate Doubles," *BBC News Delhi Online*, 31 December 2010, www.bbc.co.uk/news/world-south-asia-12094360; Purba Dutt, "Divorce Rates Climbing Up in Bangalore?" *Times of India*, 20 February 2013, http:// articles.timesofindia.indiatimes.com/2013–02–20/man-woman/37180369_1_divorce-rates-divorce-applications-marriages; Anand Holla, "How Men Are Coping with Their Marriages," *Times of India*, 1 October 2012, http://articles.timesofindia.indiatimes. com/2012–10–01/man-woman/34163042_1_couples-marriage-nuclear-families. Most of the articles cite the rise in the number of cases in family courts (rather than population data)—that is, they measure an increase against a recent (and partial) baseline.

31. While I use a simple fraction of population in the tables, Indian demographers Ajay Kumar Singh and R. K. Sinha cite the "divorce rate" as 7.1 percent ("Growing Incidence of Divorce in Indian Cities: A Study of Mumbai," http://iussp2005.princeton.edu/papers/50689), using the formula "refined divorce rate = number of divorce /total number of married population × 1000" (the crude divorce rate = total number of divorce/total population × 1000). Singh explained in a personal communication that the multiplier of one thousand is mathematically used to calculate a rate "determined by the level of occurrence," i.e., added when the occurrence is very low; similar multipliers are used to measure maternal mortality and abortions.

32. The number of households with widowed female heads is almost double that of male widowed heads (6.8 percent compared to 3.5 percent).

CHAPTER 2

1. Jyotika Virdi categorizes the film as "a deeply conservative version of marriage and man-woman relationships" (2004, 76).

2. The organized women's movement gathered momentum in the 1920s, with a focus on building women's organizations and entering political positions at various levels (Sinha 1998, 39–40). There has been an increase both in elite and middle-class women's participation since the 1920s and in the number of nonelite politically organized women who challenged hierarchies of caste and livelihood (Sinha 1998, 39–40, 56; Sreenivas 2011, 71–72). Ironically, while feminists are repeatedly undermined in popular discourse, they are praised in nationalist accounts (Sinha 1998).

3. Other key documents and debates dealing with women, family, and violence include the 22nd Law Commission of India Report on Christian Marriages and

Matrimonial Causes Bill (1961), the 59th Report of Law Commission of India on Hindu Marriage Act and Special Marriage Act (1974), the 84th Law Commission Report on Rape and Allied Offences (1980), and the Criminal Law Second Amendment Bill (1983).

4. Personal law pertains to individuals, in contrast to territorial law, which applies to everyone in a nation-state.

5. Even the Special Marriage Act (1954), which made marriage into a secular and civil contract, was structured in terms of Hindu upper-caste marriage rules and protected Hindu joint family property for men (Agnes 2005, 117).

6. The Muslim Personal Law (Shariat) Application Act of 1937 overrode "custom or usage in matters of marriage, divorce, inheritance, and succession for Muslims" (Williams 2006, 84). It mentioned divorced Muslim women's natal inheritance rights (Jain 2005, 213), but not their entitlement to matrimonial property or alimony.

7. Constituent Assembly of India (Legislative) Debates, Legislature of India, 9 February 1939; 14 February 1939, 881.

8. Sircar represented the colonial state but was personally Hindu.

9. Prominent topics of debate included transforming the Mitakshara coparcenary system of Hindu property, including making women equal heirs of ancestral property, creating civil marriage and intercaste marriage, and providing for divorce.

10. Following calls for change from reformist groups, the Rau Committee (1941–46) solicited opinions across the country recommending that a new, comprehensive code (rather than individual laws) be written. A select committee of the Constituent Assembly and Law Minister Ambedkar then drafted the Hindu Code (Som 1994, 170; Williams 2006, 102; Guha 2007, 235).

11. New provisions included widows' absolute ownership of marital property and single and widowed women's right to adopt. But gross inequalities remained, such as the continuation of the Mitakshara coparcenary (which effectively denied daughters shares in ancestral property), the primacy of fathers as "natural" guardians of children, and married women's inability to adopt children without their husbands' permission.

12. These included the All India Anti-Hindu-Code Committee and a petition by sixty male members of the Delhi bar (Guha 2007, 236–37).

13. The RSS, established in 1925 and still active, is notorious as a Hindu nationalist conservative organization.

14. The first (failed) bill on Hindu women's divorce, introduced by Deshmukh in 1938, was the Hindu Women's Right to Divorce Bill. The debate was dominated by doubts about the consequences of "interference" in Hindu personal law and whether Hindus could have a blanket "right to divorce." The colonial government, represented by Law Member Sircar, opposed the bill on the grounds that the "preponderance of Hindu opinion" was against divorce, and the government "interfered only when 'the ordinary sense of morality was impinged on' despite majority opinion" (Basu 2001, 101). Deshmukh argued for the bill as being in line with the "spirit of Hinduism which was in favor of change" and providing Hindu women a choice, such that "those who were willing to bear with the agony and the wrongs of a married life were free to do so" (Basu 2001, 103). The closeness in timing and the political anxieties similar to MDM are notable.

15. Constituent Assembly of India (Legislative) Debates, Legislature of India, 24 February 1949, 832.

16. Ambedkar referred to himself as Shudra, emphasizing the political abjection of the word. He was from the Mahar community. *Shudra* fits within the fourfold designation of caste, or *varna*; *Mahar* refers to subcaste, or *jati*, which is the more colloquial and broad understanding of caste. In political discourse, Ambedkar has been commonly associated with the empowering term *Dalit*, meaning "oppressed."

17. Govinda Das objected to having a Hindu rather than a uniform civil code in a newly secular state, arguing that the changes had not gone far enough and mirroring the Mahasabha's attack that the HCB was communal (Som 1994, 173). V. S. Sarvate, simultaneously a Socialist and a religious conservative, argued that things should be left as they were unless private property could be abolished and communism established (Jones 1974, 78).

18. The mythological heroine Shakuntala, most famously depicted in the epic Mahabharata and the fifth-century poet Kalidasa's Abhigyanam Shakuntalam, is the subject of an erotic love story with King Dushyanta, later abandoned and rejected by him in a misrecognition drama. She is deemed to be the mother of Bharat, from whom one of the names for India is derived, hence a mythical mother of the nation. Feminist rereadings of Shakuntala, such as Vaidehi's "Shakuntale Yondige Kaleda Aparahna" (An afternoon with Shakuntala, 1993), depict her desire and intelligence and Dushyanta's arrogance and distance, reversing the usual trope of conjugal forbearance.

19. Constituent Assembly of India (Legislative) Debates, Legislature of India, 24 February 1949, 862–63.

20. Constituent Assembly of India (Legislative) Debates, Legislature of India, 1 March 1949, 996.

21. Constituent Assembly of India (Legislative) Debates, Legislature of India, 9 April 1948, 360.

22. Constituent Assembly of India (Legislative) Debates, Legislature of India, 24 February 1949, 868–71.

23. Nehru's later strategic revisions are seen by some scholars as a successful "victory of symbol over substance" (Som 1994, 180, 184–88) and by others as an expedient "eclectic" incorporation of varying interests (Subramanian 2010, 785).

24. Hindu Succession (Amendment) Act (2005).

25. The UN General Assembly directed member states to submit reports on the "status of women" in their countries, following the "Declaration on Elimination of Discrimination against Women" (1967). A reminder to India, sent in 1975 in the context of the International Women's Year to the Ministry of External Affairs, from the UN Commission on the Status of Women (Gopalan 2001, 1) eventually led to the formation of the committee, consisting of politicians, scholars, and activists and chaired by Phulrenu Guha, the minister of state in the Department of Social Welfare.

26. These recommendations include adding parity between partners in Muslim and Christian law and parity in grounds of divorce to Jewish and Christian law; adding cruelty and desertion as grounds of divorce in Hindu law and disallowing consideration

NOTES   ◆   225

of a woman's separate place of work as a ground for desertion; eliminating men's uni-lateral right of divorce in Muslim law and adding the wife's right to divorce on the husband's failure to maintain her, irrespective of her conduct; and disallowing conver-sion as a ground of divorce in all laws (CSWI 1974, 118–24).

27. Lok Sabha Debates, 27 August 1984, 237.

28. The bill's proposal that family court judges have at least seven years of experience was unpopular (Lok Sabha Debates, 227).

29. Communist Party of India (Marxist); see chapter 1 for its significance in India.

30. They argued that the act was also shortchanged in legislative process, and was superficial rather than systematic in combating violence against women.

CHAPTER 3

1. Kidder studies law-avoidant cultures, that is, contexts where speaking legalistically is a form of transgression.

2. According to the 2001 census, 8.11 percent of people in India (83,369,769) report Bengali/Bangla as their mother tongue, of whom 82 percent (68,369,255) live in West Bengal. Nationally, 41.03 percent (422,048,642) report Hindi as their mother tongue, of whom 7.34 percent (5,747,099) live in West Bengal (www.censusindia.gov.in /Census_Data_2001/Census_Data_Online/Language/parta.htm). Hindus constitute three-fourths of the total population of West Bengal, with Muslims a little less than one-fourth (23.6 percent), and Christians, Sikhs, and Jains together less than 1 percent, based on the 1991 census (Banerjee and Mukherjee 2005, 23).

3. As discussed in chapter 2, personal law pertaining to marriage, maintenance, adoption, and custody has slightly different provisions by religion.

4. Naples's cogent summary (2003, 46) cites superior "linguistic competence" and "deeper understanding of cultural practices and beliefs" as advantages of the "insider" position, and greater objectivity as the advantage of the "outsider" position.

5. Zavella (1996, 141) ponders the dilemma of speaking as a Chicana feminist while trying to explore Mexican-American women's subjectivities; Hsiung (1996, 129) describes resisting workplace patriarchies through feminist talk. Much feminist schol-arship on methodology has pondered the impossibility of transcending power hierar-chies of "Western" feminism (Stacey 1991), but Hirsch (2002) suggests that forms of participation may mediate these forms of power.

6. In Sarah Lamb's research, older Bengali women foregrounded their powerlessness and abandonment as mothers in stories about the "old and devoted mother who comes to be forgotten and turned into a beggar by her only and beloved son" (1997, 54).

7. Raymond Williams's formulation of "structures of feeling" is cogently illustrated by Ring (2006, 28).

8. Leys usefully summarizes the work of a range of affect theorists, offering the definition that "affects must be viewed as independent of, and in an important sense prior to, ideology—that is, prior to intentions, meanings, reasons, and beliefs—because they are nonsignifying, autonomous processes that take place below the threshold of

conscious awareness and meaning" (2011, 437), paralleling Mazzarella's definition of affect as "presubjective without being presocial" (2010, 291) and Shouse's as "prepersonal, . . . a nonconscious experience of intensity" (quoted in Leys 2011, 442).

9. Echoing McGuire's phrase, quoted in Ingram 1997, 215.

10. According to the 2001 census, 85.34 percent of people in West Bengal report Bengali as their primary language, and 7.17 percent Hindi as their primary language, making Hindi the second most widely spoken language in the state other than English, for which no data are available in these census categories (www.censusindia.gov.in /Census_Data_2001/Census_Data_Online/Language/Statement3.htm). Hindi and English are national languages (and hence languages of legal record).

11. See Ng (2009) for an account of bilingualism in Hong Kong courts, with a dissonance between formal legal terms in English versus affective and performative confusion in Cantonese.

12. Berti (2010) provides some rich examples of such transliteration in a criminal trial involving dowry in Himachal Pradesh.

13. There are, of course, plenty of slang terms that refer to having sex with little ambiguity, but they seem not to be considered appropriate in formal venues.

14. As Baxi (2014) and Berti (2014) vividly demonstrate, documents are used to shape subsequent verbal testimony or to contradict it, meaning that verbal testimony and written testimony are deliberately used as separate strategic tools. Differences between the two forms of testimony may produce space for negotiation and meaning (Berti 2010).

15. Berti (2010) demonstrates that criminal trials may rely on a similar process of looking to previous written (or narrated) testimony to hold verbal court testimony to account.

16. Ingram describes the "translation trinity" of Jacques Derrida, Paul De Man, and Walter Benjamin as being at the core of this field (1997, 213).

17. An apt example of such enunciatory creation is the *Temiko* case (*State of Maharashtra vs. Joyce Zee alias Temiko, Bombay Law Reporter* 77, 218), in which a Mumbai bar dancer was accused of sex work. Accusations and their repeated denial in highly charged sexual language, per standards of cross-examination, generated pornographic sexual excitement: for example, the record of the defendant's testimony reads, "It is not true that I was striking my breasts in a violent manner. It is not true that I inserted my nipples in the mouth of the customers or I pushed them with breasts or hips, it is true that when I came to the floor, I removed my top gown."

18. Cases discussed pertained to Hindu laws, but other personal law codes also have provisions for impotence-related divorce.

19. The standard of fraud in marital dissolution cases is slightly different than in the Indian Contract Act (1872, S. 17), mediated by questions of marital sacrament (Uberoi 1996, 330).

20. Justice Dharmadhikari famously said, "A marriage may not be a contract only but it is a contract also" (Uberoi 1996, 332). Contract issues date back to the Rakhmabai case pertaining to consent to child marriage (324–25).

21. *All India Reporter* (AIR) 1988 Calcutta 210.

22. AIR 1985 Bombay 103.

23. AIR 1989 Bombay 220.

24. AIR 1988 Rajasthan 180.

25. AIR 1991 Bombay 8.

26. AIR 1979 Delhi 93.

27. The judge's advice here faithfully renders case law on insanity, that mere allegations cannot be raised without substantive medical evidence (Dhanda 1995).

28. Some of the case law on potency does consist of evaluations of the male body. However, often the emphasis in cases such as assault is on reading the body for the presence of intercourse, while blatant custodial violence to the male body goes unrecorded in medical reports (Baxi 2014).

29. Bangladesh and India share the colonial legacy of having different religious personal law codes by community.

30. Monsoor (2008, 65–73) provides an overview of maintenance law, including salient differences with the Indian jurisprudential trajectory.

31. In 2000, the California-based nongovernmental organization Institute for the Study and Development of Legal Systems (ISDLS) identified the backlog of cases as a primary impediment in law and recommended mediation, suggesting the family courts as the ideal venue for implementing it.

32. Bangladesh also has Narishishu courts (women and children's courts) which are criminal courts dealing with sexual violence, such as acid burnings and rapes.

33. Information drawn from fieldwork interviews; see also Monsoor (2008, 142–46).

34. Monsoor reports 63 percent of cases cleared in Dhaka in her study period, equivalent to the recovery of Tk 1, 02, 81, 301 (2008, 144–46). The exchange rate was 1 USD = approximately 50 taka at that time.

35. See Monsoor (2009, 63–68) for the legal landscape of polygyny in Bangladesh.

36. Chapters 4 and 5 include other examples of judges using religious and cultural expectations in their negotiations. Both in Bangladesh and India, judges consider cases under all personal laws but may situate themselves as insiders or outsiders to the community. Here the judge speaks as an insider to Muslim belief.

CHAPTER 4

1. "Breaking Free," *The Telegraph* (Kolkata), 30 November 2001, 19.

2. "Family Court Act Change Flayed," *The Hindu*, 24 April 1996, Anjali, "The Pathos of Family Courts," *The Pioneer*, 9 April 1995, 16; P. Das, "For and Against Family Courts," *The Hindu*, 30 September 1996, 4; K. Singh, "Family Courts," *The Pioneer*, 17 April 1996, 6.

3. This group, whose demands dated back to pre-independence civil disobedience movements, argued that with indigenous systems, "faction and conflict, bred by colonial oppression, would be replaced by harmony and conciliation" (Galanter 1972, 55–56).

4. Most judges came to the Kolkata Family Court as their last assignment before retirement, as a special job with visibility and perks. Between sixty and sixty-two, they cease to be under the High Court and fall under the state government, which Agnes argues makes for "lack of supervision and accountability" (2011, 291).

5. Judge Ganguly recalls that the demonstrations went on for a few days, but the court stayed open with police protection from the High Court (interview, 29 June 2009).

6. The Kolkata metropolitan area generates 37 percent of the state's matrimonial cases, the rest being heard in the Alipore district courts, where matrimonial issues are undifferentiated from the larger roster of civil district court cases.

7. Agnes's (2004b) report on the Kolkata court is notoriously negative, compared to other cities, but other courts have similar problems of administration and access (see Vatuk 2006).

8. The number of restitution cases is small because many of these are converted either to divorce or mutual consent petitions (Agnes 2004b).

9. When I began fieldwork at the court in 2001, the staff reported that 1,869 of 2,243 (83 percent) matrimonial cases and 803 of 1,081 (74 percent) maintenance cases filed since 2000 had already been "disposed" (733 cases were originally transferred from the city civil courts and the rest were filed in the family court).

10. See Agnes (2011, 311) for a different account of backlog.

11. Figures from other cities show similar numbers, although Pune appears atypical. Maintenance was given or enhanced in 17.7 percent cases in Bengaluru, 15.8 percent in Mumbai, and 51.9 percent in Pune. Reconciliation was effected in 3.2 percent of cases in Bengaluru, 5.4 percent in Mumbai, 22.4 percent in Pune (Agnes 2004a, 65). In the Hyderabad/Secunderabad Family Courts, 14 percent of cases ended in reconciliation, and 21 percent with maintenance (Vanka and Kumari 2008, 121).

12. See Agnes (2011, 282–85) on concurrent jurisdiction of high courts.

13. *Family Courts Act 1984, Bare Act 2001* (Allahabad: Law Publishers, 2001), 1.

14. According to Pratibha Gheewala, retired chief counselor of Mumbai Family Courts, this interpretation is followed in the Mumbai courts (personal communication, 15 December 2002).

15. The term *conciliation* has a long history in the United Kingdom: while originally interchangeable with *reconciliation*, "the distinction between intervention aimed at reducing conflict upon the breakdown of a marriage and intervention intended to repair a failing relationship" developed clearly in the 1970s, as "a modernization of the concept of reconciliation" (Dingwall and Eekelaar 1988, 3, 15).

16. Presumably the amount of blood is part of the narrative hyberbole.

17. Interview, 29 June 2009.

18. Berti's ethnography of a drug trial in Himachal Pradesh vividly documents the ways trials were shaped by judges' questioning and translation: witness statements in police reports needed to be confirmed orally before the judge, and the judge summarized trial testimony (2014, 8).

19. Agnes reviews roles for lawyers and counselors across various Indian cities (2011, 294–304), arguing that each can be useful to gender justice when placed within creative alternatives for legal access and support.

20. Judicial service payments, i.e., judges' salaries, come from the state government, but other family court funds come from the national government, making reimbursements remote and complicated.

21. Anthropologists have suggested that discourses of corruption signal people's sense of legitimate interactions and exchanges (Gupta 2012, 14).

22. Each state in India has a women's commission to "protect and promote the interests of women" on a variety of issues, in addition to the National Women's Commission.

23. Interview, 3 September 2001.

24. Interview, 16 September 2001.

25. *Leela Mahadeo Joshi vs. Mahadeo Sitaram Joshi* (AIR 1991 Bom 195) set the appellate norm for lawyers being able to represent clients in family court. While the Kolkata judges did not mention the precedent they favored, the *Sarla Sharma vs. State of Rajasthan* I (2002) DMC 409 Raj decision held that the court can appoint a legal practitioner "in the interests of justice" (Agnes 2011, 296–97).

26. Personal communication, 23 December 2004.

27. Interview, 20 December 2005.

CHAPTER 5

Epigraph: D. Mahapatra (2008). "Is Hindu Marriage Law Breaking Homes?" *Times of India*, 23 June, 19.

1. Tapas Ghosh, "More Marriages on the Rocks," *The Telegraph* (Kolkata), 29 October 2010, www.telegraphindia.com/1001030/the_east.htm.

2. The corresponding Bangla honorific address would be *apni*; the middle-level *tumi* is most common for married couples.

3. G. S. Radhakrishna, "Cook Up a Story and Offload Your Spouse," *The Telegraph* (Kolkata), 12 September 2005, www.telegraphindia.com/1050912/asp/frontpage /story_5227175.asp.

4. Varuna Verma, "Gimme More," *The Telegraph* (Kolkata), 6 February 2011, www. telegraphindia.com/1110206/jsp/7days/story_13542608.jsp.

5. Radhakrishna, "Cook Up a Story and Offload Your Spouse."

6. Nuclear households account for 70.1 percent of total households—69.6 percent in rural areas, and 71.2 percent in urban. C. Chandramouli, Registrar General & Census Commissioner, India, Ministry of Home Affairs, "Housing, Household Amenities and Assets—Key Results from Census 2011."

7. Subodh Verma, "Cities Buck the Trend, Joint Families Are Back," *Times of India Online*, 8 April 2012, http://articles.timesofindia.indiatimes.com/2012–04–08 /india/31308182_1_rural-areas-urban-areas-households; Madhavi Rajadhyaksha, "56%

More Joint Families in City Than 10 Years Ago," *Times of India Online*, 24 March 2012, http://articles.timesofindia.indiatimes.com/2012–03–24/mumbai/31233329_1_joint-families-nuclear-families-households.

8. The phrase *love-marriage* is commonly used to refer to self-arranged marriages, the antonym being *arranged marriage* or, more accurately, *family-arranged marriage*. As these sources show, the presence or absence of love has little correlation with the mode of arranging the marriage. Arranged marriage spans a wide range of practices, with varying degrees of familiarity and choice with regard to future spouses, and should not be equated with coerced marriage.

9. See chapter 7 on domestic violence.

10. My profuse thanks to Dr. Amita Dhanda and her students at the Centre for Disability Studies at the NALSAR University of Law, Hyderabad, for an energetic discussion that helped clarify many of the issues framing this section.

11. The decree of nullity is given if "the respondent was unable to know the nature and consequences of his/her act at the time of contracting the marriage and was incapable of understanding the normal responsibilities of marriage" (Agnes 2011, 18).

12. See Agnes (2011, 18–19) for an overview.

13. Courts have urged compassionate support in cases of women's mental illness (Agnes 2011, 19).

14. *Banani Ghosh vs Arun Kumar Ghosh* (Kolkata High Court, 17 September 2009).

15. *Vidyadhar Chodankar v Malini Chodankar* II (2006) DMC609 Bom on extent of curability.

16. *Ram Narain Gupta vs Smt. Rameshwari Gupta*, AIR 1988 SC 2260.

17. Kolsky (2010b) argues that medical jurisprudence arose when professional expertise came into favor during colonial governance, as a result of the distrust of verbal testimony.

18. Of 208 petitions regarding men's violence, 205 of the men had committed bodily harm, 123 toward relatives, 59 of these being their wives.

19. Feminist anthropologists (Rubin 1975; Bossen 1988) have urged us to look beyond Lévi-Strauss's suggestion that the circulation of women and bridewealth is a fundamental building block of cultural systems; in that vein, I posit the traffic in marriage as a system of flows of labor, goods, and relationships working across genders and generations, not as the "trafficking of women."

20. A rice and milk dessert, rice pudding of sorts.

21. *Alka Sharma vs. Abhinesh Chandra Sharma*, AIR 1991 MP 205.

22. Translated idiomatically. A *potol* is a small green vegetable, not an onion.

23. In the very different context of religio-political violence, Veena Das characterizes the silences of women who cannot be placed back in normal circuits of kinship in terms of the traumatic aporia of "drinking poisonous knowledge" (2007, 57).

24. Women's spirit possession, often occurring in early years of marriage, has also been interpreted as diffused or internalized dissatisfaction with gender norms (Freed and Freed 1964; Moore 1999). Boddy (1994) provides a critical reading of such perspectives.

25. In *Kuldip Kaur vs. Surinder Singh* (AIR 1989 SC 232), the Supreme Court held that a jail sentence for failure to pay maintenance was "a mode of enforcement and not a mode of satisfaction of the liability," meaning the defaulter still had to satisfy the debt. The maximum sentence is a month of jail for each month of default (*A.Satheesh Kumar vs. Durga Devi Madurai Bench of Madras High Court*, 19 October 2010). In the family court, much confusion prevailed over how much of the defaulted amount went to the person making the maintenance claim and whether there were costs to be paid to the civil jail.

26. Tapas Ghosh, "Post-Divorce Upkeep Scales New Heights," *The Telegraph* (Kolkata), 4 April 2003, www.telegraphindia.com/1030404/asp/calcutta/story_1838534.asp.

27. "Dump Spouse, Shell Out: NRI Doctor Forced to Pay Rs 40 Lakh in Calcutta Court for Disposal of Divorce Case," *The Telegraph* (Kolkata), 7 March 2007, www.telegraphindia.com/1070307/asp/calcutta/story_7479952.asp.

28. "Dumped Your Partner? Pay Palimony—Court for Contract to Protect Deserted Live-in Pal," *The Telegraph* (Kolkata), 5 October 2010, www.telegraphindia.com/1101005/jsp/nation/story_13019806.jsp; "Nation Briefs: Live in Cash," *The Telegraph* (Kolkata), 21 April 2011, www.telegraphindia.com/1110421/jsp/nation/story_13882728.jsp.

29. Husbands can ask for maintenance under the Hindu Marriage Act and the Parsi Marriage and Divorce Act, wives under the Protection of Women from Domestic Violence Act and most divorce laws other than the Muslim Dissolution of Marriage Act. Maintenance is also available to children, adult daughters, daughters-in-law, and parents under other laws. See Agnes (2011, 118) for a useful chart.

30. *Chandana Guha Roy vs. Goutam Guha Roy* (AIR 2004 Cal 36).

31. *Lalit Mohan vs. Tripta Devi*, AIR 1990 J K 7; *Mugappa vs. Muniyamma* II (2003), DMC 2003 188 Kar.

32. *Anil Kr. v. Lakshmi Devi* AIR 1994 NOC 61 (Rajasthan); similarly, *Urmila Devi v. Hari Parkash Bansal* AIR 1988 P H 84; *Meenu Chopra vs. Deepak Chopra* AIR 2002 Del 131; *G. C. Ghosh vs. Sushmita Ghosh* I (2001) DMC 469 Del; *Rajathi vs. S. Ganesan* (1999) 6 SC 326. See Agnes's analysis (2011, 171–77).

33. *Chandana Guha Roy vs Goutam Guha Roy*, AIR 2004 Cal 36.

34. *Rita Raj Kunt vs. Anita* II (2008), DMC 827 Del; see Agnes (2011, 172).

35. Based on a national sample of 405 cases.

36. Rema Nagarajan, "86% of Women Are Left with Children but No Home," *Times of India Online*, 8 March 2011, http://articles.timesofindia.indiatimes.com/2011-03-08/india/28667734_1_cases-survey-findings-women; Smitha Verma, "Divorce Dues," *The Telegraph* (Kolkata), 2 February 2011, www.telegraphindia.com/1110202/jsp/opinion/story_13523674.jsp; "Divorced Women in Dire Straits: Survey," *Deccan Herald Online*, 20 December 2010, www.deccanherald.com/content/122210/divorced-women-dire-straits-survey.html.

37. Section 125 of the Indian Penal Code provides economic support for spouses, parents, or children under penury. Maintenance for Muslim divorcées falls under the

Muslim Women's Act, ostensibly limited to "fair and reasonable provision" for three months or the *iddat* period only. The Supreme Court held in later decisions that Muslim women could use S125 to seek "maintenance" before divorce (*Iqbal Bano vs. State of UP* (2007) 6 SCC 785) and until remarriage, removing the limitation of the three-month *iddat* period (*Shabana Bano vs. Imran Khan*, AIR 2010 SC 305). Before that, wealthier women often sought to recover *mehr*, *iddat*, and "fair and reasonable provision" amounting to tens of thousands of dollars through the Muslim Women's Act, while poorer women sought small amounts under S125 (Vatuk 2008).

38. *Mehr* may be paid in part right after the marriage ("prompt") and in part at a later time ("deferred"), but it must be paid up on the occasion of death or divorce.

39. Tripti Nath, "Lies and the Law in Divorce Battles," *Navhind Times Online*, 30 July 2010, www.navhindtimes.in/ilive/lies-and-law-divorce-battles.

40. Flavia Agnes, "Bill without Benefits," *Asian Age*, www.asianage.com/columnists /bill-without-benefits-043; Bina Agarwal, "A House Divided," *Indian Express*, 2 September 2013, 10; Namita Kohli, "Law with Loopholes," *The Hindu*, 1 October 2013, www. thehindu.com/features/metroplus/society/law-with-loopholes/article5186386.ece.

CHAPTER 6

1. See Arondekar (2009) for the colonial use of tests of "habituation" to particular sex acts on men's bodies, taken as consensual sexual activity.

2. My narrative of the situation is pieced together from subsequent scant accounts in the media ("Buddha Rap on Academy Operation," *The Telegraph* (Kolkata), 16 January 2005; "Stage Bloc Flays Cop Forced Entry," *The Telegraph* (Kolkata), 15 January 2005) and my fieldwork sites, including the Women's Grievance Cell at Kolkata Police Headquarters, and organizations that offered help with marriage mediation and violence (chapter 7).

3. "Buddha Rap on Academy Operation."

4. "Opinion—Life Chasing Art," *The Telegraph* (Kolkata), 16 January 2005.

5. Section 375 of the Indian Penal Code defines rape, while 376 defines punishment for rape. S375 is similar to many other sexual assault statutes in its definitions: it specifies gender, rape being a man's "sexual intercourse" with a woman "against her will," "without her consent," by threat of harm, under the false belief that she is having sex with her husband, if she is incapable of giving consent because of having been drugged, or if she is below sixteen. Moreover, rape is defined as particularly heinous in the following circumstances: when she is pregnant or under twelve, or in cases of gang rape or custodial rape.

6. "City Page," *The Telegraph* (Kolkata), 7 February 2005.

7. Baxi (2014, 1–60) provides a detailed reading of the Mathura case and its legacy for feminism, as well as previous notorious trials that did not spur reform.

8. Shefalee Vasudev and Methil Renuka, "Sexual Crimes: Rape!" *India Today*, 9 September 2002, 48.

9. While the judge ultimately dismissed the case, citing improbability, the event became a prominent platform in organizing against rape in the women's movement in

India. "Rape Case Shocks Women in India," *New Internationalist* 277 (1996): 5, provides one of numerous accounts of the case.

10. "Probe into Bihar Dalit Women's Rape," *India eNews.com*, 3 September 2006. *Dalit* indicates low-caste, "untouchable" groups.

11. "Rape Cases We Forgot: Soni Sori, Chhattisgarh's Prisoner of Conscience," IBN Live, 4 January 2013, http://ibnlive.in.com/news/rape-cases-we-forgot-soni-sori-chhattisgarhs-prisoner-of-conscience/313817-3-235.html.

12. Shuddhabrata Sengupta, "Justice for Soni Sori: Gathering at Jantar Mantar, 02/01/13," *Kafila.org*, 2 January 2013, http://kafila.org/2013/01/02/justice-for-soni-sori-gathering-at-jantar-mantar-020113/.

13. Soma Marik, "Barasat Rape, Murder and the Culture of Rape in West Bengal," *Kafila.org*, 17 June 2013, http://kafila.org/2013/06/17/barasat-rape-murder-and-the-culture-of-rape-in-west-bengal-soma-marik/.

14. Sandip Roy, "Kolkata Gangrape: How the 16-year-old Victim Became a Political Football," *Firstpost*, 3 January 2014, www.firstpost.com/politics/kolkata-gang-raped-twice-burned-to-death-victim-now-a-political-football-1319165.html.

15. Snehamoy Chakraborty, "Envy Becomes Savagery," *The Telegraph* (Kolkata), 24 January 2014, www.telegraphindia.com/1140124/jsp/frontpage/story_17859762 .jsp#.UuKLm_tOnal.

16. Caesar Mandal, "Woman Raped in Moving Car in Kolkata," *Times of India Online*, 8 June 2012, http://articles.timesofindia.indiatimes.com/2012-06-08 /kolkata/32123583_1_woman-driver-car.

17. Mandal, "Woman Raped in Moving Car"; Monideepa Banerjie, "Kolkata's Park Street Rape Case: 10 Big Facts," *NDTV*, 20 February 2012, www.ndtv.com/article /india/kolkatas-park-street-rape-case-10-big-facts-177930.

18. Arjun Chatterjee, "Kolkata Rape Victim Accuses Police of Humiliation, Inaction; CM Orders Probe," *India Today Online*, 16 February 2012, http://indiatoday. intoday.in/story/kolkata-gangrape-victim-mamata-banerjee/1/173915.html.

19. "Katwa Rape Staged: Didi," *Indian Express Online*, 29 February 2012, www .indianexpress.com/news/katwa-rape-staged-didi/918105/.

20. The woman's admission that her husband had belonged to the (now) opposition party (though he had died eleven years before) was cited as evidence of a politically motivated accusation, a transparently thin claim. Monideepa Banerjee, "Another Bengal Rape Is 'Concocted,' According to Mamata," *NDTV Online*, 29 February 2012, www.ndtv.com/video/player/news/another-bengal-rape-is-concocted-according-to-mamata/225010?v.

21. Marik, "Barasat Rape, Murder and the Culture of Rape in West Bengal"; Shiv Sahay Singh, "Protest against Mamata's Surprise Visit to Barasat," *The Hindu*, 18 June 2013, www.thehindu.com/news/national/other-states/protest-against-mamatas-surprise-visit-to-barasat/article4823354.ece.

22. Flavia Agnes, "Opinion: Why I Oppose Death for Rapists," *Mumbai Mirror*, 5 April 2014, www.mumbaimirror.com/mumbai/cover-story/Opinion-Why-I-oppose-death-for-rapists/articleshow/33250078.cms.

23. The Indian jurist Jaising Modi's *Medical Jurisprudence and Toxicology* (1920), which Kolsky contends "remains the standard authority in India today," famously "asserted that most rape cases were either concocted for blackmail or to deny consensual sex," (2010a, 114). That is, Indians have also been deeply involved in proliferating such ideologies of rape.

24. Rape was identified as a human rights violation during the First World Conference on Women in Mexico City in 1975. The most influential of international documents for monitoring gender policy, the Convention on Elimination of all Forms of Discrimination against Women (CEDAW), which was prepared for the mid-decade UN Women's conference in 1980, did not contain an explicit statement against violence (Edwards 2010, 94). However, CEDAW clauses on antidiscrimination and equality have routinely been applied to demand accountability for gendered violence.

25. To the consternation of some feminists, the eventual Criminal Law Act (2 April 2013) is not gender neutral, does not include marital rape (other than for married couples who are separated), and defines consent through problematic associations with marriage, knowledge, and ability.

26. Raji Rajagopalan, "Incest, Sexual Abuse of Children," *Herizons* 18, no. 2 (2004): 13.

27. Utkarsh Anand, "Of 1 Lakh Pending Cases in '12, Only 14 Pc Disposed Of," *Indian Express*, 26 August 2013, 2.

28. "Report Confirms Marine Drive Rape," *Times of India*, 17 June 2005.

29. Vasudev and Renuka, "Sexual Crimes: Rape!"

30. Both these accounts appear in "The Rapes Will Go On," *Tehelka Magazine*, 14 April 2012, www.tehelka.com/story_main52.asp?filename = Ne140412Coverstory .asp.

31. Sewell Chan, "'Gray Rape': A New Form of Date Rape?" *New York Times*, 15 October 2007, http://cityroom.blogs.nytimes.com/2007/10/15/gray-rape-a-new-form-of-date-rape/.

32. Himanshi Dhawan, "'Pink Chaddi' Campaign a Hit, Draws Over 34,000 Members," *Times of India*, 14 February 2009, http://articles.timesofindia.indiatimes.com /2009–02–14/india/28037274_1_pink-chaddi-pink-chaddi-campaign-sri-ram-sene.

33. "'This Is Justice,' Say His Victims," *Global News Wire—Indian Express*, 16 August 2004; "The Day of the Furies," *The Telegraph* (Kolkata), 22 August 2004.

34. "The Day of the Furies."

35. Ketan Mehta's 1987 film *Mirch Masala* (*Spices* in English version) ends with a scene where the lustful government official is brought down by chili powder, flung by the women workers of a chili powder factory (notably, they are brought from their former indifference to action by the inspiration of the male protagonist).

36. A registered marriage typically requires a month's advance notice. Bigamy constitutes a ground for divorce under the Hindu Marriage Act, and also a criminal offense by a man against a married woman's husband (S494 IPC). While only legal wives had property/maintenance claims, recent Supreme Court decisions grant some maintenance rights to cohabitees.

37. "When Rape Becomes a Reason for Marriage," *Times of India*, 29 August 2013, 2

38. "Sentence Cut as Rapist Marries Victim," *Times of India*, 22 January 2002.

39. "Man Acquitted in Kidnap, Rape Case," *The Hindu*, 17 June 2005.

40. "Rape-Accused Marries Victim in Orissa," *Indo-Asian News Service*, 28 July 2006.

41. In cases where rape sentences were reduced on exculpatory grounds that invoked *mens rea* or motivation of the defendants, there is a distinctive inversion of the common trial procedure of weighing the raped woman's state of mind in High Court decisions, with women's perceptions (including consent) being almost entirely wiped out (*State of M.P. vs. Balu*, 2005 11 Supreme Court Cases 108; *State of M.P. vs. Babu Barkare*, 2005 5 SCC 413; and *State of M.P. vs. Rameswar*, 2005 2 Supreme Court Cases 373). Several of these exculpations described the accused as "an illiterate laborer from a rural area," connoting rape as an urban phenomenon caused by confusion over sexuality and public space.

42. "I Will Not Marry Him! Hang Him: Rape Victim," *Indo-Asian News Service*, 4 May 2005; "News," *Off Our Backs* 35, nos. 5–6 (2005): 6–7.

43. Morocco's 2004 Mudawana code is touted as providing a model for gender-equitable rights for Muslim women, but issues of marriage choice remain unreformed.

44. "Moroccans Call for End to Rape-Marriage Laws," *BBC News Africa*, 17 March 2012, www.bbc.co.uk/news/world-africa-17416426; "Morocco Mulls Tougher Line on Rape-Marriages," *Al-Jazeera Online*, 17 March 2012, www.aljazeera.com/news/africa/2012/03/201231513432547/1675.html.

45. "Freed Afghan Rape Victim Gulnaz 'May Marry' Attacker," *BBC News Asia*, 15 December 2011, http://www.bbc.co.uk/news/world-asia-16201956; Lawrence Quil, "For Afghan Women, Rape Law Offers Little Protection," *NPR*, 2 December 2011, http://www.npr.org/2011/12/02/143057341/for-afghan-women-rape-law-offers-little-protection.

46. *Vishnu vs. State of Maharashtra* (2006 1 Supreme Court Cases 283: 292).

47. *Uday vs. State of Karnataka* (2003 4 Supreme Court Cases 46), 48.

48. *Economic Times*, 13 July 2003.

49. "Transporter's Fiancée Fears Threat to Life," *Times of India*, 28 September 2005.

50. "Sex on a Promise 'Equal to Rape,'" *Dominion Post*, 25 August 2003, 2.

51. *Bodhisattwa Gautam vs. Subhra Chakraborty* (1996 1 Supreme Court Cases 490).

52. *Deelip Singh vs. State of Bihar* (2005 1 Supreme Court Cases 88: 90).

53. Utkarsh Anand, "Failing to Marry not a Crime," *Indian Express* Law, 21 May 2013, 8.

54. "Rape Count Up on False Cases: Court Concerned for Falsely Implicated Men," *Times of India*, 28 July 2013, 2; Harish V. Nair, "HC Concerned about Misuse of Rape Laws," *Hindustan Times* (New Delhi), 27 May 2013, 5.

55. Neeraj Mishra, "Knot Right," *India Today*, 24 October 2005, 26.

56. "Consensual Sex with Minor not Crime: Court," *Times of India*, 26 August 2013, 1, 5.

57. *Lalta Prasad vs. State of M.P.*, 1979 4 Supreme Court Cases 193.

58. Siddiqi found the language of Bangladeshi police First Information Reports to be ambivalent (2010). It was impossible to determine whether families deliberately used

kidnapping law to block marriage choices, whether women declared that they were in a consensual relationship under coercive pressure from men with powerful connections, or whether an abduction-rape had turned into a consensual relationship.

59. In post-partition India and Pakistan, the murder of abducted women by their families to prevent their polluting the (healthy) family body may be described as "social death" (Das 2007, 79).

60. Flavia Agnes, "Consent, Age and Agency: Reflections on the Recent Delhi High Court Judgement on Minors and Marriage," *Kafila*, 12 June 2012, http://kafila.org/2012/06/12/consent-age-and-agency-reflections-on-the-recent-delhi-high-court-judgement-on-minors-and-marriage-flavia-agnes/.

61. Kiesiläinen posits these categories in the context of Nordic history in the Middle Ages and the early modern period.

62. Stevens's and Brown's conceptions of marriage depict conjugality (the couple) and kinship (family) as co-constructed and mutually beneficial. But as discussed in chapter 5, historians of South Asia have deemed the separation of conjugality and kinship to be a critical axis of emergent modernities.

63. "Fast Track Justice," *Times of India*, 6 May 2005, 18.

64. "Bihar Court Hands Out Rape Verdict in 5 Hours," *Times of India*, 20 October 2006, 12.

65. Monobina Gupta, "Rape Relief within Weeks," *The Telegraph* (Kolkata), 24 October 2005, 1.

66. "Rape Victim's Words Gospel Truth," *Times of India*, 17 May 2006, 11. Menon, "Sexual Violence," 130, lays out some problematic ways in which lack of corroboration is validated only in certain performances of femininity allied with chastity. The Supreme Court deemed in 2013 that while victim testimony "commands great respect and accept-ability," mere corroboration would not suffice if there is "any 'doubt in the mind of the court." R. Balaji, "Top Court Rider on Rape 'Victim' Version," *The Telegraph* (Kolkata), 20 September 2013, 4.

67. "SC Tells Courts not to Take Rape Cases Lightly," *Hindustan Times*, 4 October 2006, 6.

68. See also Littleton (1993) for a similar argument on equality; in contrast, MacKinnon (1988) portrays law as constitutive of the patriarchal norms (of sexuality), meaning equality is impossible.

69. Sunaina Kumar, "The Biggest Change Is That No-One Is Calling Her a Zinda Laash: Flavia Agnes," *Tehelka Magazine*, 26 August 2013, www.tehelka.com/the-big-gest-change-is-that-nobody-is-calling-her-a-zinda-laash-flavia-agnes/.

CHAPTER 7

1. Criminal Law Second Amendment Bill (1983), *Indian Lok Sabha*, 426.

2. "Dowry deaths," are most usefully analyzed as structurally similar to other domestic violence fatalities, in which demands for cash and goods serve as one justifica-tion for violence (Narayan 1997).

3. The S498A offense is "cognizable" (police may arrest without a warrant) and "non-bailable" (getting bail is not the right of the accused, and bail may only be obtained later from a court and not from the police).

4. S498A cases are recorded as 3.8 percent of total crimes under the Indian Penal Code, with a chargesheeting rate of 93.9 percent and a conviction rate of 20.9 percent. Note that the chargesheeting rate reflects cases that were finally admitted under S498A—that is, cases that could not be negotiated away in another form—and that the conviction rate recorded here is considerably higher than that reported by other researchers.

5. Arrested women are, however, rarely found guilty (Gangoli and Rew 2011, 426).

6. Some of the lowest reported numbers are in the highest educational levels and the top wealth quintile, but whether this is because education or economic resources provide some relief from violence or because reporting such violence has a higher social cost in class respectability is impossible to tell. About one in five women in these groups report violence nonetheless.

7. "A Women-Friendly Divorce Law?" *NDTV*, 18 July 2013, www.ndtv.com/video/player/the-buck-stops-here/a-women-friendly-divorce-law/283562?hp.

8. Shobha Saxena, *Times of India*, 6 January 2008, 12.

9. Praveen Kumar, "Mujhe biwi se bachao," *MidDay News*, 27 October 2007.

10. Maitreyi Chatterji, interview, September 3 2001.

11. Vinod Shukla, "The Bitter Half?" *Sahara Time*, 19 July 2008, 28–31; "HC Gives Guidelines on Section 498A," *Times of India* (Hyderabad), 22 January 2014, http://timesofindia.indiatimes.com/city/hyderabad/HC-gives-guidelines-on-Section-498A/articleshow/29173500.cms.

12. See Lodhia (2009, 114) for a detailed analysis of the statistics.

13. I draw here on my 2013–14 fieldwork involving participant observation and interviews with men's rights activists.

14. The presumed third "mistake" is that they were engaged in a child custody dispute.

15. For a roster of informal options in Mumbai, see Dave and Solanki (2001, 24–25).

16. The PWDVA or Protection of Women from Domestic Violence Act (2005), offering a civil remedy in place of S498A's criminal scope, has been deemed by some women's movement organizations to be "path-breaking." It extends beyond married couples to families, and covers marital rape as well as sexual and emotional violence. Aarti Dhar, "Torment within Four Walls," *The Hindu*, 29 January 2013, www.thehindu.com/news/cities/Delhi/torment-within-four-walls/article4354004.ece. While my fieldwork did not encompass a study of PWDVA claims, other research indicates that it is often met with similar outrage ("Feminist Media: Presenting the Agenda of the Indian Radical Feminists," http://feministmedia.wordpress.com/2007/10/30/anniversary-of-the-abomination-called-pwdva-2005/, an antifeminist website).

17. The addition of dowry charges often weakens domestic violence cases (Lodhia 2009, 111).

18. Though this would amount to about four years' income at Rs. 2,500 per month, it sounds like a lot for a middle-class person to have in raw savings. The suddenness of

the claim also indicated that it may have been a symbolically high number presented in order to negotiate.

19. Provident Funds are savings and pension schemes contributed to by both employer and employee, which can be borrowed against or even withdrawn.

20. Rochelle Jones, "All-Women Police Stations—Addressing Domestic Violence in India," *Association for Women in Development Resource Net*, 7 July 2006, www.wunrn.com/news/2006/07_31_06/080206_india_all.htm.

21. Sandeep Joshi, "States Not Keen on Women Police Stations," *The Hindu*, 24 December 2012, www.thehindu.com/news/national/states-not-keen-on-women-police-stations/article4232696.ece.

22. The move was ultimately turned down by the legislature. Among various protests about the scope and nature of authority of these units, there was a prominent concern among those not affiliated with the ruling party that the units might be overly influenced by the political connections and interests of litigants. Talwar and Shramajibee Mahila Samity (2002, 8) affirm the profound influence of political alliances in *shalishi* cases.

23. In the other settings, while an occasional family member was called to mediation sessions, the focus was on talking to the couple individually and then jointly.

24. Nagaraj (2010, 437–38) similarly describes the use of threats to deploy criminal law.

25. Talwar and Shramajibee Mahila Samity also report that activists found that fear of legal action could be used to negotiate modifications in behavior (2002, 27).

26. Ray describes it as an umbrella entity forged to counter the dominance of party-affiliated women's organizations (1999, 95, 101).

CHAPTER 8

1. Neha Bhatt, "Hear That She-Bang?" *Outlook* 53, no. 49 (December 2013): 50–61.

REFERENCES

Abu-Lughod, L. (1990). "The Romance of Resistance: Tracing Transformations of Power through Bedouin Women." *American Ethnologist* 17 (1): 41–55.

———. (2009). "Shifting Politics in Bedouin Love Poetry." In *Poetry and Cultural Studies: A Reader*, edited by M. Damon and I. Livingston, 116–32. Urbana: University of Illinois Press.

Adelman, M. (2004). "The Battering State: Towards a Political Economy of Domestic Violence." *Journal of Poverty* 8 (3): 45–64.

Agarwal, B. (1994). *A Field of One's Own : Gender and Land Rights in South Asia*. New York: Cambridge University Press.

Agnes, F. (1999). *Law and Gender Inequality: The Politics of Women's Rights in India*. New Delhi: Oxford University Press.

———. (2004a). *A Study of Family Courts Karnataka*. Bengaluru: Karnataka State Women's Commission.

———. (2004b). *A Study of Family Courts, West Bengal*. Kolkata: West Bengal Women's Commission.

———. (2005). "Law and Gender Inequality: The Politics of Women's Rights in India." In *Writing the Women's Movement: A Reader*, edited by M. Khullar, 113–30. New Delhi: Zubaan.

———. (2011). *Family Law: Marriage, Divorce and Matrimonial Litigation*. New Delhi: Oxford University Press.

———. (2012). "From *Shah Bano* to *Kausar Bano*: Contextualizing the Muslim Woman within a Communalized Polity." In *South Asian Feminisms*, edited by R. Lukose and A. Loomba, 33–53. Durham, NC: Duke University Press.

Ahmed, S. (2004). *The Cultural Politics of Emotion*. New York: Routledge.

Alcalde, C. (2010). *The Woman in the Violence: Gender, Poverty, and Resistance in Peru*. Nashville, TN: Vanderbilt University Press.

Arondekar, A. (2009). *For the Record: On Sexuality and the Colonial Archive in India.* Durham, NC: Duke University Press.

Arunima, G. (2003). *There Comes Papa: Colonialism and the Transformation of Matriliny in Kerala, Malabar, c. 1850–1940.* New Delhi: Orient Longman.

Auerbach, J. S. (1983). *Justice without Law?* New York: Oxford University Press.

Bagchi, J. (2005). "Introduction." In *The Changing Status of Women in West Bengal, 1970–2000: The Challenge Ahead,* edited by J. Bagchi, 14–15. New Delhi: Sage.

Banerjee, N., and M. Mukherjee (2005). "Demography." In *The Changing Status of Women in West Bengal, 1970–2000: The Challenge Ahead,* edited by J. Bagchi, 21–33. New Delhi: Sage.

Barrett, M., and M. McIntosh (1982). *The Anti-Social Family.* London: Verso.

Basu, A., and N. Bhatt (2010). "Justice by Death: The Self-Styled Custodians of Honour Are Out to Set Their Sisters Right." *Outlook* (New Delhi), 12 July, 56–57.

Basu, M. (2001). *Hindu Women and Marriage Law : From Sacrament to Contract.* New Delhi: Oxford University Press.

Basu, S. (1999). *She Comes to Take Her Rights: Indian Women, Property and Propriety.* Albany: State University of New York Press.

———. (2003). "Shading the Secular: Law at Work in the Indian Higher Courts." *Cultural Dynamics* 15 (2): 131–52.

———, ed. (2005). *Dowry and Inheritance.* Issues in Indian Feminism. New Delhi: Women Unlimited.

———. (2008). "Separate and Unequal: Muslim Women and Un-Uniform Family Law in India." *International Feminist Journal of Politics* 10 (4): 495–517.

Baxi, P. (2000). "Rape, Retribution, State: On Whose Bodies?" *Economic and Political Weekly* 35 (14): 1196–1200.

———. (2005). "The Medicalisation of Consent and Falsity: The Figure of the *Habitué* in Indian Rape Law." In *The Violence of Normal Times: Essays on Women's Lived Realities,* edited by K. Kannabiran, 266–311. New Delhi: Women Unlimited.

———. (2014). *Public Secrets of Law: Rape Trials in India.* New Delhi: Oxford University Press.

Baxi, U. (1986). *Towards a Sociology of Indian Law.* New Delhi: Satyavahan.

Bebelaar, K., S. Caplow, et al. (2003). "Domestic Violence in Legal Education and Legal Practice: A Dialogue between Professors and Practitioners." *Journal of Law and Policy* 11 (2): 409–93.

Behar, R. (1993). *Translated Woman: Crossing the Border with Esparanza's Story.* Boston: Beacon Press.

Benjamin, W. (2000 [1923]). "The Task of the Translator." *The Translation Studies Reader,* edited by L. Venuti, 15–25. London: Routledge.

Berk-Seligson, S. (2002). *The Bilingual Courtroom: Court Interpreters in the Judicial Process.* Chicago: University of Chicago Press.

Bernstein, A. (2003). "For and Against Marriage: A Revision." *Michigan Law Review* 102 (2): 129–212.

Bernstein, E., and L. Schaffner (2005). "Regulating Sex: An Introduction." In *Regulating Sex: The Politics of Intimacy and Identity*, edited by E. Bernstein and L. Schaffner, xi–xxiii. New York: Routledge.

Berti, D. (2010). "Hostile Witnesses, Judicial Interactions and Out-of-Court Narratives in a North Indian District Court." *Contributions to Indian Sociology*, n.s., 44 (3): 1–21.

———. (2014). "Binding Fictions: Contradictory Facts and Judicial Constraints in a Narcotics Case." In *Anthropology of Criminal Cases in South Asia*, edited by D. Berti and D. Bordia. New Delhi: Oxford University Press.

Betzig, L. (1989). "Causes of Conjugal Dissolution: A Cross-Cultural Study." *Current Anthropology* 30 (5): 654–76.

Bhattacharya, H. (2009). "Performing Silence, Gender, Violence and Resistance in Women's Narratives from Lahaul, India." *Qualitative Inquiry* 15 (2): 359–71.

Blomley, N. (1989). "Text and Context: Rethinking the Law-Space Nexus." *Progress in Human Geography* 13 (4): 512–34.

Blomley, N., D. Delaney, et al. (2001). *The Legal Geographies Reader: Law, Power and Space*. London: Wiley-Blackwell.

Bloom, D. E., and N. G. Bennett (1990). "Modeling American Marriage Patterns." *Journal of the American Statistical Association* 85 (412): 1009–17.

Boddy, J. (1994). "Spirit Possession Revisited: Beyond Instrumentality." *Annual Review of Anthropology* 23: 407–34.

Bohannan, P. J. (1957). *Justice and Judgment among the Tiv*. London: Oxford University Press for the International African Institute.

Borneman, J. (1996). "Until Death Us Do Part: Marriage/Death in Anthropological Discourse." *American Ethnologist* 23 (2): 215–35.

Bose, S., and A. Jalal (1998). *Nationalism, Democracy and Development: State and Politics in India*. New York: Oxford University Press.

Bossen, L. (1988). "Toward a Theory of Marriage: The Economic Anthropology of Marriage Transactions." *Ethnology* 27 (2): 127–44.

Brass, P. R. (1994). *The Politics of India since Independence*. Cambridge: Cambridge University Press.

Brook, H. (2000). "How to Do Things with Sex." In *Law and Sexuality: The Global Arena*, edited by C. Stychin and D. Herman, 132–50. Minneapolis: University of Minnesota Press.

Brown, W. (1992). "Finding the Man in the State." *Feminist Studies* 18 (1): 7–34.

Buchhofer, B., and K. A. Ziegert (1981). "Family Dynamics and Legal Change: Empirical Sociology in Search of a General Theory on the Effects of Law on Family Life." *Journal of Comparative Family Studies* 12 (4): 397–412.

Buddin, T. (1978). "Counselors, Lawyers and Custody Disputes in the Family Courts." *Australian Journal of Social Issues* 13 (3): 216–31.

Bumiller, K. (1987). "Victims in the Shadow of the Law: A Critique of the Model of Legal Protection." *Signs* 12 (3): 421–39.

———. (2008). *In an Abusive State: How Neoliberalism Appropriated the Feminist Movement against Sexual Violence*. Durham, NC: Duke University Press.

Burman, M. (2010). "Rethinking Rape Law in Sweden: Coercion, Consent or Non-Voluntariness?" *Rethinking Rape Law: International and Comparative Perspectives*, edited by C. McGlynn and V. E. Munro, 196–208. Oxford: Routledge-Cavendish.

Butler, J. (1993). *Bodies That Matter: On the Discursive Limits of "Sex."* New York: Routledge.

Cahill, A. J. (2001). *Rethinking Rape*. Ithaca, NY: Cornell University Press.

Calavita, K. (2001). "Blue Jeans, Rape and the 'Deconstitutive' Power of Law." *Law & Society Review* 35 (1): 89–116.

Camerini, M., R. Gill, et al. (1988). *Dadi's Family*. Boston: PBS Video.

Centre for Social Research (2005). *Stop Violence against Women: From Womb to Tomb*. Annual Report. New Delhi: Centre for Social Research.

Chakrabarty, B. (2011). "The Left Front's 2009 Poll Debacle in West Bengal, India." *Asian Survey* 51 (2): 290–310.

Chambers, C. (2005). "Masculine Domination, Radical Feminism and Change." *Feminist Theory* 6 (3): 325–46.

Chatterjee, I. (2004). *Unfamiliar Relations: Family and History in South Asia*. New Brunswick, NJ: Rutgers University Press.

Chaudhuri, M. (2004). *Feminism in India*. New Delhi: Women Unlimited.

Chaudhuri, S. (1990). *Calcutta: The Living City*. 2 vols. Calcutta: Oxford University Press.

Chowdhry, P. (1994). *The Veiled Women: Shifting Gender Equations in Rural Haryana, 1880–1990*. Delhi: Oxford University Press.

———. (2007). *Contentious Marriages, Eloping Couples : Gender, Caste, and Patriarchy in Northern India*. New Delhi: Oxford University Press.

Chowdhury, E. H. (2005). "Feminist Negotiations: Contesting Narratives of the Campaign against Acid Violence in Bangladesh." *Meridians: Feminism, Race, Transnationalism* 6 (1): 163–92.

Cohen, L. (1998). *No Aging in India: Alzheimer's, the Bad Family and Other Modern Things*. Berkeley: University of California Press.

Cole, J., and L. Thomas, eds. (2009). *Love in Africa*. Chicago: University of Chicago Press.

Comaroff, J. L., and S. Roberts (1981). *Rules and Processes: The Cultural Logic of Dispute in an African Context*. Chicago: University of Chicago Press.

Conley, J. M., and W. M. O'Barr (1990). *Rules vs. Relationships: The Ethnography of Legal Discourse*. Chicago: University of Chicago Press.

Coomaraswamy, R. (2005). *The Varied Contours of Violence against Women in South Asia*. Report Prepared for the Fifth South Asia Regional Ministerial Conference Celebrating Beijing Plus Ten, Jointly Organized by Government of Pakistan and UNIFEM South Asia Regional Office.

Cornwall, A., and M. Molyneux (2006). "The Politics of Rights—Dilemmas for Feminist Praxis: An Introduction." *Third World Quarterly* 27 (7): 1175–91.

Coutin, S. (2002). "Reconceptualizing Research: Ethnographic Fieldwork and Immigration Politics in Southern California." In *Practicing Ethnography in Law: New*

Dialogues, Enduring Methods, edited by J. Starr and M. Goodale, 108–27. New York: Palgrave.

Cowan, S. (2007). "'Freedom and Capacity to Make a Choice': A Feminist Analysis of Consent in the Criminal Law of Rape." *Sexuality and the Law: Feminist Engagements*, edited by V. E. Munro and C. F. Stychin, 51–71. Oxford: Routledge-Cavendish.

Crenshaw, K. (1996). "Mapping the Margins: Intersectionality, Identity Politics, and Violence against Women of Color." In *Applications of Feminist Legal Theory to Women's Lives*, edited by D. K. Weisberg, 363–77. Philadelphia: Temple University Press.

CSWI (1974). *Towards Equality: Report of Committee on the Status of Women in India*. New Delhi.

Cunningham, C. D. (1991–92). "The Lawyer as Translator, Representation as Text: Towards an Ethnography of Legal Discourse." *Cornell Law Review* 77: 1298–1387.

Daly, K., and J. Stubbs (2006). "Feminist Engagement with Restorative Justice." *Theretical Criminology* 10 (1): 9–28.

Das, V. (1996). "Sexual Violence, Discursive Formations and the State." *Economic and Political Weekly* 31 (35–37): 2411–23.

———. (2007). *Life and Words: Violence and the Descent into the Ordinary*. Berkeley: University of California Press.

Dave, A., and G. Solanki (2001). *Journey from Violence to Crime: A Study of Domestic Violence in the City of Mumbai*. Mumbai: Department of Family and Child Welfare, Tata Institute of Social Sciences.

Demian, M. (2003). "Custom in the Courtroom, Law in the Village: Legal Transformations in Papua New Guinea." *Journal of Royal Anthropological Institute*, n.s., 9: 97–115.

Dempsey, M. M. (2007). "Toward a Feminist State: What Does 'Effective' Prosecution of Domestic Violence Mean?" *Modern Law Review* 70 (6): 908–35.

Derrida, J. (1992). "Force of Law." In *Deconstruction and the Possibility of Justice*, edited by D. Cornell, M. Rosenfeld, and D. G. Carlson, 3–67. New York: Routledge.

Deshpande, S. (2004). *Contemporary India: A Sociological View*. New Delhi: Penguin.

de Sousa Santos, B. (2006). "The Heterogeneous State and Legal Pluralism in Mozambique." *Law & Society Review* 40 (1): 39–75.

Dhanda, A. (1995). "Insanity, Gender and the Law." *Contributions to Indian Sociology*, n.s., 29 (1–2): 347–67.

Dingwall, R., and J. Eekelaar (1988). *Divorce Mediation and the Legal Process*. Oxford: Clarendon Press.

Donzelot, J. (1997). *The Policing of Families*. Translated by R. Hurley. Baltimore, MD: Johns Hopkins University Press.

Dutta, K. (2003). *Calcutta: A Cultural and Literary History*. Oxford: Signal Books.

Eaton, M. (1986). *Justice for Women? Family, Court and Social Control*. Milton Keynes: Open University Press.

Edwards, A. (2010). "Everyday Rape: International Human Rights Law and Violence against Women in Peacetime." *Rethinking Rape Law: International and Comparative Perspectives*, edited by C. McGlynn and V. E. Munro, 92–108. Oxford: Routledge-Cavendish.

Edwards, P. E. (1997). "Gender Issues in Family Law: A Feminist Perspective." *Family and Conciliation Courts Review* 35 (4): 424–42.

Ehrlich, S. (2011). "Bounded Bodies and the Concept of Post-Penetration Rape." Paper presented at the American Anthropological Association Conference, Montreal, Canada.

Engel, D. M. (1980). "Legal Pluralism in an American Community: Perspectives on a Civil Trial Court." *American Bar Foundation Research Journal* 5 (3): 425–54.

Fineman, M. A. (1991). "Societal Factors Affecting the Creation of Legal Rules for Distribution of Property at Divorce." In *At the Boundaries of Law: Feminism and Legal Theory*, edited by M. A. Fineman and N. S. Thomadsen, 265–79. New York: Routledge.

Fisk, O. (1984). "Against Settlement." *Yale Law Journal* 93 (6): 1073–90.

Foucault, M. (1978). *The History of Sexuality*. Vol. 1. New York: Random House.

———. (1991). "Governmentality." In *The Foucault Effect: Studies in Governmentality*, edited by G. Burchell, C. Gordon, and P. Miller, 87–104. Chicago: University of Chicago Press.

Freed, S. A., and R. S. Freed (1964). "Spirit Possession as Illness in a North Indian Village." *Ethnology* 3 (2): 152–71.

Friedman, L. M. (2002). "A Few Thoughts on Ethnography, History and Law." In *Practicing Ethnography in Law: New Dialogues, Enduring Methods*, edited by J. Starr and M. Goodale, 185–89. New York: Palgrave.

Galanter, M. (1972). "The Aborted Restoration of 'Indigenous' Law in India." *Comparative Studies in Society and History* 14: 53–70.

Galanter, M., and J. Krishnan (2003). "Debased Informalism: Lok Adalats and Legal Rights in Modern India." In *Beyond Common Knowledge: Empirical Approaches to the Study of Law*, edited by E. G. Jensen and T. C. Heller, 96–141. Stanford, CA: Stanford University Press.

Gangoli, G. (2007). *Indian Feminisms: Law, Patriarchies and Violence in India*. Hampshire: Ashgate.

Gangoli, G., and M. Rew (2011). "Mothers-in-Law against Daughters-in-Law: Domestic Violence and Legal Discourses around Mother-in-Law Violence against Daughters-in-Law in India." *Women's Studies International Forum* 34: 420–29.

Geertz, C. (1983). "Local Knowledge: Fact and Law in Comparative Perspective." In *Local Knowledge: Further Essays in Interpretive Anthropology*, 167–233. New York: Basic Books.

Giddens, A. (1993). *The Transformation of Intimacy: Sexuality, Love, and Eroticism in Modern Societies*. Stanford, CA: Stanford University Press.

Glendon, M. A. (1980). "Modern Marriage Law and Its Underlying Assumptions: The New Marriage and the New Property." *Family Law Quarterly* 13 (4): 441–60.

Gluckman, M. (1955). *The Judicial Process among the Barotse of Northern Rhodesia*. Manchester: Manchester University Press.

Goldberg, S. B., F. E. A. Sander, et al. (1999). *Dispute Resolution: Negotiation, Mediation and Other Processes*. Gaithersburg, NY: Aspen Law & Business.

Goode, W. J. (1993). *World Changes in Divorce Patterns*. New Haven, CT: Yale University Press.

Gopal, S. (2012). *Conjugations: Marriage and Form in New Bollywood Cinema*. Chicago: University of Chicago Press.

Gopalan, S. (2001). *Towards Equality—the Unfinished Agenda—Status of Women in India 2001*. New Delhi: National Commission for Women.

Gough, E. K. (1994). "Brahman Kinship in a Tamil Village." In *Family, Kinship and Marriage in India*, edited by P. Uberoi, 146–75. Delhi: Oxford University Press.

Greenhouse, C. J., B. Yngvesson, et al. (1994). *Law and Community in Three American Towns*. Ithaca, NY: Cornell University Press.

Griffiths, A. M. O. (1997). *In the Shadow of Marriage: Gender and Justice in an African Community*. Chicago: University of Chicago Press.

Griffiths, J. (1986). "What Is Legal Pluralism?" *Journal of Legal Pluralism and Unofficial Law* 24: 38.

Grillo, T. (1990–91). "The Mediation Alternative: Process Dangers for Women." *Yale Law Journal* 100: 1545–1610.

Grover, S. (2010). *Marriage, Love, Caste and Kinship Support: Lived Experiences of the Urban Poor in India*. New Delhi: Social Science Press.

Guha, R. (2007). *India after Gandhi: The History of the World's Largest Democracy*. New York: Harper Collins.

Gupta, A. (2012). *Red Tape: Bureaucracy, Structural Violence and Poverty in India*. Hyderabad: Orient Blackswan.

Hale, S. (2002). "How Faithfully Do Court Interpreters Render the Style of Non-English Speaking Witness' Testimonies? A Data Based Study of Spanish-English Bilingual Proceedings." *Discourse Studies* 4 (1): 25–47.

Hall, S. (1993). "Encoding, Decoding." In *The Cultural Studies Reader*, edited by S. During. London: Routledge.

Halley, J., P. Kotiswaran, et al. (2006). "From the International to the Local in Feminist Legal Responses to Rape, Prostitution/Sex Work, and Sex Trafficking: Four Studies in Contemporary Governance Feminism." *Harvard Journal of Law & Gender* 29 (2): 335–423.

Hansen, T. B., and F. Stepputat, eds. (2001). *States of Imagination: Ethnographic Explorations of the Postcolonial State*. Durham, NC: Duke University Press.

Hasan, K. M. (2001). "A Report on Mediation in the Family Courts: Bangladesh Experience."Presented at the 25th Anniversary Conference of the Family Courts of Australia, Sydney, 26–29 July, http://siteresources.worldbank.org/INTLAWJUSTINST/Resources/JusticeHasan.pdf.

Hasan, Z., and R. Menon (2004). *Unequal Citizens: A Study of Muslim Women in India*. New Delhi: Oxford University Press.

Hautzinger, S. (1997). "Calling a State a State: Feminist Politics and the Policing of Violence against Women in Brazil." *Feminist Issues* 1–2: 3–30.

———. (2007). *Violence in the City of Women: Police and Batterers in Bahia, Brazil*. Berkeley: University of California Press.

Helliwell, C. (2000). "'It's Only a Penis': Rape, Feminism and Difference." *Signs* 25 (3): 789–816.

Hirsch, S. F. (1998). *Pronouncing and Persevering: Gender and the Discourses of Disputing in an African Islamic Court.* Chicago: University of Chicago Press.

———. (2002). "The Power of Participation: Language and Gender in Tanzanian Law Reform Campaigns." *Africa Today* 49 (2): 51–75.

Holden, L. (2008). *Hindu Divorce: A Legal Anthropology.* Aldershot: Ashgate.

Hossain, S., and L. Welchman (2005). *"Honour": Crimes, Paradigms and Violence against Women.* London: Zed Books.

Hsiung, P.-C. (1996). "Between Bosses and Workers: The Dilemma of a Keen Observer and a Vocal Feminist." In *Feminist Dilemmas in Fieldwork,* edited by D. L. Wolf, 122–37. Boulder, CO: Westview.

Ingram, S. (1997). "'The Task of the Translator': Walter Benjamin's Essay in English, a Forschungsbericht." *TTR: Traduction, Terminologie, Rédaction* 10 (2): 207–33.

International Institute for Population Sciences and Macro International (2007). *National Family Health Survey (NFHS-3), 2005–06: Vol. 1, India.* Mumbai: International Institute for Population Sciences.

Jacob, H. (1992). "The Elusive Shadow of the Law." *Law & Society Review* 26 (3): 565–90.

Jain, P. (2005). "Balancing Minority Rights and Gender Justice: The Impact of Protecting Multiculturalism on Women's Rights in India." *Berkeley Journal of International Law* 23: 201–22.

Johnson, J. E. (2009). *Gender Violence in Russia: The Politics of Feminist Intervention.* Bloomington: Indiana University Press.

Jones, R. (1974). *Urban Politics in India: Area, Power and Policy in a Penetrated System.* Berkeley: University of California Press.

Just, P. (2000). *Dou Donggo Justice: Conflict and Morality in an Indonesian Society.* Oxford: Rowman and Littlefield.

Kannabiran, K., and V. Kannabiran (2002). *De-eroticizing Assault: Essays on Modesty, Honour and Power.* New Delhi: Women Unlimited.

Kannabiran, K., and R. Menon (2007). *From Mathura to Manorama: Resisting Violence against Women in India.* New Delhi: Women Unlimited.

Kapur, R., and B. Cossman (1996). *Subversive Sites: Feminist Engagements with Law in India.* New Delhi: Sage.

Katzenstein, M. F. (1989). "Organizing against Violence: Strategies of the Indian Women's Movement." *Pacific Affairs* 62 (1): 53–71.

Kaviraj, S. (2003). "A State of Contradictions: The Post-Colonial State in India." In *States and Citizens: History, Theory, Prospects,* edited by Q. Skinner and B. Strath, 145–60. Cambridge: Cambridge University Press.

Kay, H. H. (1987). "Equality and Difference: A Perspective on No-Fault Divorce and Its Aftermath." *University of Cincinnati Law Review* 56 (1): 1–90.

Keefe, T. (2007). "Marriage in the Later Fiction of Camus and Simone de Beauvoir." *Orbis Litterarum* 33 (1): 69–86.

Kelly, L. (2005). "Inside Outsiders: Mainstreaming Violence against Women into Human Rights Discourse and Practice." *International Feminist Journal of Politics* 7 (4): 471–95.

———. (2010). "The Everyday/Everynightness of Rape: Is It Different in War?" In *Gender, War and Militarism: Feminist Perspectives*, edited by L. Sjoberg and S. Via, 114–23. Santa Barbara, CA: Praeger.

Khullar, M. (2005). *Writing the Women's Movement: A Reader*. New Delhi: Zubaan.

Kidder, R. L. (2002). "Exploring Legal Culture in Law Avoidance Societies." In *Practicing Ethnography in Law: New Dialogues, Enduring Methods*, edited by J. Starr and M. Goodale, 87–107. New York: Palgrave.

Kiesiläinen, N. (2004). "The Reform of Sex Crime Law and the Gender Neutral Subject." In *Nordic Equality at a Crossroads: Feminist Legal Studies Coping with Difference*, edited by E.-M. Svensson, A. Pylkkänen, and J. Niemi-Kiesiläinen, 167–94. Burlington, VT: Ashgate.

Koivunen, A. (2010). "An Affective Turn? Reimagining the Subject of Feminist Theory." In *Working with Affect in Feminist Readings: Disturbing Differences*, edited by M. Liljestroem and S. Paasonen: 8–28. Oxford: Routledge.

Kolenda, P. (1984). "Woman as Tribute, Woman as Flower: Images of 'Woman' in Weddings in North and South India." *American Ethnologist* 11 (1): 98–117.

Kolsky, E. (2010a). "'The Body Evidencing the Crime': Rape on Trial in Colonial India, 1860–1947." *Gender & History* 22 (1): 109–30.

———. (2010b). "The Rule of Colonial Indifference: Rape on Trial in Early Colonial India, 1805–57." *Journal of Asian Studies* 29 (4): 1093–1117.

Koss, M. P. (2010). "Restorative Justice for Acquaintance Rape and Misdemeanor Sex Crimes." In *Feminism, Restorative Justice, and Violence against Women*, edited by J. Ptacek, 218–38. Thousand Oaks, CA: Sage.

Koss, M. P., and M. Achilles (2008). "Restorative Justice Responses to Sexual Assault." National Online Research Center on Violence against Women, www.vawnet.org/Assoc_Files_VAWnet/AR_RestorativeJustice.pdf.

Kritzer, H. M. (2002). "Stories from the Field: Collecting Data Outside Over There." In *Practicing Ethnography in Law: New Dialogues, Enduring Methods*, edited by J. Starr and M. Goodale, 143–59. New York: Palgrave.

Kumar, R. (1993). *A History of Doing*. New Delhi: Kali for Women.

Kwiatkowski, L. (2011). "Domestic Violence and the 'Happy Family' in Northern Vietnam." *Anthropology Now* 3 (3): 20–28.

Lamb, S. (1997). "The Beggared Mother: Older Women's Narratives in West Bengal." *Oral Tradition* 12 (1): 54–75.

Lawyers Collective (2009). *Ending Domestic Violence through Non-Violence: A Manual for PWDVA Protection Officers*. New Delhi: Lawyers Collective.

Lawyers Collective Women's Rights Initiative and International Center for Research on Women. (2009). *Third Monitoring and Evaluation Report 2009 on the Protection of Women from Domestic Violence Act 2005*. New Delhi: Lawyers Collective.

Lazarus-Black, M. (2007). *Everyday Harm: Domestic Violence, Court Rites, and Cultures of Reconciliation*. Urbana-Champaign: University of Illinois Press.

Lazarus-Black, M., and S. F. Hirsch (1999). "Performance and Paradox: Exploring Law's Role in Hegemony and Resistance." In *Contested States: Law, Hegemony and Resistance*, edited by M. Lazarus-Black and S. F. Hirsch, 1–31. New York: Routledge.

Leys, R. (2011). "The Turn to Affect: A Critique." *Critical Inquiry* 37 (3): 434–72.

Littleton, C. A. (1993). "Reconstructing Sexual Equality." In *Feminist Legal Theory: Foundations*, edited by D. K. Weisberg, 248–63. Philadelphia: Temple University Press.

Llewellyn, K. N., and E. A. Hoebel (1941). *The Cheyenne Way: Conflict and Case Law in Primitive Jurisprudence*. Norman: University of Oklahoma Press.

Lodhia, S. (2009). "Legal Frankensteins and Monstrous Women: Judicial Narratives of the 'Family in Crisis.'" *Meridians* 9 (2): 102–29.

Luo, T.-Y. (2000). "'Marrying My Rapist?!' The Cultural Trauma among Chinese Rape Survivors." *Gender and Society* 14 (4): 581–97.

MacKinnon, C. A. (1988). *Feminism Unmodified: Discourses on Life and Law*. Cambridge, MA: Harvard University Press.

———. (1989). *Toward a Feminist Theory of the State*. Cambridge, MA: Harvard University Press.

Madan, T. N. (1994). "The Hindu Family and Development." In *Family, Kinship and Marriage in India*, edited by P. Uberoi, 416–34. Delhi: Oxford University Press.

Majumdar, R. (2004). "Looking for Brides and Grooms: *Ghataks*, Matrimonials and the Marriage Market in Colonial Calcutta, circa 1875–1940." *Journal of Asian Studies* 63 (4): 911–35.

———. (2007). "Review Essay: Arguments within Indian Feminism." *Social History* 32 (4): 434–45.

Majumder, S. (2010). "The Nano Controversy: Peasant Identities, the Land Question and Neoliberal Industrialization in Marxist West Bengal, India." *Journal of Emerging Knowledge on Emerging Markets* 2 (1): 41–66.

Mani, L. (1990). "Contentious Traditions: The Debate On Sati In Colonial India." In *Recasting Women: Essays In Indian Colonial History*, edited by K. Sangari and S. Vaid, 88–126. New Brunswick, NJ: Rutgers University Press.

Marcus, S. (1992). "Fighting Bodies, Fighting Words: A Theory and Politics of Rape Prevention." In *Feminists Theorize the Political*, edited by J. Butler and J. W. Scott, 385–403. New York: Routledge.

Mardorossian, C. M. (2002). "Toward a New Feminist Theory of Rape." *Signs* 27 (3): 743–75.

Marshall, A.-M., and S. Barclay (2003). "In Their Own Words: How Ordinary People Construct the Legal World." *Law and Social Inquiry* 28 (3): 617–28.

Mathis, R. D., and Z. Tanner (1998). "Effects of Unscreened Spouse Violence on Mediated Agreements." *American Journal of Family Therapy* 26: 251–60.

Mazzarella, W. (2010). "Affect: What Is It Good For?" In *Enchantments of Modernity: Empire, Nation, Globalization*, edited by S. Dube, 291–309. London: Routledge.

McGlynn, C., N. Westmarland, et al. (2012). "'I Just Wanted Him to Hear Me': Sexual Violence and the Possibilities of Restorative Justice." *Journal of Law and Society* 39 (2): 213–40.

McIntyre, L. J. (1995). "Law and the Family in Historical Perspective: Issues and Antecedents." *Marriage and Family Review* 21 (3–4): 5–30.

Mehra, M. (1998). "Exploring the Boundaries of Law, Gender and Social Reform." *Feminist Legal Studies* 6 (1): 59–83.

Menon, N. (2004). *Recovering Subversion: Feminist Politics beyond the Law.* New Delhi: Permanent Black.

———. (2012). *Seeing Like a Feminist.* New Delhi: Zubaan & Penguin

Merry, S. E. (1986). "Everyday Understandings of Law in Working-Class America." *American Ethnologist* 13 (2): 253–70.

———. (1988). " Legal Pluralism." *Law and Society Review* 22 (5): 868–96.

———. (1991). "Law and Colonialism: Review Essay." *Law and Society Review* 25 (4): 889–922.

———. (1993). "Sorting Out Popular Justice." In *The Possibility of Popular Justice: A Case Study of Community Mediation in the United States,* edited by S. E. Merry and N. Milner, 31–66. Ann Arbor: University of Michigan Press.

———. (1999). *Colonizing Hawai'i: The Cultural Power of Law.* Princeton, NJ: Princeton University Press.

———. (2006a). *Human Rights and Gender Violence: Translating International Law into Local Rights.* Chicago: University of Chicago Press.

———. (2006b). "Transnational Human Rights and Local Activism: Mapping the Middle." *American Anthropologist* 108 (1): 38–51.

———. (2009). *Gender Violence: A Cultural Perspective.* Sussex: Wiley-Blackwell.

Merry, S. E., and N. Milner (1993). *The Possibility of Popular Justice: A Case Study of Community Mediation in the United States.* Ann Arbor: University of Michigan Press.

Mills, J. H. (2003). "Body as Target, Violence as Treatment: Psychiatric Regimes in Colonial and Post-colonial India." In *Confronting the Body: The Politics of Physicality in Colonial and and Post-colonial India,* edited by J. H. Mills and S. Sen, 80–101. London: Anthem Press.

Minakimata, S. (1988). "Kaji Chotei: Mediation in the Japanese Family Court." In *Divorce Mediation and the Legal Process,* edited by R. Dingwall and J. Eekelaar, 116–26. Oxford: Clarendon Press.

Minow, M., M. Ryan, et al., eds. (1992). *Narrative, Violence and the Law: The Essays of Robert Cover.* Ann Arbor: University of Michigan Press.

Mirchandani, R. (2005). "What's So Special about Specialized Courts? The State and Social Change in Salt Lake City's Domestic Violence Court." *Law and Society Review* 39: 379–417.

Mir-Hosseini, Z. (1993). *Marriage on Trial: A Study of Islamic Family Law, Iran and Morocco Compared.* London: I. B. Tauris.

Mitra, N. (1999). "Best Practices among Responses to Domestic Violence in Maharashtra and Madhya Pradesh." In *Domestic Violence in India: A Summary Report of Three Studies,* edited by PROWID, 18–27. Washington, DC: International Center for Research on Women.

Mnookin, R. H., and L. Kornhauser (1979). "Bargaining in the Shadow of the Law: The Case of Divorce." *Yale Law Journal* 88: 950–97.

Mody, P. (2006). "Kidnapping, Elopement and Abduction: An Ethnography of Love-Marriage in Delhi." In *Love in South Asia: A Cultural History*, edited by F. Orsini, 331–44. Cambridge: Cambridge University Press.

———. (2008) *The Intimate State: Love-Marriage and the Law in Delhi*. New Delhi: Routledge India.

Molyneux, M. (1985). "Mobilization without Emancipation? Women's Interests, the State and Revolution in Nicaragua." *Feminist Studies* 11 (2): 227–54.

Monsoor, T. (2008). *Gender Equity and Economic Empowerment: Family Law and Women in Bangladesh*. Dhaka: British Council Dhaka.

———. (2009). *Gender Equity: Islamic Family Law and Women (A Research from Malaysia and Bangladesh)*. Dhaka: British Council Dhaka.

Moore, E. P. (1999). "Law's Patriarchy in India." In *Contested States: Law, Hegemony and Resistance*, edited by M. Lazarus-Black and S. F. Hirsch, 88–117. New York: Routledge.

Moore, S. F. (1969). "Law and Anthropology." *Biennial Review of Anthropology* 6: 252–300.

Moorhouse, G. (1974). *Calcutta: The City Revealed*. Harmondsworth: Penguin.

Mulla, S. (2011). "In Mother's Lap: Forging Care and Kinship in Documentary Protocols of Sexual Assault Intervention." *Law, Culture and the Humanities* 7 (3): 413–33.

Munro, V. E. (2010). "From Consent to Coercion: Evaluating International and Domestic Frameworks for the Criminalization of Rape." In *Rethinking Rape Law: International and Comparative Perspectives*, edited by C. McGlynn and V. E. Munro, 17–29. Oxford: Routledge-Cavendish.

Nader, L. (1993). "Controlling Processes in the Practice of Law: Hierarchy and Pacification in the Movement to Re-form Dispute Ideology." *Ohio State Journal on Dispute Resolution* 9 (1): 1–25.

———. (1997). "Controlling Processes: Tracing the Dynamic Components of Power." *Current Anthropology* 38 (5): 711–37.

———. (2002). *The Life of the Law : Anthropological Projects*. Berkeley: University of California Press.

Nagaraj, V. (2010). "Local and Customary Forums: Adapting and Innovating Rules of Formal Law." *Indian Journal of Gender Studies* 17 (3): 429–50.

Nair, J. (1996). *Women and Law in Colonial India*. New Delhi: Kali.

Nakonezny, P. A., R. D. Shull, et al. (1995). "The Effect of No-Fault Divorce Law on the Divorce Rate across the 50 States and Its Relation to Income, Education and Religiosity." *Journal of Marriage and Family* 57 (2): 477–88.

Naples, N. (2003). *Feminism and Method: Ethnography, Discourse Analysis and Activist Research*. New York: Routledge.

Narayan, K. (1993). "How 'Native' is a Native Anthropologist?" *American Anthropologist*, n.s., 95 (3): 671–86.

Narayan, U. (1997). "Cross-Cultural Connections, Border-Crossings and 'Death by Culture': Thinking about Dowry-Murders in India and Domestic-Violence Murders in the United States." In *Dislocating Cultures: Identities, Traditions and Third-World Feminism*, 81–118. New York: Routledge.

Ng, K. H. (2009). *The Common Law in Two Voices: Language, Law, and the Postcolonial Predicament in Hong Kong*. Stanford, CA: Stanford University Press.

Nongbri, T. (2010). "Family, Gender and Identity: A Comparative Analysis of Trans-Himalayan Matrilineal Structures." *Contributions to Indian Sociology*, n.s., 44 (1–2): 155–78.

Okin, S. M. (1989). *Justice, Gender and the Family*. New York: Basic Books.

Panagariya, A. (2008). *India: The Emerging Giant*. New York: Oxford University Press.

Pande, R. (2002). "The Public Face of a Private Domestic Violence." *International Feminist Journal of Politics* 4 (3): 342–67.

Parashar, A. (1992). *Women and Family Law Reform in India: Uniform Civil Code and Gender Equality*. New Delhi: Sage.

Partners for Law in Development (2010). *Rights in Intimate Relationships: Towards an Inclusive and Just Framework of Women's Rights and the Family*. New Delhi: Partners for Law in Development.

Pateman, C. (1988). *The Sexual Contract*. Stanford, CA: Stanford University Press.

Pathak, Z., and R. S. Rajan (1989). "Shahbano." *Signs* 13: 558–82.

Pearson, J., and N. Thoeness (1988). "Divorce Mediation: An American Picture." In *Divorce Mediation and the Legal Process*, edited by R. Dingwall and J. Eekelaar, 70–91. Oxford: Clarendon Press.

Phadke, S. (2003). "Thirty Years On: Women's Studies Reflects on the Women's Movement." *Economic and Political Weekly* 38 (13): 4567–76.

Plesset, S. (2006). *Sheltering Women: Negotiating Gender and Violence in Northern Italy*. Stanford, CA: Stanford University Press.

Presser, L., and E. Gaarder (2000). "Can Restorative Justice Reduce Battering? Some Preliminary Considerations." *Social Justice* 27 (1): 175–95.

Pringle, R., and S. Watson (1992). "'Women's Interests' and the Post-Structuralist State." In *Destabilizing Theory*, edited by M. Barrett and A. Phillips. Stanford, CA: Stanford University Press.

Puar, J. (2007). *Terrorist Assemblages: Homonationalism in Queer Times*. Durham, NC: Duke University Press.

Puri, A., and C. S. Dogra (2010). "Dreams Girl: Will Love Ever Find a Place in Khap Country?" *Outlook* (New Delhi), 12 July, 52–54.

Puri, J. (1999). *Woman, Body, Desire in Post-colonial India Narratives of Gender and Sexuality*. New York: Routledge.

Raheja, G. G., and A. G. Gold (1994). *Listen to the Heron's Words: Reimagining Gender and Kinship in North India*. Berkeley: University of California Press.

Rai, S. M. (1996). "Women and the State in the Third World: Some Issues for Debate." In *Women and the State: International Perspectives*, edited by S. M. Rai and G. Lievesley, 5–22. London: Taylor and Francis.

Rajan, R. S. (1993). *Real and Imagined Women: Gender, Culture and Postcolonialism*. London: Routledge.

————. (2003). *The Scandal of the State: Women, Law and Citizenship in Postcolonial India*. Durham, NC: Duke University Press.

Ramazanoglu, C., and J. Holland (2002). *Feminist Methodology: Challenges and Choices*. London: Sage.

Ray, R. (1999). *Fields of Protest: Women's Movements in India*. Minneapolis: University of Minnesota Press.

Ray, R., and S. Qayum (2009). *Cultures of Servitude: Modernity, Domesticity and Class in India*. Stanford, CA: Stanford University Press.

Reisman, W. M. (1999). *Law in Brief Encounters*. New Haven, CT: Yale University Press.

Resnick, J. (1996). "Asking about Gender in Courts." *Signs* 21 (4): 952–90.

Riessman, C. K. (1990). *Divorce Talk: Women and Men Make Sense of Personal Relationships*. New Brunswick, NJ: Rutgers University Press.

Ring, L. (2006). *Zenana: Everyday Peace in a Karachi Apartment Building*. Bloomington: Indiana University Press.

Roberts, S. (1994). "Law and Dispute Processes." In *Companion Encyclopedia of Anthropology*, edited by T. Ingold, 962–82. London: Routledge.

Roy, A. (2003). *City Requiem, Calcutta: Gender and the Politics of Poverty*. Minneapolis: University of Minnesota Press.

Roy, S. (2010). "Wounds and 'Cures' in South Asian Gender and Memory Politics." In *Global Perspectives on War, Gender & Health: The Sociology and Anthropology of Suffering*, edited by H. Bradby and G. L. Hundt, 31–49. London: Ashgate.

Roychowdhury, P. (2013). "'The Delhi Gang Rape': The Making of International Causes." *Feminist Studies* 39 (1): 282–92.

Rubin, G. (1975). "The Traffic in Women." In *Toward an Anthropology of Women*, edited by R. Reiter, 157–210. New York: Monthly Review Press.

Sack, E. J. (2004). "Battered Women and the State: The Struggle for the Future of Domestic Violence Policy." *Wisconsin Law Review* 2004: 1657–1740.

Samadhan, Delhi High Court Mediation and Conciliation Centre (2011). *Reflections of Samadhan, the Delhi High Court Mediation and Conciliation Centre: 2006–2010*. New Delhi: Delhi High Court.

Sanday, P. (2003). "Rape-Free versus Rape-Prone: How Culture Makes a Difference." In *Evolution, Gender and Rape*, edited by C. B. Travis, 337–62. Cambridge: MIT Press.

Sangster, J. (1996). "Incarcerating Bad Girls: The Regulation of Sexuality through the Female Refuges Act in Ontario, 1920–1945." *Journal of the History of Sexuality* 7 (2): 239–75.

Santos, C. M. (2004). "En-gendering the Police: Women's Police Stations and Feminism in Sao Paulo." *Latin American Research Review* 39 (3): 29–55.

Saradamoni, K. (1999). *Matriliny Transformed: Family, Law, and Ideology in Twentieth Century Travancore*. Walnut Creek, CA: Sage.

Sarat, A., M. Constable, et al. (1998). "Ideas of the 'Everyday' and the 'Trouble Case' in Law and Society Scholarship: An Introduction." In *Everyday Practices and*

Trouble Cases, edited by A. Sarat, M. Constable, D. M. Engel, V. Hans, and S. Lawrence, 1–13. Chicago: Northwestern University Press.

Sarkar, T. (2002). "Semiotics of Terror: Muslim Children and Women in Hindu Rashtra." *Economic and Political Weekly* 37 (28): 2872–76.

Schaffner, L. (2005). "Capacity, Consent and the Construction of Adulthood." In *Regulating Sex: The Politics of Intimacy and Identity*, edited by E. Bernstein and L. Schaffner, 189–205. New York: Routledge.

Sen, I. (2005). "A Space within the Struggle." In *Writing the Women's Movement: A Reader*, edited by M. Khullar, 80–101. New Delhi: Zubaan.

Seuffert, N. (1999). "Domestic Violence, Discourses of Romantic Love, and Complex Personhood in Law." *Melbourne University Law Review* 23: 211–40.

Sharafi, M. (2008). "Justice in Many Rooms since Galanter: De-romanticizing Legal Pluralism through the Cultural Defense." *Law and Contemporary Problems* 71: 139–46.

Shukla, R. (2005). "SC Upholds Constitutionality of S 498A." *InfoChange News and Features* (August), www.infochangeindia.org/analysis86.jsp.

Siddiqi, D. (2010). "Blurred Boundaries: Sexuality and Seduction Narratives in Selected 'Forced Marriage' Cases from Bangladesh." In *"Honour" and Women's Rights*, edited by Manisha Gupte, Ramesh Awasthi, and Shraddha Chickerur. Pune: MASUM.

Sieder, R., and J.-A. McNeish (2013). "Introduction." In *Gender Justice and Legal Pluralities: Latin American and African Perspectives*, edited by R. Sieder and J.-A. McNeish, 1–30. Oxford: Routledge.

Simpson, B. (1998). *Changing Families: An Ethnographic Approach to Divorce and Separation*. Oxford: Berg.

Sinha, M., ed. (1998). *Selections from Mother India by Katherine Mayo*. New Delhi: Kali for Women.

Smart, C. (1995). *Law, Crime and Sexuality: Essays in Feminism*. London: Sage.

Smart, C., and J. Brophy (1985). "Locating Law: A Discussion of the Place of Law in Feminist Politics." In *Women-in-Law: Explorations in Law, Family and Sexuality*, edited by C. Smart and J. Brophy, 1–20. London: Routledge & Kegan Paul.

Smith, B., ed. (2000). *Global Feminisms since 1945*. London: Routledge.

Smith, P. M. (1988). "Families in Court: Guilty or Guilty?" *Children and Society* 2: 152–64.

Solanki, G. (2001). "Women's Experiences through the Police Lens: Analysis of Cases Registered under Section 498(A)." *Journal of Gender Studies* 10 (1): 83–86.

———. (2011). *Adjudication in Religious Family Laws: Cultural Accommodation, Legal Pluralism, and Gender Equality in India*. Cambridge: Cambridge University Press.

Som, R. (1994). "Jawaharlal Nehru and the Hindu Code: A Victory of Symbol over Substance." *Modern Asian Studies* 28 (1): 165–94.

Spivak, G. C. (1988). "Can the Subaltern Speak?" In *Marxism and the Interpretation of Culture*, edited by. C. Nelson and L. Grossberg, 271–313. Urbana-Champaign: University of Illinois Press.

————. (1993)." The Politics of Translation." In *Outside in the Teaching Machine*, 179–200. New York: Routledge.

————. (2010). "Situating Feminism," Beatrice Bain Research Group Annual Keynote Lecture, Program in Critical Theory, University of California at Berkeley, 26 February.

Sreenivas, M. (2004). "Conjugality and Capital: Gender, Families and Property under Colonial Law in India." *Journal of Asian Studies* 63 (4): 937–60.

————. (2008). *Wives, Widows, Concubines: The Conjugal Family Ideal in Colonial India*. Bloomington: Indiana University Press.

————. (2011). "Creating Conjugal Subjects: Devadasis and the Politics of Marriage in Colonial Madras Presidency." *Feminist Studies* 37 (1): 63–92.

Srivastava, S. (2009). "Urban Spaces, Disney-Divinity and Moral Middle Classes in Delhi." *Economic and Political Weekly* 64 (26–27): 338–45.

Stacey, J. (1991). "Can There be a Feminist Ethnography?" In *Women's Words: The Feminist Practice of Oral History*, edited by Sherna Berger Gluck and Daphne Patai, 111–19. New York: Routledge.

Star, L. (1996). *Counsel of Perfection: The Family Court of Australia*. Melbourne: Oxford University Press.

Stark, B. (2001). "Marriage Proposals: From One-Size-Fits-All to Postmodern Marriage Law." *California Law Review* 89 (5): 1479–1548.

Starnes, C. (1993). "Divorce and the Displaced Homemaker: A Discourse on Playing with Dolls, Partnership Buyouts and Dissociation under No-Fault." *University of Chicago Law Review* 60 (1): 67–139.

Starr, J., and M. Goodale (2002). "Introduction: Legal Ethnography: New Dialogues, Enduring Methods." In *Practicing Ethnography in Law: New Dialogues, Enduring Methods*, edited by J. Starr and M. Goodale, 1–10. New York: Palgrave.

Stevens, J. (1997). "On The Marriage Question." In *Women Transforming Politics: An Alternative Reader*, edited by C. J. Cohen, K. B. Jones, and J. C. Tronto, 62–83. New York: NYU Press.

Sturman, R. (2005). "Property and Attachments: Defining Autonomy and the Claims of Family in Nineteenth-Century Western India." *Comparative Studies in Society and History* 47: 611–37.

Subramanian, N. (2010). "Making Family and Nation: Hindu Marriage Law in Early Postcolonial India." *Journal of Asian Studies* 69 (3): 771–98.

Suneetha, A. (2012). "Muslim Women and Marriage Laws: Debating the Model Nikahnama." *Economic & Political Weekly* 47 (43): 41.

Suneetha, A., and V. Nagaraj (2006). "A Difficult Match: Women's Actions and Legal Institutions in the Face of Domestic Violence." *Economic and Political Weekly*, 14 October, 4355–62.

———— (2010). "Dealing with Domestic Violence towards Complicating the Rights Discourse." *Indian Journal of Gender Studies* 17 (3): 451–78.

Talwar, A., and Shramajibee Mahila Samity (2002). "The Shalishi in West Bengal: A Community Response to Domestic Violence." In *Women Initiated Community Level*

Responses to Domestic Violence: Summary Report of Three Studies, 14–30. Washington, DC: International Center for Research on Women.

Tamanaha, B. Z. (2000). "A Non-Essentialist Version of Legal Pluralism." *Journal of Law and Society* 27 (2): 296–321.

Tellis, A. (2014). "Multiple Ironies: Notes on Same Sex Marriage for South Asians at Home and Abroad." In *Marrying in South Asia: Shifting Concepts, Changing Practices in a Globalising World*, edited by R. Kaur and R. Palriwala, 333–50. New Delhi: Orient Blackswan.

Trinch, S. L., and S. Berk-Seligson (2002). "Narrating in Protective Order Interviews: A Source of Interactional Trouble." *Language in Society* 31: 383–418.

Tsai, B. (2000). "The Trend towards Specialized Domestic Violence Courts: Improvements on an Effective Innovation." *Fordham Law Review* 39: 1285–1327.

Uberoi, P. (1996). "When Is a Marriage Not a Marriage? Sex, Sacrament and Contract in Hindu Marriage." In *Social Reform, Sexuality and the State*, edited by P. Uberoi, 319–45. New Delhi: Sage.

Vaidehi. (1993). "Shakuntale Yondige Kaleda Aparahna (An Afternoon with Shakuntala)." In *Women Writing in India*, edited by S. Tharu and K. Lalita, 2:535–45. New York: Feminist Press.

Vanka, S., and M. N. Kumari (2008). "Sustaining Democracy within the Family through Family Courts: An Exploratory Analysis." In *Democracy in the Family: Insights from India*, edited by J. Deshmukh-Ranadive, 113–27. New Delhi: Sage.

Vatuk, S. (1972). *Kinship and Urbanization: White Collar Workers in North India*. Berkeley: University of California Press.

———. (2001). "'Where Will She Go? What Will She Do?': Paternalism toward Women in the Administration of Muslim Personal Law in Contemporary India." In *Religion and Personal Law in Secular India*, edited by G. J. Larsen, 226–48. Bloomington: Indiana University Press.

———. (2006). "Domestic Violence and Marital Breakdown in India: A View from the Family Courts." In *Culture, Power, and Agency: Gender in Indian Ethnography*, edited by L. Fruzzetti and S. Tenhunen, 204–26. Calcutta: Stree.

———. (2008). "Divorce at the Wife's Initiative in Muslim Personal Law: What Are the Options and What Are Their Implications for Women's Welfare?" In *Redefining Family Law in India: Essays in Honour of B. Sivaramayya*, edited by A. Parashar and A. Dhanda, 200–35. London: Routledge.

Virdi, J. (2004). *The Cinematic Imagination: Indian Popular Films as Social History*. New Delhi: Permanent Black.

Visaria, L. (1999). "Violence against Women in India: Evidence from Rural Gujarat." In *Domestic Violence in India: A Summary Report of Three Studies*, edited by PRO-WID, 9–17. Washington, DC: International Center for Research on Women.

Visweswaran, K. (1994). *Fictions of Feminist Ethnography*. Minneapolis: University of Minnesota Press.

von Benda-Beckmann, K. (1981). "Forum Shopping and Shopping Forums: Dispute Processing in Minangkabau Village." *Journal of Legal Pluralism* 19: 117–59.

Wadley, S. S. (2002). "One Straw from a Broom Cannot Sweep: The Ideology and Practice of the Joint Family in Rural North India." In *Everyday Life in South Asia*, edited by D. P. Mines and S. Lamb, 11–22. Bloomington: Indiana University Press.

Wardle, L. D. (1991). "No-Fault Divorce and the Divorce Conundrum." *Brigham Young University Law Review* 1991 (1): 79–142.

Watson-Franke, M. B. (2002). "A World in Which Women Move Freely without Fear of Men: An Anthropological Perspective on Rape." *Women's Studies International Forum* 25 (6): 599–606.

Weber, M. (2004). "The Three Pure Types of Legitimate Rule." In *The Essential Weber: A Reader*, edited by S. Whimster, 133–45. London: Routledge.

Westmarland, N., and G. Gangoli, eds. (2011). *International Approaches to Rape*. Bristol: Policy Press.

Weston, K. (2004). "Fieldwork in Lesbian and Gay Communities." In *Feminist Perspectives on Social Research*, edited by H.-B. S. Nagy and M. L. Yaiser, 198–205. New York: Oxford University Press.

White, L. E. (1990). "Subordination, Rhetorical Survival Skills and Sunday Shoes: Notes on the Hearing of Mrs. G." *Buffalo Law Review* 38: 1–58.

Whitehead, A. (1982). "'I'm Hungry, Mum': The Politics of Domestic Budgeting." In *Of Marriage and the Market: Women's Subordination Internationally and Its Lessons*, edited by K. Young, C. Wolkowitz, and R. McCullagh, 93–116. London: Routledge & Kegan Paul.

Wiegman, R. (2012). *Object Lessons*. Durham, NC: Duke University Press.

Williams, B. F. (1996). "Skinfolk, Not Kinfolk: Comparative Reflections on the Identity of Participant Observation in Two Field Settings." In *Feminist Dilemmas in Fieldwork*, edited by D. L. Wolf, 72–95. Boulder, CO: Westview.

Williams, R. V. (2006). *Postcolonial Politics and Personal Laws: Colonial Legal Legacies and the Indian State*. Delhi: Oxford University Press.

Williams, W. W. (1997). "The Equality Crisis: Some Reflections on Culture, Courts and Feminism." In *The Second Wave: A Reader in Feminist Theory*, edited by L. Nicholson, 71–92. New York: Routledge.

Wolf, D. L. (1996). "Situating Feminist Dilemmas in Fieldwork." In *Feminist Dilemmas in Fieldwork*, edited by D. L. Wolf, 1–55. Boulder, CO: Westview.

Yalom, M. (2001). *A History of the Wife*. New York: Harper Collins.

Yi, Z., and W. Deqing (2000). "Regional Analysis of Divorce in China since 1980." *Demography* 37 (2): 215–19.

Young, K., C. Wolkowitz, and R. McCullagh, eds. (1982). *Of Marriage and the Market: Women's Subordination Internationally and Its Lessons*. London: Routledge & Kegan Paul.

Zavella, P. (1996). "Feminist Insider Dilemmas: Constructing Ethnic Identity with Chicana Informants." In *Feminist Dilemmas in Fieldwork*, edited by D. L. Wolf, 138–59. Boulder, CO: Westview.

INDEX